That Summer in Sicily

BALLANTINE BOOKS

NEW YORK

That
Summer
in Sicily

✦

A LOVE STORY

Marlena de Blasi

Copyright © 2008 by Marlena de Blasi
Photograph © 2008 by Grafica, Inc.

Published in the United States by Ballantine Books,
an imprint of The Random House Publishing Group,
a division of Random House, Inc., New York.

BALLANTINE and colophon are registered trademarks
of Random House, Inc.

LIBRARY OF CONGRESS CATALOGING-IN-PUBLICATION DATA

De Blasi, Marlena.
That summer in Sicily : a love story / Marlena de Blasi.
p.   cm.
ISBN 978-0-345-49765-9 (hardcover)
1. Sicily—Social life and customs—20th century.   2. National
characteristics, Sicilian.   3. Country life—Italy—Sicily.   4. De Blasi,
Marlena—Travel—Italy—Sicily.   I. Title.
DG865.6D4 2008
914.5'804929092—dc22   2008002774

Printed in the United States of America on acid-free paper

www.ballantinebooks.com

2 4 6 8 9 7 5 3 1

FIRST EDITION

Book design by Carole Lowenstein

As I write this, it is early November 2007.
Sometime late in January or early February 2008,
a baby girl will be born to Robin Rolewicz and Matthew Duchnowski.
And it's to her, to this yet unborn child that I dedicate my book,
with prayers and love for the beautiful life of

Marlena Pi Duchnowski

And for my own beautiful babies,
Lisa Elaine and Erich Brandon

per Fernando Filiberto Maria, l'amore mio

That Summer in Sicily is the story of actual people and actual events, but it is also a tale woven together from scenes that were described to me—often in Italian, more often in dialect—with all of the blanks and lacunae that characterize such accounts. In the way of storytellers everywhere, I have exercised some poetic license: events have been merged or enlarged, names have been changed, time frames collapsed or expanded to suit the needs of the narrative. In addition, to protect my protagonists and their way of life, I have placed the narrative at a geographic distance from the place where these events in fact unfolded.

BIRTH DATES

Simona: 1905
Leo: 1912
Cosimo: 1919
Tosca: 1930
Yolande: 1931
Charlotte: 1932
Mafalda: 1933

A NOTE ABOUT
THE ORIGINS OF THE TERM
Donnafugata

Ayn as Jafat is Arabic for "fountain of health." Under the Saracen dominion of Sicily, this term was dialectically corrupted into *Ronna-fuata*. Over the centuries, the term was further corrupted into the modern *Donnafugata,* at which point its original significance was lost to its literal translation of "fleeing woman." The term *donnafugata* has since been used as the name of various properties, both real and fictional, as well as the name of products and businesses in Sicily and elsewhere in the world. *Donnafugata* is the name of the summer villa in Lampedusa's *The Leopard.* Additionally, it is the trade name of the Sicilian wines produced by the Rallo family, fourth-generation wine-makers of Belice, Pantelleria, and Marsala.

CONTENTS

PROLOGUE

This could only be a story about Sicily. And Sicily could only be an island, less by the caprice of nature than by her own insolence. As though she might have quit Italy had she not already been born separate from it. Yet this is not a story about *only* the island but of a hamlet in the middle of that island. At the top of the island. A hamlet made of heaped-up stones and huddled in the cleft of an anchoritic mountain beneath the ruins of a temple. Above and all 'round the hamlet is a high plateau planted almost everywhere in wheat. On parched meadows, sheep and goats graze. The only water thereabout is a metallic smudge where the white sky meets the yellow earth and the only waves are of that wheat, the shuddering golden stalks of it roaring like the sea and crashing in the goddess-blown winds. Stone Age tangles of myrtle and broom and wild marjoram and wild thyme clutch at the steeps, and the only chink in the towering silence is the foul whispering of the scirocco.

Here, the substance of life lived three millennia ago or in the mid-nineteenth century or, as in this case, some seventy years distant, can seem essentially the same as that which formed the incidents of the day before yesterday. Nothing much has been lost or forgotten or left to languish from the time before now so a stunning tribal continuance prevails here. The ancient past, the more recent past, and the present congregate, abide together in that continuance. And apart from the evidence of a vacillating fancy for some fashionable goods and ideas, one might be hard put to divine a particular historical moment for the way it looks and feels and sounds here. Especially of an evening's wandering in the fallow of Demeter's broken temple. Tramping among the great fluted columns, supine, lustrous under the moon, our boots bruise the wild thyme and weeds tear my dress. A scrap of white linen on a rock rose.

It was here in these mountains that the Greek's goddess of grain and fertility and motherhood once held forth. Where she does still, the locals will tell you. It was Demeter who illumined the magic of sowing seeds beneath the earth, protecting them, feeding them, growing them up into ripeness. Resonance of the female condition, of other seeds planted in the dark velvet corners of a womb. Under Demeter's will, the local tribes' harvests flourished, she conjuring the sun and the rain and the breezes on their behalf, and they, in turn, honoring her with great fires under the drenching light of a full moon and ritual offerings of bread and wine. All was Elysium until the day when Demeter's daughter, her Persephone, was seized by Pluto. The child had been gathering flowers by the Lake of Pergusa just outside the walls of Enna when the god of the underworld saw her, was enchanted by her. He would have Persephone as his bride. Pluto carried the child to Hades and, tempting her with the seeds of a pomegranate, won Zeus's permission to keep her. Demeter gnashed the sun, keeping the mountain villages and the fertile fields—and the world itself—in darkness until she'd made her pact with Zeus: for half of each year, her daughter would be restored to her. With Persephone again by her side, the goddess rekindled the sun and tipped down the warm rain over the earth only to suspend them each time her child returned to Hades.

The villagers and the farmers here tell the story of Demeter and Persephone with all the fresh wonder and anguish of a thing only just happened. They tell it in the same way they tell the story of Mary and Jesus. They believe the stories with equal fervor, resonant as they are of their own stories. Allegiance does not shift but only enlarges its endearment to hold both mothers—one with her crown of woven corn husks, the other shrouded in a rough woven veil. *Why must we pray to only one? To us, they are the same. Le addolorate.* Grieving women. In Sicily, the sacred and the profane are kin.

INTRODUCTION

As it has been with other adventures in my life, this one began with an assignment. It was the summer of 1995—I'd been married to the Venetian for nearly nine months—when I was asked by a scholarly monthly magazine to write a seminal piece on the interior regions of Sicily. By then I'd written extensively of the glories in the coastal cities and towns. The lustrous footfalls of the Greeks. The splendored epitaphs impressed by Saracen sheiks and Norman kings. More even, had I written of the archipelagos where Aeolus's winds still whine and screech among the violent crags of these unornamented outposts of the world as she was. Now it would be to the high fastness of the mountains that I would go.

I'd suspected that I was not the editor's first choice among the qualified journalists writing in the English language, and even before my departure, my suspicions were summarily confirmed. Several people had already turned down the job, including one staff writer who'd lived in Sicily longer than a decade. The reason? It was the same as the warning railed down upon me by other colleagues and friends: *The center of the island is an aloof and pathless place and the colossal silence of it all is reflected in its people.* But I said that silence is the admission of mystery. And mystery is good. Unshrinking, the caveats served only to intrigue.

But it was not just Sicily that was on our path that summer. My husband and I would spend three, perhaps four, months roaming all the regions south of Lazio, south of Rome. Exploration and research for a book. All along the southern routes we met with an almost sacrosanct kindness. There was beautiful food at the humblest tables, people who laid down their shovels or mops, who descended from tractors or the backs of mules, to guide and inform and encourage. Swept away by this generosity, we approached the mountains, unguarded.

I'd set some fundamental plans by telephone and post with museum docents, with professors of art history and archaeology, with writers and journalists, cooks and bakers. Or so I'd believed. My professional welcome seemed relatively assured. Once I'd arrived at the first destination and taken the most perfunctory measure of the place and those few of its inhabitants who showed themselves, I understood my error. At appointed hours in appointed places, I sat alone. Numbers dialed rang into infinity. Not to worry. There was the next place. And the one after that. But the next place was always the same as the place before it.

Nearly two weeks had passed when, having purposefully left my once precious roster of names and numbers behind in a hotel room, I began a spontaneous campaign directed at the locals. Elegant business cards from a celebrated American magazine proffered to tourist office workers, or museum guides or cleaning ladies or baristas or old men playing cards beneath the scrawny shadows of a clump of eucalyptus roused nothing more than mumbles. Primal grunts. From young men who leaned against church walls, thumbs cradled in their belts, eyes at half mast like ancient lizards deep in the torpors of the drugging sun, they raised no sound at all.

Even those pivotal interviews that had been arranged by my editor were ignored or forgotten. The meticulously drawn route was marked only by misanthropic silences, closed doors, and epic heat. I surrendered. I telephoned the editor to tell him so. There was silence then even from him.

The weight of the work put aside, Fernando and I say we'll wend our way down from the mountains and head southwest toward Agrigento. Or perhaps southeast toward Noto. Almost anywhere away from here. First, a day or so to recover, to rest in an even minimally cordial atmosphere. In a bar one morning, I risk posing a question to a pair of military policemen whom we'd seen—same time, same place—for several days running. Could they suggest a place where we might stay out in the countryside? A small hotel or *pensione*? Unexpectedly, they say yes. There is a woman they'd heard of who receives guests—when she chooses—offering room and board and hospitality. The concept of hospitality in this unchivalric desert makes us smile. We take directional notes from the policemen.

"Arrivederci," one of them says, twisting his body away from the bar, raising his half-ration of breakfast grappa—reduced for duty's sake—in salute as we leave.

"The woman is called Tosca. Her place is *Villa Donnafugata*. Although there's no sign to tell you so," he shouts.

The road is paved with sun-bleached stones and whorls of yellow sand are gritty, blinding veils upon the windows. The July heat is vicious heat. Strangling heat. After more than two hours of a tormenting pilgrimage up goat paths and across great gashes through wheat fields masquerading as roads, we can't tell if we are progressing or only circling back upon land we've already traveled. Illusion, the sliding panel. The dupe. Another substance of Sicily.

Leaving the car in a rocky niche, we climb a stony path up into the hamlet that we think is the one indicated by the policemen. We'll find someone who can help us. Panting, feverish, we come upon a small piazza. There is a fountain shaped like a sleigh and trickles of water fall from its four baroque curlicues into a basin where women are washing clothes, slapping the wet things rhythmically against the stone and wailing some vestigial Arab chant. There is no one else about save an old sheepdog who sleeps near their feet. No children. No men. We greet them and wait to be greeted in return. They stop their singing. They look at us but no one speaks.

"We're looking for *la signora* Tosca," I say again and again, each time employing different hand movements and intonations. "*Villa Donnafugata.* Can you tell us how to find it?"

Nothing. Believing my speech to be unintelligible to them, Fernando steps closer in toward the group, languidly lights a cigarette, takes a few puffs before he says, "*Ci serve il vostro aiuto.* We need your help."

As though Fernando's words were a cue, still looking straight at us, they resume their chant. We turn away, begin to walk back across the piazza to the downward path. I look back and, at chest height, wave good-bye. I understand what a foolish sight we must have been to them. Especially me in my big hat and dark glasses. If we'd scaled the hill in white muslin britches, flailing scimitars, we would have been more familiar. More welcome. Still, I would have liked to have washed my own soiled shirt in that fountain, to have bent over the murky water and slapped the cloth against the stones, the glint of long gold earrings caressing my face. My wave connects. With her chin, one woman gestures toward a hill that sits behind the hamlet. The same hill over which we have just traveled.

Fernando refuses not only to drive but to speak. I retrace the route back through the wheat fields, easing the car once again between the stalks. The overheated chassis, sensing danger, chokes, then bravely shimmies inside the dense growth. Our only view is of the bronze curtain the wheat makes, and we must either raise the windows or be slashed by the knife-sharp fronds that swipe at us as we move along. We lurch inside this suffocating dream until, with no warning, the field ends scant centimeters from a stand of poplars. A shy wind moves the crisp leaves of them and we heave open the car doors, breathless as from a chase, to let the air touch us. Beyond a meadow grown in purple vetch and beyond that to what seem like acres of gardens, we see turrets and crenellated towers and juliet balconies and a red and yellow porcelain-tiled mansard roof that, lit by the climbing sun, seems ablaze. We see what looks like a castle. As we walk toward it, a gaudy scent of roses and rotting oranges agitates the breeze.

PART I

Villa
Donnafugata
1995

CHAPTER I

HOLLYHOCKS DON'T GROW IN THE DESERT. YET HUNDREDS AND hundreds of their red satin blossoms line a wide stone path to a flung iron gate. I know this is a dream. Through the gate lie astonishing, sweeping gardens. There are roses. Ivory and white and the color of burnt cream, they climb trellises and sprawl in beds, spill and ramble and entwine. Boxwood parterres, hedges of yew, clumps of lavender, fat and tall, and white foxgloves nod among white dahlias, among white peonies. I know that the castle and the roses and the holly-hocks are sun-stroke illusions. The hallucination will pass. We'll climb back in the car and drive away from this madness of silence and mockery. But while the hallucination endures I want to look over there, where gnarled trunks of wisteria and jasmine and grapevines tent a pergola, make a dark, shady room from whose depths laughter comes. How many days has it been since I've heard laughter? Even my own? I walk toward the pergola, and stand at the opening to see a clutch of women in long black dresses who sit 'round an oilclothed table. Tremulous light insists among the leaves, spangles the women's fingers flurrying over a heap of yellow beans.

"Buongiorno," they say before we can.

We wish them a good day in return, and somehow the greeting is sufficient. I need nothing more than to look upon these fantastical figures, and they seem to need nothing more than to be at their work. Dreams can be so simple. Though she knows nothing of who we are or what we might want, one of the women—perhaps the eldest—rises and points the way toward the castle. A welcome. It is a long walk past groves of lemons and oranges, an orchard of almond trees, smaller stands of plum and cherry. I hear Fernando saying over and over again, *"Where are we? Where in hell are we?"*

Imposing, rhapsodical, the castle with the red and yellow roof soars up from a quivering crystalline mist and another garden, stone-walled, draped in more wisteria and more roses and haphazardly grown in flowers and vegetables and herbs, lies before it. In the center of the enclosure, a second covey of black-clad women are at work. Tentatively, we walk through the open gate and they look up from scrubbing chairs and tables, one from the quiet task of slitting the throat of a very small goat, catching its blood in a chipped white basin. Another peers from behind a great pot set over a gas burner resting on a tree stump. She stirs onions in hot fat. There's the scent of something else that's good, too. Pig charring over wood. A group sits in a circle to loop the dried stalks of purple garlic into braids. In the low cleft of a gigantic magnolia tree, one woman sits and writes in a black leather book. As did the women at the fountain down in the hamlet, these women softly chant. Seeming neither surprised nor disturbed by our presence, beatifically they greet us, then continue with their work. Their singing. Uncertain but not uncomfortable, we stand there quietly. Every few moments, one whispers to another and they all giggle, their eyes on us. Just as I have dreamed the hollyhocks and the roses and the laughing women shelling beans, surely I dream them. I listen carefully to their chanting and, sotto voce, I am trying to echo the hollow, vacant sounds they make when a woman appears from the far end of the garden.

Neither young nor old, she, too, is in costume, if of a different sort: Wellingtons and jodhpurs and a suede riding coat. For a moment she pauses under an oak tree, and the shadows of the leaves make a black lace shawl about her head and shoulders. Magisterially, then, she goes among the women, observing what they do, nodding or shaking her crown of gray braids according to her pleasure, her displeasure. Surely she is Tosca.

"They're singing of the inevitably unequal proportions of grief and rapture in a life. Did you know that?" asks the woman.

I wonder if the disdain in her bearing, in her voice, is a cover for timidity. As she approaches us, I nearly gasp at her beauty. "Did I know that they were singing about that or do I know that it's true?" I ask.

"Perhaps I meant both. I'm Tosca Brozzi."

"Buongiorno, Signora. Noi siamo de Blasi da Venezia."

"I know. I know. There'll be time to talk about your journalistic failures at table. I suspect we'll get 'round to 'grief and rapture,' as well. We'll be sitting down at one. I'll let you know later if there's room for you to stay. You can wash and rest in there," she says, gesturing toward the great black doors of the house or the villa or the mansion. The castle. Whatever it is.

We hesitate, and she says, "Agata is there to show you the way." Fernando and I look at each other, the look asking, *Do you want to stay? Do you want to see this through?* He takes my hand and pulls me toward the open doors.

Yet another woman in black is this Agata. She shakes our hands and speaks less assuredly in Italian than did Tosca, mixing it with dialect, but not so thickly that we cannot understand her. Be understood by her. She smiles and chatters, leading the way down a dark corridor lit by the flame of a single candle set in a wall sconce, then opens a door upon a large square room that smells faintly of fresh paint. Yellow walls, a paler yellow sofa, and a pair of blue damask love seats. A mottled gold-framed mirror leans out over a small white marble fireplace. Lavender is massed in great rope-bound bunches and sits in corners on the marble floors, beside the chairs, on a peeling gilt table, in the lap of the hearth.

"*Si accomodi.* Be comfortable."

She opens a door to a small bathroom and takes fresh towels from a cabinet.

"*Vi porto un aperitivo tra poco.* I'll bring you an *aperitivo* in a while."

When she closes the door, I expect it will be the end of the dream.

"Is this real?" we ask each other at the same moment.

Now we hear our own laughter.

"I don't know where we are or with whom, but I know we're safe. We're in the right place," Fernando says.

"Journalistic failures. How does she know about . . ."

"Because no one spoke to us doesn't mean that they don't speak to one another."

"Are they all widows out there?"

"I think so."

"Is this a rest home with a duty roster? Or a commune? I mean, they can't all be her relatives?"

"No, it's not a rest home. The women are all much too vibrant.

Some of them are relatively young. I don't think it's a commune, either. I don't know what it is."

With lemon soap and squares of rough white linen, we scrub our faces and upper bodies, anointing and splashing ourselves with the contents of a jumble of apothecary bottles with hand-wrought labels. *Neroli oil, neroli water, lavender water, rose oil.* We rub the dust of Sicily from our feet, from our sandals, smooth our hair, button our shirts back in place, and, fearing a deep sleep should we sit, we stand in the freshly painted yellow room and shake our heads in wonder.

"I want to look about the place. I want to see more of it, don't you?" I say.

"This is a private home. We'll be shown what they would like us to see, when they would like us to see it. Patience."

"Let's go back out to the garden, then. And to the car. Clean shirts and . . ."

"I think we'll be going back to the car soon enough. After lunch, I mean. I doubt we'll be staying long afterward."

"I don't know what to think of this Tosca. She seemed like an extra from the set of *Quo Vadis* as she came striding through the garden, bursting in upon the enchantment."

"Actually, she is more *Felliniana*. Yes, Fellini would have cast her in *La Dolce Vita.* But she speaks. I'm indebted to her for that."

We gather our things and walk back down the candlelit corridor, headed for the garden, when Agata opens a pair of wide carved doors and sweeps her hands in a welcoming gesture. We enter not into a room but into the declining sumptuousness of a regimental hall. Fragments of frescoed gods and goddesses—plump flanked and rolling eyed—hurtle across the high crumbling walls, giving erotic chase up onto the great vault of the ceiling. And under the frenzy of this cupola, three massive tables are set. The underwater silence of the gardens, gently penetrated by the women's chants and their laughter, has given way to domestic pandemonium. This is Tosca's dining hall.

Five or six or more of the widows float in and out of the space, porting platters and trays and covered tureens, placing them on the side tables and buffets that line the walls. They all shriek at once, most often addressing someone in the farthest reaches of the hall or in far-flung rooms. Unseen doors are repeatedly slammed; unskilled, unshy hands pound scales on a piano located somewhere on an upper floor. In cussing pursuit of a newborn orphan lamb escaped from the kitchen where it had been brought to be bottle fed, two older men search the premises, discover the tiny creature in peaceful sleep, nearly invisible among the worn cushions on a velvet chair. One of the men places the now-protesting lamb 'round his neck like a scarf, says he'll carry him back to the kitchen. I want to go to the kitchen.

Keeping a few paces behind the man with the lamb collar, I follow him out of the house, through the walled garden, and past two small beehive-shaped stone outbuildings, one of which houses a wood-burning oven. On a long marble-topped table in front of it, neat rounds of flour-dusted dough have been set to rise in the sun. I have never seen dough set to rise in the sun. I am still inside the dream. Though I want to stop the dream here, at least for a while, to stay with the dough and the sun and the good smells that linger from an earlier bake, I run to catch up with the man and the lamb. Down a wide white graveled path lined with yews, he is heading for what looks like a barn that sits close by the edge of a wheat field. I crunch along the gravel behind him and I know that he knows I am following him. In fact, he half turns every so often and smiles, as though in encouragement. The man and the lamb disappear into the barn, and when I arrive at the threshold of the open doors, I stand before the most splendid kitchen I've ever seen.

For this past year—this first year of my life in Italy—I'd cooked in the tin-can Playskool kitchen of Fernando's bunker by the sea. Or not cooked, as it usually turned out, since my new husband—despite the truth that he knowingly, willfully married an impassioned cook— prefers to dine as he'd always dined: One hundred twenty-five grams of spaghetti cooked halfway to flexibility and slathered with two soupspoonsful of bottled sauce. A salad with no vinegar or salt. And if he was celebrating, a slate-thin cut of a chicken's breast hardened in a Teflon skillet. A slice of lemon. I rock on the dusty heels of my old boots at the door of paradise.

Yet more of the black-dressed women are at work. Or are they the same black-dressed ones who were under the pergola with the beans or in the walled garden? Do they simply shift geography? No, these are most definitely women I've not yet seen. White aprons to the ankle, black scarves wrapped pirate-like, hiding their crowns of braids, exposing faces, exalting black Arab eyes. They all seem to have the same eyes.

Massive dark wood beams hang low over what must be more than two hundred square meters of dark red tiles. Rough plaster walls are washed in the same color as the parched wheat blowing in the field outside the door. The great stone paws of some mythic beast rest on the hearth floors of two stupendous fireplaces that, like flaming sphinxes, crouch at either end of the room. There are three ancient marble sinks, one of them fashioned from a baptismal font. There is an ancient cast-iron, wood-fired stove and a sparkling dark green Aga, the latter seeming to be out of use since the cooks all hover about the old one as well as in the environs of a six-burner gas range. There are no machines in evidence, but rather racks and racks of knives and utensils and culinary battery. Two long worktables are positioned in disparate parts of the space and four or five women are at work behind each one of them. I step inside, say *permesso* in a voice that no one hears above the collective din. Some look at me and smile; most go about their business. I step farther inside.

Baronial armoires and dressers and cupboards are stashed with porcelain, ceramics, terra-cotta pots and dishes, glassware, silver, copper, pewter, linens, candlesticks, pitchers, serving platters, and stacks and stacks of bowls. The dresser drawers hang open and show linings of old fabric—faded, torn, marked with unsharp knives. In one of the dressers, a deep long drawer is kept open just wide enough to form a perfect vise in which to secure a vertically placed three-kilo round of bronze-crusted, wood-charred bread while a widow carves thick, rough slices of it, letting the crumbs fall in upon the velvet. In another dresser with the same sort of very long drawers, cheeses—already aged and ready for the table—are kept swaddled in white linen. Like a great, tall jewel box, the interior walls and shelves of one armoire—devoted to the keeping of sweets—are upholstered in torn, faded yellow brocade. On the deep shelves sit tins and glass jars and yard-long rectangular tarts spread with jams or chunks of caramelized fruit. On one shelf there are silver trays laid with tiny pastries shaped like peaches or oranges, glazed in barely pink icing and ornamented with perfect stems and leaves cut from candied angelica. I hear my own barely contained gasps of delight as I watch the women ready plates and baskets and trays to be carried to the dining hall. My hands itching to touch something, I keep them behind my back. Keep the hopeful smile upon my face.

"*Posso aiutarvi?* May I help you?" I ask in several ascending registers.

Their efficiency is complete, though, and all the goods are in hand or ensconced upon the folded white cloths that they place over their pirate headdresses to cushion the burden of a wash basket full of bread or one of biscotti or of peaches and plums still nodding on their branches. And the parade begins. Out the door they walk, hips swaying, backs and shoulders arched, breasts thrust. Chanting, praying. Alone, I bring up the rear, try to walk the way they walk, swish my hips under my jeans, hold my head as though an amphora of wine rests there. It feels good. The sun is torrid upon us, the scents of the food are glorious, and as I run my hand along the prickly leaves of the yews lining the white gravel path I feel so grateful to be inside this dream of Sicily.

CHAPTER II

IN THE DINING HALL THERE IS A PREPONDERANCE OF WOMEN. Perhaps there are forty of them with twelve or so men scattered among the three tables. Freshly slicked hair, some sort of jacket over buttoned-to-the-throat shirts, three of the men might be under thirty, while the others—prepared in equally elegant fashion—might be a generation or so older. Save Tosca and I and two others, all the women wear mourning.

Agata shows Fernando and I to our places—his next to the lamb rescuer and mine near a woman who she presents as Carlotta. We are introduced as *i Veneziani*. The marked skin on Carlotta's hands says she might be sixty, yet her great black fawn's eyes and small-boned thinness make her seem a girl. Both Carlotta and a somewhat older-looking woman called Olga, who sits opposite from us and shakes hands with me across the table, wear dark print dresses of a vintage 1940s' style. Every woman in the room wears her hair in some construction of intricate braids. I try to smooth my loose, long, too curly hair and feel barbaric.

"Where have you been?" Fernando wants to know.

"I went to see the kitchen," I tell him grinning.

Everyone seems to be seated except Tosca and the tall, stout man with whom she confers near one of the tables. Though their backs are to us, the way they stand, almost touching, and lean to listen to each other makes them seem a couple. So Tosca has a husband, I think, and yet, when they turn to take their places at table, I see that the man, a magnificent Christopher Plummer look-alike but with those same black Arab eyes, is wearing a cleric's collar. A priest. He seats Tosca, remains standing, and strikes a glass with a knife handle. Closes his eyes, opens his arms wide, palms upward, and begins to pray. Everyone takes the hand of the person next to her or him. Heads are bowed and lips move in loud personal thanksgiving. Pitchers of wine and water are passed and laden serving plates fly in all directions, *buon pranzo.*

"Allora, come si chiama questo posto?" I ask Carlotta, pretending to have forgotten the villa's unforgettable name.

"Non ha un nome veremente ma la gente locale l'ha sempre chiamata Villa Donnafugata. É una lunga storia. It doesn't really have a name but the local people have always called it Villa Donnafugata. The house of the fleeing woman. A long story."

I don't tell her that it's precisely a long story that I'd like to hear but only smile and say, *"Ho capito, ho capito."* I understand.

Carlotta continues, though. In a quiet, aristocratic voice that contrasts with the lusty dialect of the others 'round us, she tells me that the villa is an eighteenth-century Anjou castle built originally to be that noble family's hunting lodge in this part of Sicily. *La signora*— as she refers to Tosca—inherited the villa from an Anjou prince whose ward she once was. She acknowledges my widened gaze.

"Yes, *la signora*'s life has often been a very romantic one," she says, lustrous eyes flashing and, perhaps, about to spill tears.

She tells me that, bit by bit, *la signora* restored the place. For more than thirty years, *la signora* has lived here with—and at this point

Carlotta hesitates as though even she is not certain who all the residents might be—a number of her friends and friends of friends.

"People in need. Of other people, mostly," she says. "When villagers, local farmers, find themselves alone—widows, widowers—many of them come to make their home here. If they have grown children, some prefer to live together with them, but for others, well, they find that the sort of communal life we have here helps them to stay well, to stay young. And if need be, we have a health-care facility and staff nurses, visiting physicians. The women are like sisters; I'm sure you've already noticed that. In fact, many of them are related by blood or by marriage. Most of them were neighbors in the village or worked side by side in the fields all their lives. We are all related by affection. We are part of one another's history. We are Sicilian."

She says this last as though there is nothing more to say.

Wanting her to tell me more, after a while I ask her, "How many people live here?"

"It changes. People die, but also babies are born here."

"Babies? Here?"

"Yes, babies. We have a birthing clinic here. A beautiful facility, very small, though, with room for only three or four women. Two of our widows were midwives, and they are training some of the younger women to take their place. Obstetricians from the city visit weekly, but often I think they come because they like to be here. Because they like to dine with us. By the way, we're a bit excited today since one of our expectant mothers is very close to her time. Very close, indeed. You can imagine how many aunties and uncles and surrogate grandparents each of our babies has. Mother and child can stay for as long as a year if they like. Until they can get situated more permanently."

I note that Carlotta does not speak of unwed mothers, of home-lessness, of poverty. Rather she has said: *People who need other people. We are all related by affection. We are part of one another's history. We are Sicilian.*

My gaze is drawn over and over again to a woman who sits to the left of the priest. Carlotta looks at me looking at the woman.

"She, the one sitting next to Don Cosimo, is *la signora* Tosca's sister. She is *la signora* Mafalda."

So Christopher Plummer is called Don Cosimo. And to his left, the small woman with the blond braids and the beautiful profile is Tosca's sister, the one who'd been sitting and writing in the cleft of the magnolia when we arrived. *Mafalda. Carlotta. Olga. Agata. Don Cosimo.* I look from one to the other. I want to ask Carlotta if she knows whether we'll be staying beyond lunch but the question, any way I could pose it, might be awkward for her to answer. I must wait for word from *la signora* herself.

Instead I ask, "But how does the household function? Does everyone have a specific job?"

"We all do what we're good at doing. And since there's so *very much* to do to maintain a place as vast as this," she says sweeping her arms, throwing back her head in laughter, "with so much land, the animals, the gardens, our work is almost constant. Sometimes I think the truth is another, though. That the work is only an *intermezzo, un divertimento,* to fill the scant hours between meals. We eat often and well here, *signora. . . . Io non ricordo il suo nome, scusatemi.*"

"*Mi chiamo Chou-Chou e mio marito è Fernando.*"

I don't know if Carlotta has heard me, since she's begun speaking in dialect with another of the women about, I think, the imminent birth of the baby. But perhaps it's not that, since their faces demonstrate sorrow rather than happy anticipation. Carlotta excuses herself, rises, and together with another woman leaves the dining hall. I take a moment to look about the room. To study the people. Never have I seen or imagined anything like this. Like them. I hear the woman called Olga telling Fernando that thirty-four widows are presently in residence in the villa. Further, she tells him that during the harvests of wheat and grapes and olives, twenty or more women from neighboring villages join the widows in their work. Day by day, she says, the thirty-four resident women perform all the cooking, baking, preserving, serving, cleaning, scrubbing, polishing, sewing, mending, washing, ironing, and the tending of flower, herb, and vegetable gardens, as well as the tending of the courtyard animals. She says that the household presently counts well over half a hundred souls within its walls. Fernando asks about the men who live here.

"*Adesso ci sono ventidue uomini.* Now there are twenty-two men who live and work here, but, like the women, their numbers increase during the harvests, the threshing, the sowing, the olive pressing, the winemaking seasons. They care for the fruit orchards, see to the dairy cows, the cattle, work the land. Some tend the small herds of sheep and goats and pigs. During this season, baskets of food are brought to the men who work the land farthest from the villa, but you'll see them all at table this evening," Olga explains. "The men you see here now are mostly all full-time gardeners."

"Gardeners, and also the artisans who work at the restoration of the villa," says another of the women.

"And there are always one or two itinerant artisans who come to our table each day. The shoemaker spends every other Saturday here."

"And the knife and tool sharpener comes on Mondays."

"The men who come to fleece the sheep."

"And don't forget Furio," says the youngest and perhaps prettiest of the widows.

"Ah, Furio," they say in chorus. All the women laugh and shake their open hands at chest height in a gesture of extreme admiration.

Everyone at the table adds the name of another support player to the list of rotating guests and I'm already wishing the dream would last long enough so that I might know all of them. I like it here inside Tosca's place.

Slowly, the hall is emptying. Each person methodically piles plates and silver onto large trolleys. Some gather whatever food remains on the serving pieces onto sheets of thick white paper, the ends of which they skillfully fold and twist, then pass the goods down to a widow who identifies the contents of each package with a bold black pen. She piles the packages then into wooden fruit crates, which she places on a different sort of wagon or trolley. Everyone knows his or her part in the play. No wasted steps. No wasted time. Two of the men who were at table wheel the marked packages out of the hall and I look after them, wondering the destination of all that beautiful food.

Fernando is still in conversation with Olga, and so—without asking if I might—I begin to take up one of the cloths as I see women doing at other tables. It's Carlotta, back from her mission, who takes it from me, saying I shouldn't bother. I stand awkwardly by until she consents, gesturing for me to take the other ends of a cloth that she has begun to remove. Together we shake and snap and carefully fold the long, magnificently embroidered piece with easy precision. It ends up in my hands, and when she takes it from me, Carlotta smiles. I see that she has been crying.

Pretending not to notice, I ask her, "Where will they take that food?"

"To the church of San Salvatore in the village. At six-thirty each afternoon, the food is distributed to the villagers. Only the people who have need come to take it. I think it's been nearly twenty years since we began this program. In the beginning, *la signora* and Don Cosimo would deliver the food directly to the families, but now that there are so many more, it's become necessary for the families to come fetch it. Actually it's better this way since, before the distribution begins, everyone gathers in the church to say the rosary with Don Cosimo. He blesses them, blesses the food, the angelus rings, and everyone goes home to their suppers. I go to help whenever I can. It's my favorite part of the day."

Carlotta is crying openly now, wiping tears from her thin cheeks with the back of her hand, blotting her eyes with a crumpled handkerchief pulled from the bosom of her dress.

I venture, "Is it the baby?"

"No. No, the baby seems to have decided to rest where she is for a while longer. One of our women is, well, she's very sick. *Lei, non ce la fa.* She's not going to make it."

"*Capisco, mi dispiace.* I understand, I'm sorry," I say and she looks at me, brushing my cheek with the hand that brushed her own so that now my face is wet with her tears. Agata is racing toward us.

"I'll show you to your room now, if you like," she says.

"But we haven't spoken with *la signora* yet, and I don't know if . . ."

"It's all arranged. If you would care to stay, you are welcome. *La signora* will speak with you later about the details. *Venite.*"

Touching Fernando's arm, nodding at him to follow her, Agata leads the way out of the hall, over the uneven stone floor of another hall, and we mount a wide marble stairway. On the third landing, Agata stops.

"*Ecco,*" she says in front of a beautiful if very ruined wooden door. Taking a long, flat iron key from the ring on her belt, she inserts it into the lock, flings the door wide, hands the key to Fernando. "*Buon riposo,*" she says and softly closes the door.

The room meanders over a space larger than our Venetian apartment. There are a series of short corridors, anterooms, and alcoves that are sparsely, artfully furnished with a small bench or an immense sheaf of lavender or a collection of gilt candlesticks set upon a rickety table. Up three steps made of round flat stones, the white-walled space opens upon a high-ceilinged area with a white bed, two winged chairs covered in white linen, a table with a small wrought-iron lamp, an armoire. The tips of the pines in the garden sway and creak in the hot African winds just outside a long, paned open window.

"What do you think?" I ask him.

"Of the room? It's wonderful."

"This *place. These people.*"

"It's all wonderful. As much of it as I can understand, since I still don't know *what* this place is."

"They're all so beautiful. Have you ever seen so many beauties in one room? Did you notice the priest? And Carlotta looks like a China doll. And the woman who was telling you about the place, what was her name?"

"Olga. It was difficult for me to follow her dialect . . ."

"No, I mean she was beautiful, too. Maybe it's only that they all look well and peaceful. Happy. Except for Carlotta, who was worrying over one of the widows who she thinks is dying. Did you know that there's a birthing clinic here?"

"I can't imagine it gets much use, what with the average age of the women being sixty-five or so."

"It's for other women. Women who need help, Carlotta said. Women from the nearby villages. I saw the kitchen, Fernando."

"Yes, you already mentioned that," he says through his thin letter-box smile.

"Enormous. Two fireplaces. And they chant when they cook, too. Do you think we can stay for a while?"

"I don't know. *La signora* may not be willing to extend her pity for more than one night. Besides, this isn't exactly the place that came to mind when we talked about where we'd like to go next. I agree that it's a fascinating sort of retreat, but might it not become difficult to bear all this excess? So many people, so much food, so much mystery. So many roses, for Christ's sake."

"I think this Tosca woman has made a sanctuary rather than a retreat. Actually it's a small universe, contained, utopian in its way, I think. A rarefied refectory and boarding house and working farm where people who want to be together come to live. And, from time to time, to die."

"Was it the kitchen?"

"Was what the kitchen?"

"You're smitten, my love."

"Who's smitten? It's only that this has been a joyful revelation. I mean, this is a society that I would never have believed could exist."

"You walk through a garden or two, wash your face with orange-blossom water, sit down to lunch with fifty Sicilian widows, all of whom wear their hair in braids, and you've been transformed. I know that look. It's the same one you get after you've been to the Rialto. I saw it for the first time when we were in the water taxi on the way to the airport. That time you were smitten with me."

"Thirty-four. Thirty-four widows live here. Are you jealous of thirty-four widows?"

"More confused than jealous. I thought it was only Venice and I who could affect you so. Please don't tell me you want to begin braiding your hair and wearing black."

"I'd make a fine widow."

"I thought you made a fine bride."

We undress, fold down the covers, and fall upon the bed.

"Did you see that emerald necklace she wore?"

"What emerald? Who?"

CHAPTER III

THE WHINNYING OF HORSES, THE HOLLOW, EVEN CLUMPING OF
hooves upon stone awaken me before dawn. More spent than we'd
realized, we have slept through our first evening at the villa. I go to
the still open window and look down to see two men formally
dressed for riding. I think one of them is the priest, and as I look
more closely, I see that perhaps the other person is not a man at all
but Tosca herself. Branches of pine and the barely thinning darkness
conceal them, making a conspiracy of their soft voices. They mount
and ride off. Taking on the clandestine flavor of the scene, I wash and
dress and, with my boots in hand, tiptoe along the narrow corridors,
through the alcoves to the door. Furtively I open and close it. Put on
my boots. And now?

   I walk downstairs and outside and follow perfumes of wood
smoke to the bakehouse. The ovens must have been lit hours ago but
there is no sign of rising bread here. No sign of a baker. On the worktables there are flat pans of skinned pistachios and almonds, a bowl
of yellow raisins and one of glistening crystallized clementines. What
must be two kilos of butter in a stoneware crock. A tin of dark sugar.
A jug of olive oil, a two-liter bottle of black rum, and a kilo-bar of
pastry-maker's chocolate. Pastry-making day. Sweet Jesus, I'm back

inside the dream. If I could find a few eggs, I could put together a pair of clementine tarts drizzled with rummed black chocolate, a batch or two of pistachio biscotti, a few olive oil cakes stuffed with almond paste. Nearly snorting with covetousness, I look up and down the gravel paths hoping to see where the widows might be but there is no one. Surely they're in the kitchen. As I start up the path I hear their chanting floating up from the villa garden. I turn back.

Bending into the fountain, a group of widows are washing their hair. Washing one another's hair. Laughing, screaming, they pour jugs and pitchersful of cold water over foaming heads, and the scents of lemon and neroli are sharp and strong. Heads swathed in thick white towels, they go to join the other widows who stand near the magnolia in two long rows, each one braiding the hair of the widow in front of her. Pulling combs and pins from apron pockets, their fingers fly, slicing swift perfect parts, pulling, twisting the hair into braids and coils and mounting them, fastening them into loops and crowns. When the hair of the widow who is first in line is finished, she goes to the back of her line to work on the hair of the last widow. When they are finished, they sign the cross on one another, take up their chanting, and disperse every which way to whatever work is theirs. The ceremony has taken perhaps ten minutes and, like a Mass, every movement had significance. Though they'd noticed that I stood quietly just beyond, only now do they greet me. One wants to take me into the dining hall for breakfast; another asks after Fernando. I would like to have my hair braided. Looking from one to another of them, I ask the question, but they are all speaking at once and do not hear me. I take hanks of my hair and begin twisting it, asking the question again with my eyes and, without a word, one of the widows takes my hair in her hands, pulls it and me out of the fray, and sets to work. Fearing I am too tall for her to easily reach the top of my head, I want to ask if I might sit for the operation, but her solution is to stand behind me, to pull my head sharply down and back, curving my torso to her working height. Silently I submit. Chanting, she parts my hair with the side of a thumbnail; chanting, she yanks and plaits and twines the hair, riveting each braid to my scalp with a long, sharp pin. Still chanting, she rubs something waxy or oily between and over the braids and comes to stand in front of me. I straighten myself to face her and she says, *"Bellissima,"* and summons the few others who are still nearby to look at me. There is gleeful and positive accord. I don't say that my temples are so taut that I see double or that I feel twenty head wounds where the pins went in. All I say is thank you as they sign the cross over me, lead me into the dining hall. I like it here, I say to myself. I say it over and over again.

I sit and drink the bowl of good coffee that a widow pours out from shoulder height, French style, from a white porcelain pitcher at the same time she pours steaming milk. The potion splashes a little on my fingers, and I lick the hot, creamy stuff, suck the burn away. Thick slices of wood-roasted bread are piled into baskets, pots of butter and jams and preserves of every color and texture line the tables. I break my toast into small pieces and dip them into the coffee and look about to see if there is someone whom I recognize from the afternoon before. Where is Tosca? I find myself wondering this as though the scene could not be complete without her. This surprises me. I wander back out into the garden, where two groups of widows have set up 'round worktables. At one, four widows are sewing by hand the final stitches and hems upon what look like ball gowns or some sort of fancy costumes. When I ask about them, they say they are making their "final" dresses. Elegant, ornate, they would never permit themselves such dresses in life. In death, though, well, that's another matter, they say. There is ebullient discourse and a trading of prayers and chants with the widows at the second table.

There the widows sit with bushels of artichokes, the six- or eight-inch stems of which have already been trimmed and peeled. The great, round thistles are wonderful to see. Holding them by the stems, the widows slice away the evil points of the leaves with short, sharp knives, then whack the things against the large, flat stones that each one has by her work space. With a single fierce twist of the knives, they remove the chokes, stuff the empty maws with fistfuls of mint pulled from a great pile of it in the center of the table. Standing behind the mint, one widow has been smashing endless heads of purple-skinned garlic and smearing the paste into a marble bowl. The others take heaps of it onto their knives and rub it into the mint, onto the inner surfaces of the artichokes. Tightly packed into shallow pans then, the stems all pointing one way. Swirls of good green oil, a shower of sea salt, splashes of white wine, lemons—sliced thinly— heaved over all so that almost nothing of the green shows through. So many lemons. More oil. But sparingly this time. I am breathless at the ease and speed and beauty of their motions. Other widows come to collect the artichoke-filled pans—two widows to each pan—to carry them off to the ovens. I step forward to ask if I might help with the transport. Smiles. Back-handed fluttering of fingers. I should be waking Fernando, bringing him some coffee, but I don't want to miss a moment of any of this. I tell myself he'd prefer to sleep as I follow the artichokes to the kitchen.

I try to count the widows who move about there, but they move so swiftly and look so much alike that I can't say. Twenty perhaps. Weren't some of them just in the hair-braiding lines? Twenty pirate headdresses, forty hands, twenty registers of chanting, praying. I watch as the first pan of artichokes is shoveled into the oven of the wood-burning stove and then move along the back wall closer to one of the fireplaces where a widow is shaping flat breads, baking them on hot stones laid in the embers, stacking them into cloth-lined tubs. In the hearth at the other end of the room and over a much quieter, barely burnishing fire, terra-cotta dishes of wine-soaked lamb are set down among the embers, covered with inverted lids over which more embers are shoveled, so that by supper time, the flesh will be charred and smokey, velvety enough to eat with a spoon.

Two men carry in bushels of eggplant. Long, slender, tight-skinned purple ones with leaves and stems intact. I think they say something like *let us know if you'll need more, otherwise we'll leave them for tomorrow.* Long, slender, tight-skinned, *just-harvested* eggplants. A quick rinse in the baptismal font, then onto the worktable to be dried, stems trimmed. Leaving them whole but making deep cross-hatch cuts over the entire surface of them, the widows roll the eggplants in a bin filled with a blend of flour, bread crumbs, sea salt, and grated pecorino. They roll and pat and roll again, pressing the dry mixture into each tiny crevice, and then lay the strange-looking beasts onto paper-lined trays, port them across the room to the gas burners where other widows wait to plunge them, a few at a time, into boiling oil, then leave them to float about undisturbed until the inner flesh of the eggplant is softened and collapsing and the outer, exposed flesh and the skin are darkly bronzed and crisped. Pulled out with a skimmer, set back on the paper-lined trays, great crystals of gray sea salt are rubbed between the palms over the blistering-hot things. Whisked off to the dining hall. I will learn that these eggplants are served nearly cold and still crisp with a wild marjoram-sharpened raw tomato sauce. I will learn that they are purposefully not served hot from the pan but left to cool so that the flavors mingle and intensify. Too, I will learn of my alarming capacity to gorge upon them.

I am crazed by now with the need to get in there and cut and pat and plunge myself. I lean fetchingly against the doorway, scuttle about the perimeters of the room, daring to enlarge my advance but never entering the main territory. I am invisible. The widows interrupt their chanting and praying only to laugh or to weep. They pray over each other, over the worktables, over the fires. They pray over the eggplants and the knives and the flat-bread dough rising outside the kitchen door. Incantations, exhortations. Curses. As widows and farmers pass to and fro before me, I ask if there's anything I might do. I ask twelve thousand times. More smiles. More back-handed fluttering of fingers. They don't understand me. I'm sure they simply don't understand. I mount a campaign to communicate with mono-syllabic cries of joy and curiosity and hand gestures of rolling, stir-ring, chopping. This brings two of the widows to where I stand near the door. Gently they push me out into the greater light, look hard at my face. Shaking their heads, they leave me there and go back to work. What is it? What did they see? I am the new girl in town, even with my crown of braids. I start back on the path to the villa, hardly glancing at the pastry-making widows along the way. They'll never learn my *truc* for pistachio biscotti. Nor the one for the olive-oil cake with the heartful of almond paste. I touch my braids. I try out the chant that they sing most often. I sing it louder. It hardly matters not being able to participate. Being here is everything. I do not notice that Tosca stands in the main doorway of the villa as I approach it.

"Are you menstruating?"

Rather than her riding clothes, she wears a lovely black dress made of something like faille, I think, a sheath that ends just above the ankles, no sleeves, her smooth, muscular arms darker even than the tawny skin of her face. Bare feet in silk sabots with a thin, high heel. Coiled and plaited more extravagantly than it was the day before, her hair smells like orange blossoms. The emerald is at her throat. We meet, nearly head-on, as I am entering and she is leaving. Now it's I who doesn't understand.

"Are you menstruating?" she repeats crossly.

"Do you mean right this moment?"

"Yes, right this moment. The women will neither permit you to touch the food nor do they want you to pass through the kitchen. They believe you're menstruating. If you are, your presence will bring down a curse upon the food and perhaps even upon they who are foolish enough to admit you into their sanctum in such a state."

The awkwardness I'd felt moments before has escalated to hot embarrassment.

"That's medieval."

"It's much older than that. Still valid, though. So, are you menstruating?"

"Well, not exactly. Sometimes, lately, my menses are, you know, *irregular.*"

"They could tell by looking into your eyes. I admonish you to please stay out of the kitchen. Here there is no trifling with the sacred."

She walks past me, stops a few meters out into the garden, turns head and shoulders 'round to say, "A chant comes from the back of the throat rather than the diaphragm. It's not at all like singing. You're gorgeous with the braids, by the way."

The least she might have done was to point me in the direction of the red tent, I think as I watch the long black figure of her until she's out of sight. I think further: Here I am twice expatriated. First from America. Now from Venice. Here is like no other place. Once again, I am a beginner.

CHAPTER IV

IT WAS GOOD THAT I HADN'T WORRIED FOR FERNANDO. IT SEEMS that Agata had gone to fetch him soon after I'd left our room. Sat him down to breakfast with some of the men, the second shift on their way to the orchards. The Venetian boy had spent his morning among the almond trees. Made friends with a red-haired farmer called Valentino who is the son of the former caretaker of the villa. Fernando says that Valentino was born at the villa in 1939, that he's lived and worked here for most of his life. Since long before Tosca's era. He tells me all this with a fresh enthusiasm, a rare flush of joy. He takes a breath then, looks at me as though I've just arrived, stretches his lips into the letter-box grin, kisses me hard on the mouth, pulls me in the direction of the dining room. "I knew it," he says fixing his gaze upon my hair.

"Oh, my braids. I have double vision but I love them. I've been banned from the kitchen."

"Excellent. You won't mind so much then that we're leaving after lunch, will you?"

"Why? We've just arrived. Has someone told you we must?"

"No. No one has said a thing. Which is one of the reasons why I think we should go. I still don't know the first thing about this place and it makes me uncomfortable. For instance, what does it cost to sleep and dine here? There are no tariffs posted; there seem to be no other 'guests,' if that's what we are. I have this eerie sense that everyone here was someone else before they arrived. You know, like the island where all bad boys are turned into asses. I expect to look in the mirror and find I've become a crusty old farmer. And you, with the braids, are already halfway to widowhood. Let's get away while we can, my love." He laughs then at his own cleverness. "Besides," he continues, "we've had the rest we needed. Our plan was to *escape* from these mountains. Here we've only gone into a deeper isolation, albeit one where people speak. But it's time to get on with our journey." Another letter-box smile. "I do like the braids."

He's holding me softly by the shoulders and, in his way, making perfect sense. But I'm not going anywhere.

"I saw them making these magnificent eggplant and, for supper, they've braised lamb in the embers of the hearth. Let's ask about the details—the financial ones, I mean—and then we'll see. We'll talk about it again later. Okay?"

"Okay. Okay for the eggplant and the lamb. But no widow's weeds."

"No widow's weeds."

Though no one whom we ask directly answers our questions about tariffs, we stay that day. We stay the next day and the day after that. We never *decide* to stay but simply get caught up in the imperishable rituals and rhythms of the villa. There are bells to wake us, bells that announce prayer and work, bells that summon us to table, back to prayer, back to work. Back to table. A rejoicing, harmonious, sometimes solemn life, the boundaries of acquaintance, friend, and family are as tightly woven as the widows' hair. No one seems to count upon one person's attentions but on the benevolent vigilance of the tribe. They seem to fare well. There are moments that do indeed recall *The Red Tent;* others—especially when Tosca is present—recall *The Leopard.* Most often the scenes are straight from *Cinema Paradiso.*

The unassailable matriarch and protectress of all who rest in her embrace, Tosca holds benign, unconditional sway. Mystery is almost palpable about her. Never appearing at breakfast, she—dressed in the old, exquisitely cut men's clothes she was wearing when we first saw her—rides out to the farthest fields in the early mornings and, when she returns, retires to some private place until nearly noon. Her hair freshly twisted into its coils and loops, she struts about the villa and the gardens in one or another of an endless repertoire of good black dresses, the square-cut emerald hung from a short braided chain of rose gold resting in the hollow at the base of her throat. In the garden or in a corner of the dining hall, Tosca conducts much of the house business with Mafalda, her sister, who is the land overseer, and with the two widows who perform as account supervisor and general house manager. There are always others who join them, those who have been to the village or to Enna or even farther afield and thus have gossip and reportage to offer. They discuss the more efficient production of cheese, the rebuilding of a barn, the reconstruction of yet another unused space within the villa into bedrooms, the wholesaling of the orange crops, the harvesting of *neroli*—the fragile blossoms of the orange tree, for which perfume makers are willing to pay extravagant sums. Always there is talk of food. With delegates from the cooking and baking widows, Tosca writes menus, speaks of what's coming into ripeness in the garden, wonders how to serve the tomatoes that evening, agrees to the collective desire for a Saturday lunch of spit-roasted baby goat pierced with cloves and turned over a fruitwood fire. All 'round them—as it is all 'round every visible, discernable corner of the villa—there is no truce in the mayhem. It's not until the evening hours, after the household has dined, after everyone's work is finished, that the villa settles into a pearly kind of quiescence. It's then that Tosca hosts a sort of open house.

Villagers climb the hill to the villa to join the householders. Hair neatly tucked under kerchiefs, fresh aprons over their work clothes, the women come up to sit under the pergola with Tosca and the widows while their men, Sunday-best wool vests buttoned against the sultry night, come to play cards down in the wine cellar with the farmers. "Just like cream, women always rise to the top," Tosca repeats each evening as the men separate from their consorts.

Most all the women take one of Tosca's long, thin cigars from the proffered box, each one lighting another's, the way the faithful light one another's candles in a procession. The women choose their poison from the bottles lined up on a table on the far side of the pergola. Mostly they pour out whiskey or a potion brewed from honey and lemon verbena into thimble-sized cups, just enough to wet their lips. Sometimes they just sit there in the hot, wet perfume of the sun-crushed jasmine, smoking and sipping, not wanting or needing to talk. When they do speak, it's nearly always about men. About falling in love and making love and professing love, about the difference between infidelity and disloyalty. Sometimes they sing the same song I'd heard the widows singing on the first morn-

ing we arrived. The one about grief and rapture. When they're finished—for the moment—with talking about men, they speak of
their children.

A woman called Nuruzzu speaks of her worries for her just-
married daughter.

"She's a woman. Like a chameleon does, a woman quietly blends
into all the parts of her life. Sometimes you can hardly tell she's there,
she's so quiet going on about her business. Feed the baby. Muck the
stables. Make soup from stones. Make a sheet into a dress. She
doesn't count on destiny for anything. She knows it's her own hands,
her own arms, her own thighs and breasts that have to do the work.
Destiny is bigger in men's lives. Destiny is a welcome guest in a man's
house. She barely knocks and he's there to open the door. *Yes, yes. You
do it,* he says to destiny and lumbers back to his chair."

As each woman ends her story or her thoughts, they all take up
their chants for a few moments. Then another woman begins.

"Our babies cried when we left them and we cry when they leave
us. Echoes. Proud almost to arrogance then, we pushed them about
in their carriages. Dutifully, wearily now, they push us about in our
chairs."

"Our children don't know us as we are now. Less do they know us
as we were. Oh, how I wish they could have known us as we were. Do
you think they would recognize their young selves in our young
selves? I wish they could have seen us in all our clumsiness and selfishness, which is so like their own clumsiness and selfishness right
now. There's another echo for you."

"We believed the fairy tales we told our children and we loved
them beyond reason even when we were green and bungling about

it. We were children loving our children. And that's, who we are still."

Rather than meeting in the pergola, one evening all the women gather in and near the door to the birthing room. Though I don't understand the reason for the change of venue, I follow along, walking more or less alone. The birthing room is positioned in a first-floor wing of the villa that I've not yet seen. Not at all the clinical space I'd imagined, the room seems more a chapel, save the hospital beds and a few practical accessories. Long, wide windows with heavy silk curtains are open to the soft night. A gently lit *Tiziano* Saint Anne—Roman saint of expectant mothers—hangs on one ochre wall and a reproduction *Raffaello* Madonna who cradles her sleeping son against her red-robed breast hangs next to it. A small, ruined marble Demeter, Greek goddess of fertility and motherhood, stands on a pedestal in front of the two paintings. Passive against contrast or contradiction, the widows' reverence of and familiarity with these three images is equally fervent. They chant and pray and bless one another. "We are all women," Nuruzzu says to me, saying everything.

In the far and darkened corner of the room, two beds, side by side, are occupied. In groups of two or three, the widows go to the beds and speak softly to the women who lie in them. Once again, they chant and pray and then quietly move on so the next group of widows can make their visit. I wait for Nuruzzu to come back to the place where I stand in front of the paintings and the statue and then walk out of the birthing room with her. Without my asking her to, she tells me the story of the two women in the beds.

One is a widow called Cosettina, she begins. Already I am confused that a widow lies in the birthing room, but I say nothing.

Cosettina has lived at the villa for ten years or more and, along with her kitchen duties, she held informal classes for those other widows who had never learned to read or write. And for those who enjoyed sitting of an evening while Cosettina read aloud. Cosettina had been a schoolteacher in Enna for much of her life. And a friend of Tosca's for longer than that. If not her desire for it, her capacity to work had been steadily decreasing over the past year. Fainting spells. Mild heart attacks. One attack that was not so mild. *Dottoressa* Rosa, the young *Palermitana* who'd come to practice general medicine in the mountains, diagnosed, medicated, watched over Cosettina with hope until a few weeks earlier when, after other episodes and complications, she told Tosca it was time for Cosettina to be transferred to the hospital in Enna. Cosettina refused to leave the villa. And Tosca agreed. It was "at home" where Cosettina would wait for death. A room was arranged for her close to the dining hall so, with her door open, she would feel almost as though she were dining with the household. Tosca and the other widows lavished Cosettina with love. She became their collective child, each of them spoon-feeding her, surprising her with a sweet. With a flower. Each evening, by candlelight, they bathed her shrunken limbs with soft cloths and warm olive oil. Dressed her like a doll in embroidered shifts and tied her braids up with ribbons cut from someone's old pink nightdress.

On the day we'd arrived at the villa, Cosettina was very near the end of her life. I understood that it was Cosettina for whom Carlotta had cried that first day. Nuruzzu explained that the widows took turns keeping vigil over her through each night. And that *Dottoressa* Rosa continued her daily visits. When Tosca took her turn by

Cosettina's bed, Cosettina used the occasion to lobby for one more move.

"Let me be in the birthing room," Cosettina had asked Tosca. "Let me stay there. It won't be long and I'll be quiet about my leaving. No fuss. Nothing. I promise. I want to give up my old soul to the next baby who'll be born here. I think it's just that you let me be there."

I guess Cosettina had been expecting Tosca to refuse or at least to put up a fight but, Nuruzzu said, this morning she was carried to her bed in the birthing room where she would lie in company with St. Anne and Demeter and *la Madonna* herself. And in the next bed, a young village woman called Viola awaited the birth of her first child. Both women were approaching their time, said Nuruzzu.

After the visit to the birthing room, all the women stood or sat or milled about the garden. Tosca passed about the cigar box, saw that refreshments were served, and then walked past where I stood with Nuruzzu and some others and went back into the villa. When she returned only a few moments later, she quietly announced that Cosettina had gone. All was peaceful, she said. And, by the way, she said, Viola's daughter, though she had not yet consented to appear, seemed to be making preparatory motions in that direction. Tosca passed among the women quietly, inviting all of them into the dining hall to say the rosary together for Cosettina. The men were called in to join us. Electricity is little used in any case at the villa, but that evening Tosca called for the lights to be spent, for the candles to be lit. She shut certain windows, opened others, turned the mirrors to face the walls. Finally she sat, and someone began saying the beads. Partway through the third group of Hail Marys, a shuddering wind blew through the long cavern of a room, and Tosca smiled.

"*Ciao, Cosettina. Ti voglio tanto bene.* Good-bye, Cosettina. I love you very much."

No one had been crying until then, at least not so you could hear it. But by now they were all crying. Sobbing and weeping and repeating the same farewell to Cosettina. There was so much noise about us that it's a wonder we heard that first great squealing, screeching bellow from the birthing room. Viola named her daughter Cosettina.

The next day is Saturday. Long awake, I lie in bed waiting for the light. Waiting for the angelus. Rather than its jaunty clanging out into the mists, a fretful, tinny bell whines. For Cosettina. And with the lament still riding the air, there came then a jubilant thundering of bells. For Cosettina.

There are fewer people at breakfast, since some have ridden or walked into the village to hear the funeral mass at San Salvatore. Many of those who remained have set to work, in one way or another, preparing for the baptismal ceremony that will take place at noon. In these mountains, there is time lost neither in sending off a soul to paradise nor in washing a new one clean for its walk upon earth. Everything is taut, clear. Embraceable.

I rise to leave the breakfast table but then stay put. Antonio Banderas is walking my way. Walking past me. He smells of yeast. A widow rushes toward him and says, "*Ah, Furio. Hai già finito? Vieni a mangiare qualcosa adesso.* Have you finished already? Come to eat something now."

The itinerant baker. So Antonio Banderas roams the Madonie mountains pretending to be an itinerant baker. A magnificent cover.

Where else, how else, could he find peace from that grappling Melanie Griffith? In a thin white T-shirt, jeans, work boots, a black cotton stocking cap covers his hair, stops just above the Arab eyes.

Until now I'd wondered why the household needed another baker.

I sit back down, lean on my elbows, drum the fingers of one hand slowly on my cheek. Carlotta comes to sit with me.

"Have you met Furio?" she wants to know.

I smile and shake my head, and she begins to tell me about him. Says that he arrives before dawn each Saturday, descends upon the villa in a sputtering *cinquecento,* trailing a wagon that holds his kneading machine and sacks of the only flour with which he will bake. Stuff that is raised and water-milled by a friend near Caltanissetta. Like a holy relic, she says, he keeps a glass jar of furiously bubbling yeast on a black velvet cushion on the seat next to him. Conflicting emotions play upon Carlotta's face, and I think she sits here with me speaking of the baker as a distraction. I move my chair closer to hers. She says that Furio travels about the most remote of the villages and hamlets, wherever an old stone oven has survived. He is hosted in each place, she says. Paid a pittance for his labors if he is paid at all. He dines and sleeps wherever he stops to bake. A folkloric kind of saint, she calls him. Of course he has a woman in every village, she says. Children, too, she thinks. Though not here, she assures me, sweeping her arms wide. At least his women have good bread and they see their man— happy and loving and gentle—once a week. I think it's more than many women have, she says.

"Are you faring well? Fending for yourself, are you?" she asks.

"I'm fine. Fernando, too. Though I do feel, you know, in the way a bit. All these *family* events."

"Yes. Of course. It's why no one asked you to come along this morning. An awkward moment for you. But . . ."

Carlotta stops. Looks down at the pattern of red roses and green leaves stitched onto the tablecloth. Traces it with a forefinger.

"I've just come from Mass. Actually, I always feel just a little ashamed of myself when I go to a funeral. No matter how I try to prevent it, there always comes that moment when I say—even through the sincere weeping for the one who is gone—*I'm fine. It's she who's gone. It isn't me there in the fine polished box. It's okay. It will never happen to me. The world will end before it will happen to me.*"

"Unless it's our own child who's gone, I think we all cheer silently for our own survival. It's nothing to be ashamed of."

She doesn't seem to have heard me.

"Only once. A very long time ago. There was a funeral during which that moment never arrived. Only once."

I stay quiet.

"I do hope all of this, all of us, won't drive you away. I mean, please do stay a while longer. You will, won't you?"

"Of course she's staying." Tosca has approached the table from behind us. She walks to the other side of it, comes to sit across from us. A widow brings her coffee.

"I've noticed that you are enamored with the frescoes in this room. Am I right?"

"I guess I do look up a great deal when I'm here," I concede.

"I've been meaning to invite you to come see them in the early evening light. The colors somehow become softer *and* more intense as the sun shifts. At this time of year, I think they're loveliest at about six or so. You're welcome to take a look."

At least there is no fear of menstruating women laying waste the plump-flanked, rolling-eyed gods and goddesses under the shifting sun. "I would like that. Thank you."

Tosca and Carlotta must have things to discuss. I excuse myself. The truth is not that I'm so sensitive to their needs as I am to my own. I feel uncomfortable in Tosca's presence. There's an austerity to her that seems so out of place here. Her gaze pierces, unnerves. And yet, as I'd felt from the first day, unless she's near, something always seems missing.

CHAPTER V

IN HIS CONVINCING GUISE AS RURAL PRIEST, IT IS, MOST UNEX-
pectedly, Christopher Plummer who seeks us out most often at table,
who stops me in the halls on my way to and from our room to ask
after my comfort.

"Would you like to see the chapel?"

"La signora and I will be in the blue salon at four, if you'd like to join us for tea."

"I would be pleased to show you the library."

"Do you ride?"

When Don Cosimo corners me for a moment or two, it's always
to trill out some Ciceronian jewel about the history of the villa.
When it was built. That its principal architect was a descendent of
the designer of the fifteenth-century hospices in the Burgundian
town of Beaune. That its particular architectural amalgam of
fifteenth-century rural French and seventeenth-century Italian mo-
tifs makes it rare. Perhaps unique. The priest seems eager to speak.
He invites me to join him in the gardens where he reads every afternoon at five under the magnolia tree. Promises that it's there and
then that offers the only quiet hour of daylight about the villa.

· · ·

As the angelus rings five the next afternoon, Cosimo, like a tall black ship ploughing a calm sea, approaches the table under the magnolia where I sit expecting him. Neither of us says a word of greeting. He settles himself into a chair, pushes out a long sigh through a broad smile, and I slide my green glass bottle of water toward him across the pits and scars of the marble table. He has his own refreshment. In a single swift movement from a place under his skirts, he brings forth a flat, leather-wrapped bottle and loosens its cap. Tilting it to his lips, he takes long, gurgling pulls of something that smells more like spinach or grass than whiskey or wine.

"Pot liquor from boiled chard" are the first words he says as he secrets the bottle back in place.

He has brought no book that I can see. I close mine. Wait. He tells me that he is seventy-six years old. He must know that his face and form demonstrate at least fifteen years less—perhaps twenty less—since he pauses after his announcement, waiting for my compliments. I do not disappoint him. He says he'd been ensconced as the household's resident cleric and as the prince's chauffeur when the prince took Tosca to live in the palace fifty-six years previously.

"This palace?"

"No, no. This is not a palace. Tosca lived in the Anjou palace with the prince and his family. A baroque palace that his ancestors raised up in the middle of endless lemon groves. Hasn't anyone offered to take you there? A few hours' drive from here," he says.

Having yet had little traffic in my long life with castles and villas and hunting lodges and palaces, I have belied the truth to the priest that I am hard put to define their differences. I shall try not to let on, too, that I do not know the fundamental story of Tosca and the prince, which, it seems, he thinks I must have learned through some other auspices. I do recall, though, during that first lunch, Carlotta saying, *La signora inherited the villa from an Anjou prince whose ward she once was.* I shall not tell the priest that I have been privy to anything beyond that piquant admission. I will listen to him. My listening will be rewarded, for I will learn that he has seen everything, that he knows everything, that he remembers everything. I will learn that should there be a fray in that knowledge, in that memory, the priest will work the threads together with the prowess of a Flemish weaver.

"She was, even then, of that splendid arrogance—haughty, proud. She wore thick black braids like a crown. No one was ever certain if she was cursed or blessed, but surely there was something of the sorceress about Tosca. Leo claimed her when, I think, she was nine. Her beauty was already fearsome. It was mostly about her eyes. Pale wet jade they were, and set in skin the color of almonds burnt by the sun. Green eyes so long they seemed to intrude upon the high, sharp bones of her cheeks, and I used to think they were the eyes a mermaid would have. Tosca's eyes were a siren's eyes. Yes, she was ten or maybe still nine when he brought her to live in the palace. A common enough feudal custom, this noble, sanctioned purloining of the children of one's peasants or of anyone else, for that matter, who lived inside or on the fringes of an aristocratic province. It was an honor of sorts for the family of the child and an auspicious stepping-stone for the child herself. Despite any misuse along the way. At the very least the child would be fed and clothed. Schooled. Misuse, the child would know wherever she lived. You might ask, was this custom spurred by goodness? Spurred by lust? The motives fluttered, blended. Who could know one from the other? And so, normally

enough, everyone—including me—believed that the prince had 'requested' Tosca. As it turned out, it was Tosca's father who'd offered
her to the prince. He was a horse breeder. A horse thief, from time to
time, I guess. Anyhow, the prince had a stallion that Tosca's father
wanted more than he did his daughter.

"That morning when the prince went to fetch Tosca—an event
carefully arranged between him and the girl's father—he settled her
in the back of his great open Chrysler, arranged her down in the small
space behind where he and I sat. You see, I was his driver. A young
priest, locally born and freshly ordained from the Jesuits in Palermo,
I'd been taught to drive so I might conduct my bishop to and fro, engagement to engagement. I believe it was my driving skill rather than
my spiritual gifts for which the prince originally requested my presence at the palace and arranged for my posting to San Rocco, the
nearest village church. As confessor-chauffeur, one duty made me
privy to the imperatives of the other. A most efficient use of my time.
In any case, I remember that morning of Tosca's courtly abduction
by the prince. I remember the way she sat there in that little well
of sun-baked leather, a small brown hellion contemplating battle.
When her father leaned, with false affection, into the car to embrace
her, she bit him. Spat at him then with the force and speed of a born
blackguard, and I think that must have been Tosca's first open rebellion. I will tell you that it was not her last. She may not have wanted to
go away with the prince but she most certainly did not want to stay
with her father. In a wide grin of heart-warming vendetta, that
unloved and unloving father then heaved a great bloody sack of birds
and rabbits down onto the thin bare thighs of his little girl. The animals' heads lolled about over the top of the sack and rested on her
chest, the just-killed flesh of them already stinking of rot. Booty signi-

fying his appreciation to the prince for relieving him of the burden of his first-born daughter. A morning's hunt was Tosca's dowry. *And good riddance to you,* he'd said in a voice he thought only Tosca could hear. After all, he had the other daughter—younger, obedient, if not as beautiful as Tosca. The younger one would take decent care of him. Carry and fetch and muck. She was more likely to stay quiet in the night. Of course, if Tosca's mother had been alive . . . but that's another story.'"

The priest is quiet then. Considering, I think, "the other story." How things might have been if Tosca's mother had not died.

"Though I've told this story before, it was a very long time ago. I'm not even certain if it was only to myself that I told it. Shall I proceed?" he asks, looking at me as though I've just arrived.

It's he who had bid me here; it's he who has begun, unprompted, to speak of the past, and yet it's I—as I have at almost every juncture of these days here at the villa—who feels like the encroacher. Still, the truth is that I do want him to proceed.

"Only if you wish to," I tell him.

He closes his eyes.

"When we arrived, the prince relieved the little girl of her bloodied sack—the cruel placement of which he'd not seen before—and threw it to the ground. He lifted Tosca from her seat, wiped her dress with his handkerchief, and, as though she were a lady he was courting, showed her the way through the palace gardens. Oh, those gardens. A beguiling commotion of roses and lilac and wisteria and camellia grown so entwined as to seem all of the same root, it was a garden where bronze goddesses spat water from the nipples of their high, proud breasts and where the upper branches of oaks were fanned by the drooping fronds of old palms. It was there that Tosca would be schooled, with the prince's daughters, by a French governess. Tosca of the pale green eyes and the Saracen skin would be tamed, formed. Refined. But it would be a long time before much princely sway took hold of her.

"Days after her arrival at the palace, Tosca scaled the lemon-grove walls, took herself a horse from the stable—a just-broken mare who'd never been ridden, or so the grooms would later tell the story. She mounted her bareback. Tosca was bent on her father's place to fetch her goats. And, as it turned out, to gift her little sister the new black boots with the buttons up the side and the now torn, horse-sweat-smelling white silk pinafore she'd been dressed in that morning by a maid called Agata. Even though Tosca knew these undreamt-of treasures would be far too big for her little sister, she wanted her to have them. Amulets for the future, I think. And maybe proof of her love, though surely Mafalda must already have had rich evidence of it.

"Barefoot then and wrapped in her dead mother's housedress, Tosca rode dutifully back to the palace, her goats—which Mafalda feared and loathed—trailing along on ropes held tight in her hand. Tosca knew it was the palace where she must stay at least for a while. Until she could finesse some other plan. Besides, the palace was flush with spoils to pillage for Mafalda. That was reason enough for Tosca to stay. She watered and fed the horse, closed the stable door. Tethering her goats, for the moment, to the ankles of one of the nipple-spitting goddesses, Tosca wiped her face with a handful of fallen magnolia blossoms—a beauty secret learned long ago from her mother—and presented herself on the veranda in time for lunch."

I needn't have worried about my perceived encroachment since the priest seems to have, once again, told the story to himself.

"It all sounds familiar somehow," I say. "It's *Lampedusa,* if with more *tenderness.*"

"Familiar? I hope it's familiar. It's the human story, which repeats itself endlessly if only to prove that the past is not dead. That the past wears different costumes. Sometimes. Especially in *Sicília*. There's always a prince and a palace. Always a priest. And there's always a girl. The protagonists are eternal. With each performance the characters proceed as if they were the first ones to ever act it out. As if they didn't know how the play would end. Yes, shades of *Lampedusa*. It was he who said that all lovers play the parts of Romeo and Juliet as though the facts of the poison and the tomb had been concealed from them. He reminds us of the power of lust over the misery it can bring about. Yes, *Lampedusa*. Among others."

He looks at me then, says, "Time has obliged Tosca. Her face is much as it was on the day when I drove the prince to fetch her from her father save that now she is more lovely, more terrifying. More lovely and more terrifying than she was at eighteen or than she was on the night when I brought her the prince's riding jacket."

He says this last in a voice that comes from farther away. I don't understand about the riding jacket.

"When was that? When was it that you brought her the prince's riding jacket?"

He rises gingerly, as though in pain, steadies his hands on the table. He says, "It was long ago and in another life. Maybe in a dream."

I think that Christopher Plummer has long been in love with Tosca.

Wanting to keep him, I say, "*Lei é una creatura affascinante.* She is a fascinating creature. Did you love her, too?" I look down at my hands, the last words slipped out in a whisper.

"Sometimes an 'unlived' love can be the best kind of love. One has only to put a face to love to be happy in it. It's not knowing who your love is or where to find her that makes for madness. Having been her best friend, witness, confidante, advocate since she was ten years old, I will say that, yes, in my fashion, I was in love with her. I might say that I am in love with her still."

CHAPTER VI

I DON'T RECALL WHETHER IT WAS ON THE EVENING OF THE SAME day that Cosimo told me his story or an evening soon afterward when I'd decided to accept Tosca's invitation to see the frescoes in the changing light. I know it was a Friday, and that Fernando and I had set the next morning as our departure.

When I enter the dining hall at six she is there sitting by a spent hearth, a book opened on her lap. We greet each other, she resumes her reading, and without further discourse, I begin my tour. I wander about the vast room, head thrown back, marveling at the exalted beauty of the frescoes in the softer light. I stay for perhaps twenty minutes, during which time we say nothing more. I want to ask her about the artists, the epochs of the work. About the allegories themselves. About why there are so many blank spaces in the frescoes. I stay silent, though, sensing she is a reluctant docent. Lost in a last look, my back turned to Tosca, an Italian voice speaking in rather tentative English asks, "Do you drink gin? I have some good Genever gin if you'd like me to fix you a drink. It's about that time, isn't it? I mean for you English."

Perplexed, I stay fixed, my back still turned to Tosca. And to the voice. It can't be her speaking and yet, as I turn to her and understand that it *is* she, I begin to laugh.

"Why didn't you tell me you could speak English?"

"Why should I have done that?" she asks in mock smugness. "I also speak French and read in Greek. What's more I dance and sing, play the pianoforte. I've yet to tell you about any of those accomplishments. I neither felt nor do I feel now the need to impress or comfort you with the sound of your own language. We *are* in Sicily, after all. I simply wanted a gin tonic and thought you might, too. That I offered it to you in your own language was fairly involuntary. An impulse."

She speaks English splendidly. A Sicilian contralto singing the role of a Berkshire matron, I think. "Did you once live in England?"

"No. Never. I've never set foot off the island even once in my life."

She says this with neither pride nor regret and leaves no pause for my response. I find it curious, though, that she answers much more than my question asked. She proceeds. "I studied English and French when I was young and have read the nineteenth-century English writers over and over again for most of my life since. I don't like them in translation."

"I see. Actually, I'm not English but American, and I prefer vodka."

"I have that, too."

She rises, walks her mannish walk to a far corner of the *salone,* pauses before a narrow armoire, the rough wood of it painted a pale yellow-green like the heart of a celery. She opens its doors to reveal a bar—mirrored, upholstered in midnight-blue velvet—that would rival the lobby bar of any good small hotel in Manhattan or Vienna or Rome. From a small black enamel refrigerator she takes a bottle labeled in red Russian script. With a heavy hand, she pours from it into a cut crystal wineglass. Offers it to me.

"I have no ice," she says without apology.

"I don't take ice," I tell her in an icy tone. Tosca's refined scorn has something of mockery about it this evening. A stylish disdain that causes mine. She putters about with her gin tonic while I stand behind her. She turns to me, then raises her glass.

"To your health, *signora*," she says. Once again that counterfeit gentility.

"*Alla vostra salute, signora,*" I wish back at her. One less cube in my voice.

We remain standing, looking at each other, appraising each other. I suppress a laugh. At myself, at her. At us standing in the *salone grande* of a glorious villa set among the barren mountains at the center of an island where only the past seems present. A black faille sheath, an emerald at her throat, long brown fingers twined about the Baccarat stem, she sips and I think she, too, wants to laugh. At me, at my jeans, my three-day-old T-shirt, my great head of hair, once again unshackled. She walks back to her chair and motions for me to sit across from her.

"I rather do like speaking in English. I haven't done so in years. I fear all that's left are phrases from Dickens or the Brontës which, by now, I can parrot. I don't know if I could find the words for a spontaneous conversation with you, but I might like to try."

"But I think we'll be leaving tomorrow or the day after . . ."

She steps quickly, resolutely, upon what she does not want to hear. "Yes, of course, you're right. We'd only just have begun and then off you'd go."

As further proof of her Anglo-Saxon penchants—or only to prolong the moment—she says, "There's a *New York Times Magazine* over there in the top drawer of that console. Perhaps you would like to look at it."

"Thank you. I'll take it up with me if you don't mind," I tell her, and go to fetch it from the tall French Empire chest she indicates.

"Ah, here it is. Lovely," I say but notice how faded, wrinkled it is. I look at the date. January 1969.

Now I do laugh. "But *signora,* this is a museum piece."

Resuming Italian, she says, "Not at all. What do you suppose has changed in twenty-five years or so? I found the journal to be well written back then when someone or other left it behind. I thought it set things out rather nicely, addressing the events of the day, which are, of course, the same events of this day. Think of it. Even if its theater and its motives are being played out in a different geography, there's still war, isn't there? Still avidity and hate and violence and fear. Poverty and righteousness are still thriving. As are revolution and arrogance and lies. There is always perversion and torment, of course. What I particularly admired about this paper was the shrewd touch of pathos and poignancy strewn among the squalor and the filth. You know, The Good News. So, should I wish to be informed of events outside these mountains, I read *The New York Times Magazine.* I've perhaps reread it every two or three years just to be certain I've not missed anything. I have also been known to thrash about in that same console where I keep a Sony television. Black-and-white and with its own antenna and a twenty-two-centimeter screen on which, should nostalgia move me, I can view the nightly news broadcasts from Rome or Milan. As I might an old movie. But unlike when I watch an old movie, the news broadcasts leave me empty, angry, and I must tell myself yet again that one need tune in only once in a lifetime to the nightly news to know the chronic story of man. To know how wrong the world is. How *wronged* it is. I don't hide from the wrong. Surely I don't deny it. It's only that the wrong has yet to find its way up here. And I do my best to confound its path."

Still standing with the magazine in my hand, I say, "I do appreciate the thought, *signora.*"

I turn back to the "media chest," open the archival drawer, and gently replace the magazine, then return to my chair across from hers.

I understand that her device is sarcasm and that her message is visceral. The past is the present. The human condition endures. A venomous reading of Cosimo's same dictum. Perhaps I prefer his. We say nothing. I look at her, wondering why I resist her. The authenticity of her. The wisdom. She repels me. She enchants me. There is so much sadness just beneath her skin. Like so many of us, perhaps she is greedy about her sadness. And the scorn, the mockery, are confines that she sets out to protect it.

We are still silent when three widows enter to set the table for dinner and Tosca, distracted by their presence, perhaps dismayed by it, begins to fidget with her glass, smooths her perfect corona of braids. Smiles fitfully. I rise, place my drink, unfinished, on a small table, and thank her. Tell her I've some work to do before dinner.

As though she hasn't heard me, she asks, now reverting again to English, "Have you brought other clothes? Something elegant, I mean."

"A nice dress. Gray tulle." I tell her, wondering why she would be interested in my wardrobe.

As though "nice gray tulle" did not signify *elegant* to her, she says, "Maybe I have something that Agata could fix up for you. In fact, I think I do. Sometimes we have outside guests to supper and we all dress up a bit."

"As I said, I believe we'll be leaving tomorrow . . ."

Again, she will not hear what she does not want to hear. "It's not often there's someone new to present, you know."

"*Agata, vieni qua, tesoro.*" Agata arrives trotting, breaking only long enough to take her orders to look at whatever's left in the trunks in the old dressing room. And to take me with her.

Trunks? Dressing room? I follow Agata up three flights of wide, worn stone stairs. At the top we follow a corridor scented with mold to enter a room furnished all in armoires and dressers and trunks, accessorized here and there with mousetraps, those sprung, those still baited. The mold is masked by the perfume of decaying rodent. Backstage at some decrepit theater. Agata bends into and riffles through a large trunk. I see only her prosperous black-silked derrière and hear her mutterings and beseechings to the Madonna. Holding up some sort of dress or gown in what might be a silvery-brown color, she declares it *quella giusta*. The right one.

"*Spogliati*, take your clothes off," she commands.

Moments later, wearing what must have been a lovely pre-war tea gown, I am being twirled about by Agata. The bodice is too tight and the skirt is too long, but Agata begins a ruthless pinching of the seams, roughly gathering the hem and draping it here and there, telling me to hold it exactly the way she places the stuff in my hands. She stands back for the effect.

"*Non é male*," she says. "*Potrebbe essere molto carino.* Not bad. It could be very sweet."

So abruptly disturbed after its long repose that, when I let go of it, there are two large, jagged holes in the fine old tea gown where my hands had held it. This time Agata calls upon Santa Rosalia.

"*Toglilo adesso e dammelo.* Take it off now and give it to me," is the next command. Still zipping my jeans, smoothing my hair, I run to catch up with Agata, who has the wounded silvery-brown thing under her arm, but she disappears down one corridor or another, and when I arrive back at the dining hall, Tosca is no longer there among the widows who prepare the tables.

Later, as we dress for dinner, I tell Fernando of my visit to see the frescoes and of Tosca's thoughts about current world events. I tell him that she spoke to me in English.

"After all these days—how long has it been, nearly two weeks that we've been here?—what do you think of Tosca? What will be the impression you leave with tomorrow?" I want to know.

I'm crisscrossing the thin suede ropes of my new black sandals 'round my ankles, my calves. I've also taken out the gray tulle ballerina dress that has been rolled up in my lingerie bag since Venice. A shawl. Tosca's question about my clothes has inspired me.

"First of all, I don't think we'll be leaving tomorrow after all. When I went to settle up our account just a few moments ago, she reminded me that *ferragosto* is not the prudent time to be on the road. She's right, of course. Whatever direction we take, we'll be among the raging hordes of vacationers. She says that in a few days, perhaps another week, the roads will be clear. Even the weather is due to break, according to her."

I hobble on one sandaled foot into the bathroom, sit on the edge of the tub behind where he shaves. "So easily has she convinced you to stay for *another week*? It wanted only a traffic report and a weather prediction? Such an easy mark you are."

"Not so. She hardly set out to *convince* me of anything. She only presented additional information that caused me to change my mind. And why are you so dressed up this evening?"

"Tosca. She wanted to know if I'd brought elegant clothes. I thought I'd demonstrate my collection."

So easily has she convinced you, he mimes.

For the next day or two I don't see Tosca, save in purposeful flight about the villa and the gardens or glimpses of her at lunch and dinner. She never stops to mention the state of the silvery-brown tea dress or if or when the outside guests would come to supper. I remain mildly curious about both.

One evening as we enter the dining hall, Agata rushes up to escort us away from our regular places at table, takes us to sit with Tosca and Cosimo. Almost at once, Tosca begins speaking to me in English.

"Have you had a lovely day? Tomorrow will be somewhat cooler."

She tries out little niceties. She asks me if this form or that grammar is correct. Cosimo has commandeered Fernando's attention and I am left to Tosca's will.

"I'd like to tell you a story, Chou," she says. "Oh, I don't mean right now, of course. But soon. It's a long story, you see. I wouldn't be able to tell it to you all at once. It might take a few days. A week. I don't know. But it's a good story, I think. I've never tried to tell it from beginning to end but I want to tell it to you and I want to tell it to you in English. I suppose I'm thinking that if I tell it in a language other than my own I will still feel as though I haven't really told it at all. Does that make sense to you?"

She knows it does.

"I know that Cosimo has been telling you tales out there in the garden every day, and . . ." She smiles. Throws up her hands in a gesture of uncertainty. "Maybe it's just a desire to speak in English while I have the chance. No, it's not that. Not only that. I think it's because you're someone from the outside. Yes, I want to try out my story on someone from another place. I want to tell it to you, *leave* it with you, I guess, knowing that you'll go away. Knowing that your return here to us is *improbable* and, since my preferred method of travel is on horseback, the chances of our ever meeting again in your territory are equally *improbable* . . ."

In the space by the side of her plate, Tosca rolls her napkin into a tight cylinder, then unrolls it, smooths it flat upon the table. She repeats this business several times, then begins rolling it from a single corner, gathering up the other edges and folding them toward the center to fashion a pouch of sorts. A pocket. A place to save her story? I look at her and understand why, a few days earlier, she'd daunted Fernando's resolve to leave. Tourist hordes and traffic notwithstanding, it was because Tosca was not *ready* for us to leave. I recall Fernando's early take on villa life. *I have this eerie sense that everyone here was someone else before they arrived. You know, like the island where all bad boys are turned into asses.*

Why does Tosca want us to stay? Can it really be so that she can tell this story of hers? And if it is, why would she want to tell it to me? Oh, I heard her reasons: I'm an outsider, she won't ever see me again, the story will be told yet remain as though it was never told at all. Still. Perhaps this desire of hers will fall away like the old taffeta of the silvery-brown dress. Perhaps not, though.

The next afternoon, it's Tosca rather than Cosimo who waits for me at the table under the magnolia.

PART II

Tosca's
Story

CHAPTER I

"*SE STAI ASPETTANDO UN RACCONTO DI UNA CENERENTOLA Siciliana . . .* If you're waiting for a story about a Sicilian Cinderella . . ."

"I'm not waiting for any sort of story at all," I say, still standing, uncertain whether I want to stay. "I usually sit with Cosimo at this time. To read, to talk."

From her high-backed white iron chair with the red velvet cushion, she tugs at the less regal one next to it, beckons me to sit. I do. An assent. Into a thin, tall glass she pours out a cloudy stream of almond milk from a small pitcher, adds water from another pitcher, unscrews what looks like a medicine bottle, and with a dropper, doses the whitish swirling mixture with a few drops of neroli. Essence of orange blossoms. She stirs the drink with a long silver spoon, stirs it ferociously, removes the spoon, and lays it, bowl down, upon the table. A high priestess in full ceremony, her movements seem liturgical. She places the glass in front of me.

"The elixir of Sicily. Bitter. Sweet," she tells me. Warns me.

I run my finger along the rim of the glass. I smile at Tosca.

"It's like you, then. Also you are the elixir of Sicily. Bitter. Sweet."

She begins to laugh and, I think, to blush, though it may be only a lozenge of light flitting about the leaves that ruddies her skin.

"I knew you were the right person. I mean, I'm glad you're here. Glad you've landed here. Exactly here."

I sip the drink. I like it and sip it again, feel it caressing the knob in my chest. A tightness I hadn't known was there until now; or is it the one to which I'd grown accustomed over these past few weeks? Longer than that. I turn to Tosca as though it's she who has the answer, but she's busy with her potion. Pouring, stirring into her own glass. She drinks nearly half the drink in one long pull. As though to leave, she rises then, walks a meter or two to where another table sits—a rusted metal one upon which pots of herbs are piled randomly—and plucks, from here and there about them, withered leaves, holding the brown, dry things in one hand, proceeding to purge the plants with the other.

"It just never works," she says, but whether to me or to herself I cannot say. "I mean, trying to domesticate wild herbs."

Surely she is talking about more than the parched marjoram. Walking back to the table where I still sit, she sinks into the faded red cushion of her chair as if into some wreckage, her own wreckage I think, and crushes the dead leaves in her hand, holding out the dust of them in her palm for me to sniff. I oblige, but sense nothing but her own perfume.

Tosca begins.

"I had two childhoods. The first was spent with my family. My mother, my father, and my sister. My sister, whom my mother called *la-piccola-Mafalda,* The Tiny Mafalda—as though it were a single word—from the moment she was born and whom I've been calling the same ever since. When my mother died, my sister and I looked after my father as well as we might have been expected to do at ages five and eight. My father was never much good at looking after anyone save his horses. Save himself. But I was good at it and The Tiny Mafalda was good at it and so, together, we were fine. Fine enough. In our village, eating at least once a day and sleeping less than six to a broken bed and with no one beating or raping you on a regular basis meant you were fine. It was only with the perspective of the next childhood that I began to understand how poor I'd been, how poor my family had been. Not with space or silver or brocade or feather beds did that perspective come. It came with food.

"I'd never understood how hungry I'd always been until the time when I sat at the prince's table and ate and ate until I was full. Oh, that didn't happen on the first day and maybe not in the first week. But I'll get to that.

"I suppose it's true that, on the day when the prince came to fetch me from my father's house, I acted the nine-year-old savage. I know Cosimo told you that. I was using anger and orneriness to cover my fear. Fear of a new devil. My father was the known devil, but who was this smiling yellow-haired devil who spoke in such a soft voice? And then there were his wife and his daughters, another kind of devil. His wife. The princess Simona. Neither kind nor cruel, neither beautiful nor ugly, she was a fluttering presence who interested me far less than did the young princesses, Yolande and Charlotte. They, too, were unlike anyone I'd ever known or seen. They had names I'd never heard. They wore white stockings embroidered with butterflies and white leather shoes tied with satin ribbons and, though they were seven and eight while I'd just turned nine, they seemed to be ages older as they scurried about the grand place with such purpose, curtsying to the tall yellow-haired devil with the soft voice who was their father. As though this family had come from another corner of the earth than mine rather than from across two hills and over a few kilometers of narrow white road; yes, that's how I felt. As though they had come from another corner of the earth. We were geographical neighbors in the way Sicilians are neighbors, and yet one of their more modest drawing rooms was larger than my church, and the house where I'd lived would have been lost in the space of their pantry. And there were so many people. Not just the mother, the father, and the children but cousins, aunts, a governess who spoke even more strangely than the family, a music professor, a Latin professor, an art professor. A priest. Others whom I can't remember now. Everywhere there were servants. And guests in arrival and departure, and so it was like living in the puppet theater I'd once seen at the market in Enna. The constant entrances and exits of splendidly dressed people reciting their lines so perfectly. I watched. I watched them all and, little by little, the savage motherless green-eyed child from the horse farm grew calm. Calm enough to become curious. And then calm enough to dare join in the show myself.

"With bells and gongs and Ave Marias to mark the hours, the household regime was rigorous, compulsory. We three girls were awakened, scrubbed, combed, braided, dressed by a thirteen-year-old maid called Agata. Our Agata. Yes, it was she. The same. You'll get to know far more about Agata.

"The household gathered in the chapel for prayers and benediction at 7:45, breakfasted together in one of the smaller dining rooms at eight. We walked in the garden until nine when lessons began in the schoolroom. At one o'clock the household and guests assembled at table in another of the smaller dining rooms for lunch—a procession of tureens and platters and trays carried 'round by servants amidst the dull chink cut crystal makes as it collides in endless wishes of *salute, salute*. Never risking the bad fortune that comes with crossing arms, each one walked about the table until he or she was certain to have touched everyone's glass at least once. Twice was better. Only the yellow-haired devil stood, unmoving, at his place while all of us went to him. Even the princess Simona seemed *allegra* in her stroll about the table, wishing good health, sometimes patting a face or an arm almost affectionately. I don't recall her ever touching my face back then. I remember a gray dress of hers, though, one sewn with shiny beads at the top, and how her bobbed hair was set in tight waves and how the points of her cheeks went red and how she was almost pretty at that time of day.

"There was a mandatory *riposo* until 4:30, when tea was served in the garden or, in winter, in the schoolroom. Though lessons resumed at five, on some afternoons we girls were allowed to close our books and sit by the fire with our sewing until seven, when Agata came to rescue us, to help us dress for dinner. *Aperitivi* were served in the room where we breakfasted and then we walked, en masse—often more than twenty strong—down the long, dark corridors to the main dining hall.

"In light of the *grande bouffe* that was lunch, dinner seemed penitential—broth, cheese, glaceéd fruits, biscuits. Wine. A common, catching sulk prevailed. A whole day's worth of grievances accumulated, carried to the silk-draped table, passed about like soured milk. Simona had perhaps quarreled with the governess or the governess with the art professor and surely there were dramas among them less perceptible to me. Nevertheless they always seemed to be played out in the evening. I would sit there in my white dress, my braids coiled so tightly above my ears that my head ached, and think how very much the same the event of supper was here at the palace as it had been at home. Always having to worry if my father was angry or why, or if it was I who caused the anger. Worse was wondering if it was I who should be at work making his anger go away. Yet here among this vast polished cast, the game of mea culpa, tua culpa was played out with far more skulk. How I would long to be alone with The Tiny Mafalda in the narrow pallet of a bed that was ours. What price this thin white dress. This supper."

"I had a room in the children's wing, two rooms really; the furnishings, the walls, everything was colored pale yellow and white. Even the floors were yellow and white, great marble squares laid in a pattern that made me dizzy. And a bathroom of my own with a tub big enough to swim in, or so it seemed, though I didn't know the first thing about swimming. I didn't know much about bathing, either. I'd never had a bath in a tub except when my mother would plunk The Tiny Mafalda and me in the washtub out in the garden on the days when the washing water wasn't all that dirty. I missed The Tiny Mafalda.

"There was an alcove behind my bed where Agata slept, and I would talk to her about my sister. Sometimes that helped, but mostly all that helped were the times when I'd run away. Or ride away, back home. I'm sure that Cosimo has told you about my escapes, since I believe they are his favorite memories of me. My escapes and my thievings. Of course, the two were connected. They were connected to hunger, just as I think most crimes are connected to hunger. One hunger or another.

"Every time I sat down at table with the household, all I could think about was my sister. What was she eating for lunch? Was she eating at all? Did my father remember to leave money for her to do the shopping? I was tortured by my worries for her. Time and time again, I would wait until Agata and the rest of the household were napping and then creep out of the bedroom, step lightly down the stairs and across what seemed the immensity of the halls and the corridors and out one door or another, out one passageway or another. Free. Away into the damp, cool respite of the garden. Push open the great creaking gate and don't look back. Now run. Faster. Some sack or bag fastened to me, something good for my sister. It felt fine to run, to sweat, to feel the sack slapping against my leg. Slower, then, when I'd reached the road. Hike the white road, cross the hills back home.

"Not announcing my return as anything extraordinary, I would just pick up where I'd left off, look through the cupboard and in the baskets for whatever there was to cook and get to work. The Tiny Mafalda would be dancing 'round me, kissing me, reaching up to hold me about the waist and squeezing me with all her baby-girl's strength, and I would start in weeping and then she would and then we'd both be laughing and crying and my father would walk in and, without so much as a word from him, or him hearing a word from me, I'd be hurled down onto the bed of his truck and, with Mafalda stamping one foot and then the other on the bottom step of the porch and screaming at him with all her might to let me stay, he'd drive, pell-mell, back across the hills. Back down the white road. Back to the palace.

"After those episodes I knew that my father, having to punish someone, would be even less tolerant of my sister. I would learn that on those evenings he would sometimes eat whatever was there and not offer anything to her. I don't think he ever knew that the first thing Mafalda and I would do on those days when I came back home was to hide the food I'd thieved from the palace. Or did he? And if he did know, is that why he'd finish up the cabbage and the bread and never save a scrap for her? Did he know she was up there sitting on the little pallet, her steady nibbling keeping time with her snuffling?

"Once delivered back to the palace, desperate as only a child can be desperate, I'd take to my bed. Trembling, the raging inside my chest suffocating me until, as if from some faraway place, I would finally hear Agata's voice. Until I would feel the caressing of her cool hands through my wet matted hair. She would peel off my clothes, fill the great tub with water that was always too hot, scald and scrub me red and raw, pull a shift over my head. Lay me down to sleep.

"The next day did not bring my contrition. Truth is, I loved stealing that food to take to my sister. I don't know if it would have felt half so good if the plunder was for me, myself, but stealing for Mafalda was thrilling. I would imagine the light coming on in her big, sad eyes and I'd start right back in with my scheming and thieving. I'd take more. Always more. Oh, it wasn't as though I had to work very hard at collecting the food. Early on, Agata understood what I'd been doing and why, and she and another maid helped me. In a wooden box in the *dispensa* they would hoard cheese, dried sausages, dried fruits. Even two of the cooks became conspirators. Whatever pie or cake or biscuit they baked, they baked a Mafalda-sized version, wrapped it in a fresh white cloth, and into the wooden box it went. Whereas I'd begun by keeping apart some of my bread at each meal and supplementing it with the meager pilfering of the cupboards—a handful of rice tied up in a handkerchief, two potatoes, things like that—it wasn't long before the weekly or biweekly stash was more than I could carry. Additional accomplices rescued me.

"The cooks and Agata arranged with the stableman to let me use one of the horses. A jockey's thin, spare frame under an ancient's brown face, the stableman would be waiting on the west side, the hidden side of the barn, holding the reins of one beauty or another. Saddled, ready. I'd become something of a heroine since the day early on in my palace life when I'd stolen a barely broken mare and ridden her bareback to my father's house. Laughing and smiling and regarding me with an expression of hosannah, the stableman would help me tie down my goods, set me up there on the horse like a small warrior queen, give the hind end of the horse a good whack, yell out his blessing for the journey, and I'd trot off. Around the lemon groves. Down the white road.

"And so my plan to run away, to escape the yellow-haired devil and his candied figs and his Ave Marias and his wife with the beads on her dress and his daughters with the butterflies on their stockings, the plan to escape the palace and return to my life with The Tiny Mafalda was adjusted. If I couldn't yet manage to run away from the palace for good, then my twice-weekly run on a horse to visit Mafalda with food would suffice. I found relative peace within my nine-year-old soul as long as I was certain that my sister was not hungry. I don't know why I worried almost not at all for her safety. Why I trusted in my father's heart—black and cold as it was—not to hurt Mafalda. All these years later I still don't know why I trusted him, but I did.

"Soon I began to supplement my food gathering with the collecting of clothes for my sister. Nothing quite so blatant as I'd done during that first week when I'd left my new white pinafore with Mafalda and returned to the palace wearing my dead mother's blue housedress with the pink roses. Nothing like that. Assuming a genteel subtlety, I'd take stockings from Agata's mending basket once in a while, or a chemise. A pair of culottes. A silk undershirt with a pink ribbon woven 'round the neck. Sometimes from my own things, sometimes from the pile left in the wash basket outside Charlotte and Yolande's rooms, I'd steal the best I could find. Sweaters and shawls and lap robes, I'd steal from the salons and from the school-room and even from the chapel. I never ransacked private quarters, but rather pinched things that were left behind or forgotten or mis-placed from the rooms where we all spent time together. The pick-ings were wonderful. The Tiny Mafalda and I hid the silken, woolen, feminine treasures from our father in the little room where the washing tubs and mops and brooms were kept. Where he'd never set foot.

"And by the time my sister was seven and I was just past ten, we'd put by a veritable trousseau for her. At least in our own wondering eyes. She had food, she had clothes and blankets and books and trin-kets enough to keep a rustic breed of princess in good stead, and that's when the Arab in me began to urge The Tiny Mafalda to sell the surplus in the markets. Practicing the same restraint as I had used in acquiring the goods, she would offer a single item at a time. And only once in a while. Women began to seek her out, enquire if she had, perhaps, a nightdress. Another shawl with long silk fringe. Of course if word had reached our father, if the truth had been revealed that his daughter was unloading stolen goods in the markets and stashing lire in the hems of her petticoat, I don't know what grim jus-tice he would have meted out to her; and not because of what she'd done but because she hadn't brought her earnings home to him. Yet we hardly worried about someone telling our father. A wonderful thing about being Sicilian. One of the wonderful things. The silence, I mean. My father never found the food stashes or the clothes or the

secret pocket in the petticoat hem. Or, if he did, he neither con-
fronted The Tiny Mafalda nor disturbed her treasures.

"I arranged my visits so that I would not see my father; the high
point of my cleverness, I'd thought. Week after week, month after
month. A sober Jeanne d'Arc riding fast over the white road, potatoes
and sugar and lacy culottes were my arms against Mafalda's hungers.
Such a vainglorious little girl I was that I'd never noticed the scent of
the yellow-haired devil everywhere about my undertakings. It was
Leo. Long afterward I learned it was he who'd made the path from
me to Mafalda. It was he who'd understood that we were lonely for
each other. He who had given Agata and the stableman and others
the word to facilitate my missions. To hide the doll with the blond
braids woven with tiny ears of corn and dressed in a long white gown
in the wooden box in the *dispensa*. To strew the chapel and the salons
with shawls and sweaters. It was Leo.

CHAPTER II

"And it was Leo who, after a while, began inviting The Tiny Mafalda to the palace for Sunday lunch with—it was easy to understand—the intention of her eventual residence there. He would send a driver to fetch her in the morning and she would be enfolded into the rituals of the palace's *Buona Domenica,* Good Sunday. Soon she became a pet among the staff, and even Yolande seemed enchanted with her. A rosy mignon, *una pupetta,* as they called her. A little dolly. Yet my sister, terrorized by the sheer numbers of people moving about the palace, by the way they spoke, the way they looked, by all those faces bending down to her, the unfamiliar hands pulling at her curls, did not return the affection. Whereas I thrived upon the immoderate proportions of the palace, The Tiny Mafalda cringed, cowered. Clinging to me, speaking only to me, barely whimpering a word to anyone else, The Tiny Mafalda was shy, sullen. At Mass, she wept. At table she wept, the tears spilling through the plump, babyish hands she held tight over her eyes.

" '*Amore mio, cos' hai?* What is it, my love?' " I would ask her over and over again. She would slide herself down from the satin cushions of the pew or the red damask pillow on her chair to a safer place to weep.

" 'But don't you want to live here with me?' I would ask her. 'Here you will have *three pretty dresses and eat cakes with violet icing every morning at eleven,* just like the princess in the story. Don't you remember?"

" 'I don't like pretty dresses anymore. And I don't like cakes. I want Mamà to come back and you to come back and I want Papà to come back, too. I mean, I want him to come back from his being so mad all the time. Why did everyone go away, Tosca? Don't you see, if I go away, too, there will be no one left at home to wait for the time when everyone returns? Don't you understand that?'

"My sister's response to this time in our lives has always been a symbol for me, demonstrating that it's not the events, not the traumas or the perpetrators of those traumas that shape us. It's the stones. How the runes fell when we did. I was I. She was she. We'd been born of the same man and woman. Lived the same life. Though we loved each other mightily, we were day and night. So it was The Tiny Mafalda herself who foiled my father's and Leo's plan for her to live at the palace. She'd appointed herself guardian of the little house down the white road, over the two hills. She knew where she belonged even if the rest of us had forgotten."

"But what happened to Mafalda? Did she come to live at the palace after all? She's here now; when did she . . ."

"You must not keep interrupting me. Be patient and your questions will be answered in good time. Allow me to tell the story as I recall it."

Keep interrupting? I've hardly breathed, I say to myself. I nod my head. She proceeds.

"Life at the palace—often disciplined, harmonious, and sometimes tumultuous, perplexing—began to feel, more and more, like *my* life. Apart from the carnal pleasures of the table and the aesthetic charms of the place itself, it was the schoolroom where I first felt at home. And it was there where I was *diva*.

"You see, I'd learned to read when I was five. A rare enough accomplishment for a child in our village, rarer still for a girl than a boy. My mother had sent me to the village convent school where Suor Diana, a small, round nun with a whiskered chin and licorice breath, was *maestra*. I think there must have been no more than twenty students, collectively, in all the grades. It was she, Suor Diana, who would urge me to sit with the older children who were learning to read rather than with my own age group, who were still shouting out the alphabet. And every Saturday when I'd go with the nuns to clean the church and ready the altar for Sunday Mass, Suor Diana and I would spend an hour, two hours together, whatever time we could manage, and she would help me to read. Read aloud to me. Urge me to read aloud to her. By the time I was brought to live in the palace, I'd made my way through every textbook, every coverless, crumpled-paged book on the shelves of the children's library in the convent house, every church pamphlet about the missions in Guadalajara and West Africa. And whenever I could get one, I'd read a newspaper, front to back, marking the pages with a fat blue Crayola wherever I didn't understand something. I'd bring the desecrated document to my Saturday sessions with Suor Diana and, between mysteries and fables, she would translate the strange language of journalism for me, revealing the even more fantastical stories of politics and the arts and the misdeeds of a group of very bad men from the countryside that the newspaper called *the clan*.

"And so at nine I could read far better than Yolande, who was nearly nine herself, while Charlotte, at seven, still battled with twenty-word picture books. It wasn't that the princesses were less bright than I; rather it was that their education was so broad they'd yet to become proficient in any particular subject. In their curriculum, a smattering of French sufficed. An even lighter quota of English. There were faint allusions to world geography and Italian history. Mainly it was Latin, catechism, *The Lives of the Saints,* music, painting, and needlework—relieved by comportment and elocution—that composed the princesses' workdays. And I was to step in with their drill. Early on I began to ask for more to read. I would devour what I was given and ask for yet more. Doubting my comprehension, the teachers asked me to recount the stories of the books I'd read; *un divertissement*—as Mademoiselle Clothilde, the French tutor/governess/general *professoressa,* would call it—to color the moments of our short intervals between studies. Agata would bring us coffee-stained milk and hard sweet biscuits and I would stand and speak of one book or another. One day the yellow-haired devil was invited to hear my synopsis of *Cuore* by de Amicis and, inspired by his presence I suppose, or, more, by some stroke from the gods, I spoke at length and somehow more confidently than I had ever before, delivering my thoughts with emphatic sweeps of my arms, embellishing my talk with comparisons of other books of the genre and, here and there, quoting a passage or two, a phrase, perhaps, from the text. When I finally curtsied to Leo as I'd been taught to do by Mademoiselle Clothilde and then sat down in my place between the princesses, there was silence. No polite applause and mumbles of 'brava' coming up between bites of the sweets. The princesses sat stonily, upturned faces stiff as their shantunged bodices, and the other teachers, too, stood immutable for such a long moment that I—breathless, euphoric from the job I knew I'd done well—felt myself to be the only one still alive inside the benumbed spectacle of the schoolroom. Until Leo stood. He thanked me with a half nod, then summoned the teachers to the far side of the room, where he gave succinct, life-altering instructions for my intensified studies. And then he was gone. Once again, it was Leo."

CHAPTER III

"FROM THAT DAY FORWARD I READ AND WROTE AND STUDIED like a Jesuit acolyte, all the while retreating farther and farther from the frilly surfaces of palace life. Leo, himself, took over my Latin instruction, added lessons in Greek, piled my reading table with volume upon volume of Greek myths so that I came to know more about the lives of the ancient gods than I'd ever known about the saints. I asked him once if I was not committing a sin by studying the pagan gods when I might have been reading in my *The Lives of the Saints*. He, who had been standing, sat down next to me and said, as if in confidence, that someday I would understand there was no difference between the saints and the pagan gods, that they were quite the same personages, if with certain portions of their biographies and other certain parts of their characters more exalted in one historical era than another. His breezily if quietly spoken illumination had stunned me to slack-jawed silence, but still the prince had more to say.

" 'It was man who took the gods from Olympus and placed them in the church, Tosca. Gave them new names. Changed their histories to suit, shall we say, more contemporary needs. That's not a bad thing or a good thing, it's just what happened. As you advance in your studies of both mythology and religion, you'll find the samenesses yourself. Be open to them. I think Demeter, goddess of agriculture and motherhood, will recall events in the life of *la Madonna.* Learn all you can of Demeter, Tosca. She is very present in all our lives. Especially we who live here where she lived.'

"I am trembling with the further revelation that the Greek goddess of agriculture, who, the prince has informed me, so resembles the mother of God, lives in some far-flung wing of the palace.

" 'Where exactly are her rooms?'

" 'Her temple, Tosca. The ruins of the temple of Demeter lie on a mountain outside the walls of Enna. And there are also ruins of another of her temples right here on our land.'

"Calmed by the kilometers of distance that lie between the goddess and me, now I worry that she lives in ruins.

" 'You will come to understand the splendor of all the gods, their importance to our understanding of ourselves. They are us, Tosca. And we are them.'

"I want to ask him if Don Cosimo agrees with all this about Demeter being so much like Mary and why there is no statue of her in the chapel or why there is no Santa Demeter, but he's pacing up and down now, flinging his arms and speaking in Greek and then in Latin and then in French until he finally gets back to me and Italian.

" 'Have you found Sappho yet, Tosca?'

I cringe, thinking this Sappho must be the twin of Santa Rosalia, but I hear him telling me that she was a *poetessa.*

Leave Krete and come to this holy temple
where the graceful grove of apple trees
circles an altar smoking with frankincense

he quotes, all the dramatics gone now. He says the lines again. Asks me to repeat them with him. I try. More than I can remember all the words, I can smell the frankincense. I tell him this. He tells me he knows that I can.

"The prince constantly consulted the other teachers on my progress and steered the overall process of my education. Allowed un-limited access to his library. When I'd climb the winding stone steps up into the tower where it was housed, he seemed to always be there. I'd open the heavy doors and see him, disheveled in the chaos of his tomes. My curtsy. His nod. Aba-jours set behind each chair cast a melancholy light upon the table at which he sat. So dim and yellow was the light that the leather-bound spines towering in the stacks all 'round seemed shadows. I could smell them, though, that good, fine smell of old books, and I'd take the torch from the table, climb the ladder to fetch what I wanted. Sit back down then, always leaving a chair between Leo and me, but still close enough. Near enough to his own scent, the scent made of neroli and damp tweed and of the mud still on his boots, and in a quiet purl of joy, I'd wend my way through Sappho.

"There were days when prayers and garden walks and even meals seemed interruptions to my studies. I preferred my books to our two-hour lunches. All the dressing and undressing and dressing once again, the twitterings of admiration from guests and visiting family toward the princesses, the play of light and dark upon the moods of Simona and Leo. Too, there was an increased flurry of visitors, of people settling in to stay because of what Leo and Cosimo called *la grande guerra,* the great war. It seemed that our region of the island lay relatively out of harm's way, and thus the palace became something of a refuge. I studied more.

When it was warm, I read in the gardens or in the lemon groves, stretched out on a long marble bench, the lion-paw legs of it gnarled in tree roots and half sunk into the soft black earth. My book held above my head, I lay there on the secret baldacchino, the great oily leaves of the trees curtains that commanded dusk at noon.

"And whenever I could beg a reprieve with a sick headache, I kept my own company in my rooms. The early exuberance I'd felt at the palace was overtaken by a kind of gratitude for patronage, for my being kept, without care or obligation, so that I could learn.

The only rivals to my studies were the horses. I loved one of the Egyptian mares above all the rest in the stable and Leo saw to it that she was kept for me, readied for me each morning. I rode with whatever party was going out on a given day, Leo and Cosimo always among them, always leading. Especially when I didn't know the other riders very well, if they were recently arrived guests, for instance, I would stay close to Leo and Cosimo. Though I'd long been rescued from my bareback days, Leo knew I would just as soon do without the formalities of a saddle and so he would often dismount, check my stirrups and cinches, tell me to sit straighter. Sometimes he'd reach his hand up to the small of my back.

" 'Arch right here. Deepen the curve,' he would say, pressing hard.

"I liked that. I liked it very well, and so I would slouch all the more next morning. Wait for his hand. Though I would begin a trail with the group, I'd soon go off on my own. Longing for speed. Risk."

"One late afternoon in the winter of 1942 , Leo asked me to walk with him in the garden. A rare occurrence it was to be so summoned by him. I recall it was very cold and that I'd come out with only Agata's shawl, which she always hung on a hook by the garden door. I'd wrapped it carelessly about my long gray woolen dress and Leo pulled it tighter 'round me, chided me for leaving my coat behind. I remember he did that. I remember thinking that his wanting me to be warm must mean that he had bad news to tell me.

" 'Mafalda has been sent to live with your mother's sister, my dear. Your father came to see me this morning to tell me so that I might tell you. You see, she hasn't been well, and since your father can't be at home to watch over her and since Mafalda chose, forcefully chose, not to come here to be with us . . . '

"He breaks off, knowing that I know what Mafalda had chosen.

" 'But we've arranged a way to keep contact with her, with your aunt and the others in Vicari. I'll see that you're taken to visit her as soon as things become more secure. Meanwhile your sister is in good hands and so are you, and that's what matters. In times like these . . . '

"He talks faster and faster, inserting inanities as though I were a child. As though he'd forgotten that I was twelve, halfway to thirteen. As though he didn't know what I knew very well. That my father had been trying to pawn Mafalda upon one relative or another for a long time. Leo spoke as though he'd forgotten that I'd reconciled my father's need to live without my sister as much as I had his need to live without me. That Malfada has been reconciled to live without me, too, hurts far more. For these past three years I'd believed ours was only a physical separation. Not so now.

" 'Don't, please don't think that you can ride those eighty kilometers to Vicari as you once did those few from here to your home. I mean, your other home.'

"Awkward in even the simplest discourse about my life before coming to the palace, I help him.

" 'I won't. I could. I think I could but I won't.'

" 'I have the address so you can write to her, send her things if you wish.'

" 'Yes. Thank you.' "

"As it turned out, the address that my father gave to Leo was not at all the one where my sister was sent. Or at least was not the one where she stayed for very long. And when Leo sent word to my father that he needed to see him, it was discovered that even he no longer lived at the horse farm, the barns empty, the house abandoned."

CHAPTER IV

"It might seem strange, Chou, but neither before nor then nor on into that autumn and winter was there anything much at all in my life to suggest that the world outside the palace was at war. Save the newspaper reports, the radio broadcasts to which Leo and Cosimo and whatever males were in residence at the palace at the moment listened to with such attention, all seemed remarkably the same. In fact, I found it shocking one morning when we three girls were walking to the schoolroom and Yolande said, 'Ach, how weary I am of this war and its privations.'

"Even Charlotte seemed at a loss, and certainly I didn't know about privations. She explained that no more pastries would be coming in the weekly supplies from Palermo because there was no sugar. She said that her mother had told her so. Could we imagine such a thing? No sugar?

"Apart from the pastries, after a while there were no supplies at all to fetch in Palermo. But I never knew about that, either. I never heard about rations or bombardments or how many Italian boys were being killed or taken prisoner on the Russian front, or about those who froze to death in their Mediterranean-weight uniforms or died of hunger even before the Russian winter could take them. Save the wilderness of sugar, there was no truth to taint the punctual discharging of the events of palace life for we three girls. Even the closer-to-home truth was never spoken. The truth that, in the *borghetto,* six hundred meters from the sparkling gilt gates of the palace, children had gone and would still sometimes go to bed without supper. Or that the stores in the peasants' *magazzini* had been sorely thinned if not depleted, and that until the spring wheat could be harvested there would be no bread on their scrubbed oilclothed tables. What I did begin to understand was that Leo was somehow distracted, sad. Even more silent than usual. During that last period of the war, he and Cosimo and some small company of household men would often be gone for days. Disappear. If not without telling Simona, certainly without telling anyone else. When they'd return it would be in some strange truck or farmer's wagon loaded with oil and tins of vegetables and meat, sacks of rice, food for whatever animals were left. All of it covered with tarps and rags so that the shapes underneath looked eerily like bodies. Sleeping. Dead. They'd gone to bargain with the black-marketeers in Palermo or wherever it might have been where there were goods to be had. I would learn that Leo had unfolded astounding sums of beautiful ten- and twenty- and fifty-lira notes so that his peasants might eat. And when, in the final, most hungry weeks before the gardens and fields would begin to yield and black-market goods were nowhere to be found, Leo opened the palace storerooms to the peasants. When the peasants would hesitate over the last barrel of oil, the prince would assure them that there was more. There wasn't more. Cosimo still tells the story of Leo's cleverness in urging the palace cooks to use lard when there was no oil.

" 'But the lard is rancid, sir. Green as grass.'

" 'That's when it tastes best. Go ahead now and fix a good lard pudding. Are there any prunes left? Add some prunes.'

"How Cosimo loves to tell that exchange! Poor Simona not only had no sweets but was served prunes and lard for lunch while the peasants were blessing whatever they had with her finest virgin oil and her confessor was stifling laughs, shifting pieces of the hellish pudding about his plate. In his dedication to the welfare of his peasants during the war, Leo was triumphant.

"In 1943 the Americans debarked on the island. The Germans had already been here for more than a year, protectorates of the homeland of their Italian allies, basing their command at Enna. But when the enormous numbers of Americans with their cannons and heavy armature plunged through the waves of the Tyrrhenian Sea and onto the Sicilian shores on that day in May, the far fewer and less potently supplied troops of *Tedeschi* chose retreat. Days after the American arrival, King Vittorio Emanuele nullified the governing power of Mussolini and placed a general called Badoglio in charge of the government. Whatever government there was. Early in September 1943, Italy officially asked armistice of the Americans and hence, for us, the war was over. As I've said, I never knew it had begun.

"The only casualty that invaded the palace walls came in the form of three Americans. I don't know how many hundreds or thousands of American soldiers were billeted at Enna, first as liberators, or was it conquerors?—there are still those who dispute this point— and then as keepers of the peace after the armistice. Hotels, private homes and villas, convents, and military barracks were requisitioned to lodge them. Leo went to visit their commander, invited him to lunch. *Noblesse oblige.* Cosimo tried to dissuade him from the deed, warning that if the Americans witnessed the beauty of the palace, surely they would claim it, too, but Leo was convinced to demonstrate noble Sicilian life and culture to the Americans. Proud that his daughters and his ward might address the guests in their own language, we were extraordinarily primped and polished for the occasion. Clutching nosegays of white roses and repeating our mantra of *Good afternoon, sir, and welcome to our home,* we waited on the veranda. I don't really know what I or Yolande or Charlotte expected of these Yankee soldiers, but surely it was something other than what they were. One was very fat and tall, the one who I think was the general. Of the other two I recall only their voices, which were loud and shrill in the quiet sanctum of the great dining room. We thought them scandalous for the noises they made when they chewed, for how they laughed with their mouths open and full. Leo cringed. Cosimo snorted quietly into his cups. I don't recall whether Simona sat with us. When all was said and done, I, myself, found the Americans charming, in their way, perhaps because they were the single close-up symbol to which I'd been privy in all the hugger-muggery of that epoch. It would be a decade later and in another life before I would come to understand even some of what had been *la grande guerra*."

"Pindar and Caesare; the inevitable *The Lives of the Saints;* French, English, Italian literature. Geometry, astrology. The pianoforte. I heard Mass from the family pews, spooned my puddings at the family table, linked my arms with the princesses in the family strolls about the garden. I was one of them. I was not one of them. It must have been about then, when I was fourteen, that I began to be included in the admirations of the visitors. The extended family. The savage green-eyed motherless child had grown to be a young woman. Well-spoken, graceful, bright. There were whisperers.

 " *'Have you heard her play Brahms?'*

 " *'They say she's memorized Virgil.'*

 " *'A perfect Parisian accent.'*

 " *'A brilliant horsewoman.'*

 " *'Poverina, and to think of what her life might have been if not for Leo!'*

 " *'The prince has such a good heart.'*

 " *'The prince has such a good eye.'* "

CHAPTER V

"Soon after the peace was fixed, Leo and Simona hosted a party. Not one of our own boys or the men who had been called up or volunteered themselves to fight, not one had been lost. Eleven from among the *borghetto* had gone to war, six from the palace staff, and though three were severely wounded, all seventeen had returned.

"It was the third of May 1945, and to initiate the *festa,* Cosimo said Mass for the combined congregations of the household and the *borghetto* rather than performing the usual separate celebrations of the holy sacrament. At sunrise in the gardens, in the fickle, unconsecrated shade of the oaks, Cosimo said Mass for everyone. And afterward, we all walked, single file, upon the packed-earth paths among the wheat fields on our way to a copse of cedars by the river.

"A group of men had gone out the evening before to arrange the wood for the cooking fires, to rake the earth under the trees, pound torches into the ground. Under the sun, not yet high but already mean, we walked. Each of the men carried some crate of food—oranges, artichokes, potatoes—or parcels of linen or some bench or chair across his shoulders or led a pair of lambs or goats to sacrifice. Two had mandolins strapped across their chests and bundles of kindling tied on their backs. I remember them especially, for at the time,

I'd begun to think I was mad with love for one of these troubadours though I never could decide which of the two it was. That day both were wearing shiny black trousers with a satin stripe down the leg, the splendors of which caused their chums to claim they'd looted graves, taken the pants off dead men, so as to be smartly turned out for the *festa*. The suggestion might have been true. And the women?

"Sure as she-goats over the stones, wide, strong flanks lurching to and fro under thin cotton smocks, some with suckling babies swaddled to their breasts, they all toted jugs of water or wine upon their heads and sang some ancient song about sisterhood, about a pact to tell one another when a husband was untrue. To tell and then to help the betrayed wife to murder the betraying husband. They sang it over and over again.

"Now you'll recall that this was 1945 and there were more vehicles belonging to the palace than I could count. And by this time there was also some manner of gasoline to feed them, the trucks and Jeeps and cars, and yet we walked. Simona and the princesses walked. Everyone wanted to walk.

"By the time we'd all reached the river, the advance guard had fires leaping, had dispatched, gutted, skewered the lambs and goats, rubbed the little carcasses with oil and filled their cavities with handfuls of wild herbs. As though all seventy or eighty who composed the group were following the steps to the same primal dance, everyone got to work. I thought the scene they made was lovely. More beautiful even than the condoling dreams I would call forth as a little girl, dreams upon which I'd paint big-bosomed aunts who smelled of soap and sugar and uncles with Sunday shoes and caramels in their pockets for me. I'd invent a grandfather in whose embrace I would sit and trace the furrows of his sunburnt cheeks while he sang to me. In those dreams, my mother would never cry and my father would be the wise, reasonable *capo famiglia* who protected us all. But these characters I drew in those old dreams might have been great white snowy owls for all they resembled the real ones with whom I'd lived. Yet mine was every child's dream, wasn't it? Wasn't it yours, Chou?"

I know she seeks no answer.

"How each one of us adjusts the dream to accommodate real life. That's what separates us. One blames and wails while another gets to work. At the end of any human story, I think it's only the capacity to reconcile the dream with reality which separates characters. Well, by then, by the time I was fifteen, I'd long been finished with whatever blaming and wailing I was going to do but, from time to time, I was still wont to take out the pieces of those old dreams and give them free run over me. But the sight of that festival I came upon by the river ripped open the small place inside me where I'd hoarded the old pictures. Washed it clean and made room for something real. I understood that what I was seeing, what I was coveting in that riverside scene, was already mine. Even though I'd never lived among that race of graceful creatures, I was *of* them. Their legacies were mine, their culture was mine, and I felt that as fiercely as I did that the make-believe life in the palace was *not* mine. But I'm going too fast with this story and I know that I am. Let me get back to the *festa*.

"A group of women were smashing artichokes against flat rocks and stuffing them with a paste of oil and herbs just like we do here at the villa. Someone else was fixing sardines with great chunks of tomatoes in long, shallow pans with holes poked in their bottoms and setting them to smoke over embers of dried wild fennel stalks. Tables made of boards and barrels were covered with embroidered cloths and laid with stacks of tin plates, and the men drank in time with their work and the women sang in time with theirs, and one could hardly tell who belonged to the palace household and who to the *borghetto*. Everyone seemed happy mixed up together. I was happy. Leo seemed happy. He seemed exuberant, in fact, striding from one vignette to another, putting his hand to the preparations, tasting a sauce, filling and refilling the cups of his peasants. Shirtsleeves, riding pants, boots, all that blond hair slicked back with neroli oil and sweat, he was beautiful, and there wasn't a woman there—save his own wife and daughters—who didn't think so. And that was the second thing I'd understood on that third of May. I understood that it wasn't one of the troubadors in the tuxedo pants I wanted. I was in love with the prince."

"The *festa* went from lunch to *riposo* and on to foraging walks in the woods and fishing in the river and then back to the table. There was music all day long, but when the sun began to set and the just-lit torches glistened up in the white fog off the river, the troubadors exchanged bold, bright songs for minor-key wails, strumming them softly, the taut, tinny pings mingling with the wind. Two girls began to dance. I knew one of them. She was called Lidia and I'd seen her sometimes when she'd come to help the palace maids. I didn't know the other girl. She was different from Lidia. Different from all of us. The skin of her was the color of ripe peaches set in a red glass bowl and her eyes were long, dark Arab eyes. Her high, unbound breasts moved under her loose white dress as she swayed tenuously, her eyes looking somewhere far away. I think all she could see were the stars.

"Face to face, the girls held one another by their elbows, their bodies illumined by the two small fires that burned on either side of them. The troubadours having laid down their mandolins, there was no music. No one would have heard it anyway since everyone sat or stood or crouched in a circle 'round them, hardly breathing for their enchantment with the peach-skinned one. Lidia sat down after a while, leaving her partner to dance alone, and an old man with a mouth harp sent up a mesmerizing keen that seemed to rouse the peach-skinned girl from her trance. She moved her arms and legs as though she'd just awakened from a long sleep. Stretching herself, testing herself until, in a slow, deliberate pirouette, all the while kilting up the skirt of her dress, securing it in a knot high up on her thighs, she began to turn in place. Tight, contained turns, her neck proud, her arms arched in a wide embrace, she propelled herself slowly, seeming to listen for the next cue from the old man with the mouth harp until, hearing it, she twirled faster. Faster yet and now in the classic ballerina's pose—one leg bent, the small bare foot of it held fast against the other knee—she whirled herself upon one long, powerful leg. Faster, faster yet until it was she who commanded the man with the mouth harp and his keen became a hectic, passionate scream and still she whirled faster, flinging the mass of her dark ringlets to slap against her shoulders, always bringing her eyes back to the same critical point as she completed another turn. Faster, always faster, she hurled her splendid body until, like a dervish, she seemed to dissolve into the dark starry night. White smoke with black Arab eyes. Always she turned her Arab eyes back to him. Always back to Leo."

"There was nothing left for any of us to do after the peach-skinned girl's dancing and, little by little, the *festa* was broken down, packed up, and we walked, single file, upon the packed-earth paths among the wheat fields back home. Half crazed with envy of the girl who—even to my fifteen-year-old eyes—had surely offered herself to Leo, I refused the jasmine-scented bath Agata had drawn for me, threw myself, facedown, upon the yellow and white bed. I wept. The whole night through I wept, grieving with that envy but just as much for something else. Something that I think was an ending. You see, as the peach-skinned girl danced in the dim light of those last flames, it felt as though she'd taken something from me. With every turn, she took more. And as she spun herself fast into that black night, the whole of my childhood went with her. Broken, empty, I was less than I'd been before, or was it only that I was different? Agata kept vigil over me all that night, rocked me in her arms until dawn seeped between the shutters and, as though the new light would stay the pain, told me, 'It's over now, little one.' I remember her saying that, her tiny oval eyes swollen from sympathetic tears, her own thin body trembling with exhaustion.

"Yes, it's over, I'd told myself, too. Kept repeating the phrase. Too, I repeated what I'd told myself the day before by the river. *The scene ripped open the small place inside me where I'd hoarded the old pictures. Washed it clean and made room for something real.* But what was real? Was my love for Leo real? Was my envy of the peach-skinned girl real? Was life at the palace real? Was the *festa* by the river real? Maybe dreams are all we have. Maybe trying to live dreams is to dash them on the rocks.

"Three revelations battled for my attention. I loved Leo. I was envious of the peach-skinned girl who I began to see more as the symbol of all women, any woman who might inspire Leo's affection. I was shocked to admit that this envy must include Simona herself. As I considered this, the list of potential irritants became very long. But the third revelation was, I think, the most shocking of all. I could no longer be at home in the palace. Now that I had witnessed how the peasants lived, it was in the *borghetto* with them where I wanted to be. I didn't care about embroidered stockings or ornamented puddings or Greek or Latin or Brahms or even *The Lives of the Saints;* I wanted to work in the fields and carry wine on my head and swing my hips and sing sad songs about love. I wanted to ride bareback again, I wanted to feel that hole in my stomach at high noon and fill it with soup and bread, and I wanted to kiss Leo. Shrieking from the soul of me was the desire to kiss the prince. Each revelation battled against another until the stones fell in place. First I must get to Leo.

"I would get to Leo before the peach-skinned girl would get to him. Before he could get to her."

"By this time, Agata had washed and dressed, gone to inform the household that I was unwell on that morning after the *festa,* telling them she would look after me, keep me quietly in my rooms. I began to form my plan.

"In part, it was Flaubert who guided me that morning. Flaubert via Mademoiselle Clothilde. You see, while Charlotte and Yolande and I would be at work with our written lessons, Mademoiselle often read by the schoolroom fire or in her chair under the magnolias. During a certain period, she seemed always to be reading books by someone named Flaubert and, more often than not, one book in particular. Its title was *Education Sentimentale.* Delicate brown script on a burnt-brown suede cover and I'd longed to read it. After bouts of thieving food and clothes for The Tiny Mafalda, my skills were sharp for the unsanctioned borrowing of Mademoiselle Clothilde's books. I'd never kept any one of them long enough to distress her unduly, for in an afternoon or overnight, I'd gorge upon one or another of them and nimbly position the book just to the left or the right or under or over the place where she'd left it the day before. By the time I'd taken *Education Sentimentale* for the third time, Mademoiselle asked me what I'd thought of it. She revealed that she wasn't much older than I when she'd first 'come upon' it. I remember we laughed an almost complicit laugh, though neither of us—or was it only I?—could have imagined using certain passages from the book to seduce the prince. And yet it was exactly memories of Flaubert that cleared my head that morning after the *festa,* that set me upon my path to Leo.

"Only Agata would be privy to my plan. And once she heard it, she sat quietly, swallowing hard a few times, looking at me as though I were someone else. Appraising me.

" 'Get in the tub,' was her first directive.

"She put me in to soak and, meanwhile, scrubbed my hair with French soap, rinsed it with cold water and white vinegar and lemon juice, and then rubbed every centimeter of me with a tulle bag stuffed with crushed almond shells. Wrapped in a towel, I sat while she brushed my hair, twisted hanks of it up into strips torn from an old sheet. She rubbed me all over with neroli oil, burnishing my skin with a piece of linen until I shone like satin in the firelight, and I slept then. A cold cloth across my eyes, I slept while Agata sat beside my bed, transforming an organdy skirt into a nightdress, trimming it with lace she'd removed from a pair of Simona's pillowcases. Then, Agata slept, too, with the nightdress across her lap, and she was sleeping still when I awoke and slipped from the bed into the dressing room to look at my naked self in the big yellow-framed mirror.

"Gangly and long where she'd been plump and hard, I struck the same pose the peach-skinned girl had struck. One leg bent, resting upon the other, arms reaching out in a half circle, neck stretched, chin up, I lacked only the old man with the mouth harp to get me started. I tried a turn. Fell back halfway onto my bony derrière, re-struck the pose. Agata had come to the doorway but, rapt as I was in pursuit of the peach-skinned girl's twirls, I hadn't noticed. When she could no longer keep her laughter to herself, she threw off her dress, her slip, her camisole and culottes and joined me in front of the mir-ror. She would show me how. A less likely ballerina than even I, we left off the dancing in favor of the rose-petal kiss. A kiss like the one Roseannette gave to Frédéric in *Education Sentimentale.*

"I told Agata how Roseannette had held a rose petal between her front teeth, inviting Frédéric to nibble it, an *aperitif* before her lips. We practiced. Yes, that would work. Agata dressed herself, disap-peared out the door, and when she returned, pulled a tiny gold pot from the inside pocket of her dress. Simona's tiny gold pot. Simona's pillowcases. Simona's husband. She rouged my nipples, then the soft, fleshy part of my lower lip, told me she'd bring me some dinner, and was off to her chores. Agata had done some reading of her own, I'd thought. I lay down and reviewed the plan.

"I was to rest until the household was quiet, until Agata came to my door to tell me that Leo had gone to his rooms. She would busy herself in his wing for thirty minutes longer, determine that he re-mained in his rooms. That he was alone. She would then come back to take the rags from my hair, brush it loose, button the nightdress, and send me on my way to him. A rose petal between my teeth.

"But what would Leo think as I stood before him? What would the prince do about the rose petal? About me?

"It was true that I had grown taller than I had grown full but it was also true that my nubility had flowered. I'd seen the recognition of it in Simona's eyes. In the eyes of the princesses and of the young priest who'd come to help Cosimo, and in the eyes and the blushes of the adolescent males from the *borghetto* who I'd seen throwing coins to determine which of them would bring the firewood to the schoolroom or who would saddle my horse and, for a half second, hold me about the waist as I mounted. Nearly everyone's gaze reflected the changes in me except Leo's gaze.

"Truth was, I'd been slowly falling in love with the prince since I was nine years old. I liked everything about him. I liked his voice and the shape of his jaw and the rough feel of his coat brushing my shoulders when he adjusted my chair at table. For months, years, I'd lived in constant expectation of seeing him, if only as he passed the door to the music room, or of hearing him in discourse with Cosimo or one of the overseers or some attorney or local politician as I raced by one *salone* or another. How many errands and duties had I contrived only to put myself in his way?

"As I lay there waiting for the time to pass, I wondered about things that, before now, I'd always tried to push away. Why did Leo bring me to the palace? Why did people whisper as I left a room, or stop whispering when I entered one? Was my sense of exile—of belonging nowhere and to no one—was it real, or was it an empty husk I cherished, proof that I was once the savage motherless child? Proof that perhaps I was still? I lay there with my hard little rouged nipples and my silky skin and my lemon-smelling hair tied up in rags and, as though some phantom inquisitor had entered my rooms and made himself comfortable at the foot of my bed, I was assaulted with questions. Who was I to be contemplating another woman's husband? Were the whisperers right? Was I, among other perhaps more noble reasons, brought to the palace to be the prince's whore? And, on this first day of what I thought to be my newborn adulthood, was I be-having with the passion of a woman or only with the wantonness of a hell-bent child? I did not know.

"I heard every mournful clang of the chapel bells, my thoughts advancing and retreating with each quarter hour from four in the af-ternoon until nearly midnight, my heart shuddering at every stroke, the shame in me keeping time with the excitement.

"Agata had not returned save to leave a supper tray. Leo must have had guests, or perhaps he was in the library. Perhaps he'd gone away, but no, if that were so, Agata would have come to tell me. Yes, she would have come to tell me, and surely she'd be here at any moment to say that all was well. To brush my hair. But, no. There was no Agata as the bells tolled midnight, nor when they began their remorseless counting all over again from one. With the edges of my blanket, I rubbed the rouge from my mouth and my nipples, and I slept."

"I'd been sleeping for only moments when Agata came to wake me, to tell me it was time. Leo was in his rooms. The corridors were clear.

"*Hurry,* she kept repeating, as much to herself as to me. Fumbling with the rags and the brush and fastening the nightdress with two buttons wrong, she pushed me out into the hall, made the sign of the cross over me, and closed the door hard in my face. I began to run. At the first flight of stairs, I hesitated. No rose petals. No rouge. No shoes or slippers, and the stone was cold. Even in May, the stone was cold and I barely touched it, barely touched the banisters as I turned up the next flight. The next. I had never been to Leo's rooms, not of-ficially, though in my early reconnaissance of the palace, I'd gone up to find the prince's apartment. To walk to and fro in front of the place where he slept. To stay, for a while, where he was. To listen at his door. Now I listened at his door. Nothing. I knocked.

" '*Avanti.* Come in.'

"Frozen. Silent. I wait. I knock again.

" '*Avanti, Cosimo. Sono ancora in piedi.* Come in, Cosimo. I'm still upright.'

"I open the door and, standing by the fire, his half-dressed figure seems a kilometer distant from me.

" '*Tosca.* Are you ill? What is it?'

"He walks swiftly toward me, and I walk more swiftly to him. We are about to collide but I, daughter of a horse thief, bareback rider from the age of three, I, horsewoman superb, I leap at the prince, mount him, wrap my legs about his waist as I would a horse's belly. His shock of yellow hair is a mane. I kiss the prince. With my unrouged lips, I cover his face with kisses. His face, his head, his ears, his eyes. He is pulling at my arms, pushing my face away from his, and all the while I am kissing him. He pulls my body from his, drops me to the floor. With an open hand, he straightens his hair. Reaches for a red dressing gown. I rise. The door is still wide open and, tying the belt of the red dressing gown, he walks past me to it. Holds it wider. His eyes look somewhere beyond me. I walk to the door, halt before him. Look up at him, dare him to look back, and he does. At once vague and transfixing is his gaze, and it's I who looks away first. I walk out the door, walk imperiously down the corridor as though two pages hold the exceedingly long train of my gown. He watches me. Surely he must be watching me, but no. I hear his door shut, and then I run."

CHAPTER VI

"Next morning nothing is changed. I'd kissed Leo, even if he hadn't kissed me back. I'd calmed the envy in me over the peach-skinned girl, or pretended I had. Nothing is changed save that, dressed in one of Agata's severe cotton work dresses, my hair braided into a single plait that hangs to my waist, I sit at breakfast ravening my way through enormous quantities of bread and butter and warm milk, asking politely for more. And more. Apart from these symbols of metamorphosis itself, nothing at all is changed.

" 'Tosca, is that one of Agata's dresses you're wearing?' In my general direction and rather too brightly, Simona asks this.

" 'Yes. I've traded her some of my dresses,' I say as though it was the most reasonable business.

" 'But if yours need adjusting, the *sarta* will take care of them for you. No need to wear Agata's things.'

" 'No, it's not that mine want adjusting but only that I prefer Agata's clothes.'

"Leo says nothing. The princesses giggle. As she folds her napkin, slips it into the silver ring, Simona announces that I am never again to come to the table dressed in anything but my proper clothes. It is, of course, that very phrase that I'd hoped to elicit . . . *you are never again to come to the table dressed in anything but your proper clothes.* You see, I didn't want to come to the table. Not this table.

"After tea, I ask for a word with Leo. We walk to the lemon groves, and there I begin to tell him of my desire to move to the *borghetto*. I thank him for the fine life he's given me for six years, explain to him that I think it's time for me to get to work in another way.

" 'I believe I'm better suited to work in the fields, to help in the kitchens, to care for the smaller children than I am to *this* life.' I point in the direction of the palace. 'Mine is not an impulsive request, sir. I've considered it for a long while now. In fact, I think that, somewhere in my mind, I've been considering it almost from the beginning.' He thinks I am being false and that I want to leave the palace because he's rebuffed me. He thinks I am embarrassed. I try to address the sentiments he's yet to voice.

" 'My request has nothing at all to do with our meeting last evening.'

" 'Our meeting? Yes. I mean, no. Of course, our meeting. I wouldn't think you'd want to leave because of that.' As he'd done the night before, he runs an open hand through his hair. 'And what about your studies? You'll have precious few hours to read and I'd dare say nothing of privacy if you live down there. And what about your riding? I think you are a very romantic young woman, Tosca. And I think you see everything and everyone in a romantic way. Life is not easy in the *borghetto*.'

" 'Nor do I find it so in the palace.'

"He laughs now. Really laughs. Sits on the stone bench where I've lain so many mornings to read. 'Nor do *I* find it so in the palace.' Is he only miming me, or could he be speaking for himself? He's quiet then. Smiling a bit or trying not to, I think.

" 'You see, sir, when I first came to live here I admit that I was astonished by the palace and by all of you. I was astonished by everything. I loved swishing down the halls in my pretty dresses and I loved every ceremonious event of our days. But I want to tell you that, except when I was studying or reading, I soon began to feel as though I was playacting. You know, as if we were all reading parts from a long, long fable that didn't seem to have an ending. Not a sad ending and not a happy ending, either. Over time this life has begun to feel less and less like a *real* life. I remember how I used to live before I came here, and those memories make me feel lonely. It's not that I want to be poor again or hungry again but, strange as it might seem, I think I was happier then. Especially before my mother died. And especially when I had The Little Mafalda to care for. It was *my* life. For all these years since, I've been living someone else's life. Yours and the princesses' life. Pardon me, sir, but sometimes I don't feel so grateful to you for taking me from my old life because all I've done is to trade one kind of poverty for another. You understand, don't you, sir? About that poverty you can feel *inside*.'

"Leo is not smiling now but looking at me as though he has seen something new in my face. He studies me.

" 'Allow me some time. Perhaps there's a way that you can have both the palace and the *borghetto*.'

"I nod my head, then curtsy and begin to walk back through the garden. I think that more than the palace and more even than the *borghetto*, what I really want is for him to love me."

"For days, I think it might have been weeks even, I'd resumed my place in the schoolroom, the chapel, at table. I'd not worn any but my own clothes. I'd chosen to bide time gracefully. And then one late afternoon when I enter the library, Leo is there, as though awaiting me. No books are spread open; not even the abat-jour is switched on. I start as if to leave, as if I've interrupted him, but he invites me to take a chair next to him.

" 'I've been thinking about something that appears, now, to include you, and I believe it's time, yes, it's the right time for us to talk about it.'

"The words *something* and *it* he says with distastefulness, as though they signify something unpleasant. Or perhaps awkward. In any case, it seems strange to sit next to him with no chair between us as we usually sit. And with no pale yellow light and no books. The prince twirls a green and black fountain pen between his fingers and, in that short silence, I think I understand the nature of his intended talk. I smooth my skirts, sit straighter, hands clasped together and resting on my thighs. Leo is going to talk about sex.

" 'Do you know the meaning of the term *latifondo*?'

"Surely neither *Education Sentimentale* nor any of the other books I'd read ever addressed this *latifondo*. I consider the Latin roots and come up with 'ample bed.' I fear he is proposing some extraordinary act and so rise to leave.

"He seems not to notice my change in position and proceeds, '*Latifondo* is the term used to describe vast tracts of land. A person who owns these vast tracts of land is known as a *latifondista*. I am a *latifondista*, Tosca.'

"Well, at least he's admitted it. That he's a *latifondista*. Though I still don't understand what his ownership of vast tracts of land have to do with his liking 'ample beds.' He is talking, twirling the fountain pen. I try to listen.

" 'I inherited lands from both my father and my uncle and, over these past eighteen years since the property has been totally under my care, I've done very little to make the best use of it. We plant only a relatively small portion of the fields, use some for grazing and let the rest lie fallow. The truth is that most of my land is abandoned. I've made no investments in equipment, irrigation systems. I haven't built even the most modest of roads to facilitate the transportation of crops if there were any.'

"Certainly he is finding it difficult to get to his point. *Grazing, abandoned, irrigation* are three words that ring more loudly than the rest, but still I can't find my place in what he is saying. I am looking intently at him, though, as if I understand completely. Sagely and with pursed lips, I nod every now and then. He continues.

" 'Many *latifondisti* are against the reforms that the State is beginning to set forth as solutions to the misery so many Sicilians are trying to survive. The devastation of the war will be insoluble without reforms, but Rome is damnably slow. It will be years yet until the laws are laid down and years after that before anyone will begin to yield to them. If anyone will ever yield to them. There is no State, there is no Italian government bent on the feeding of the poor. We who *have* must change things.'

"He has my attention now. His voice is quiet, almost a whisper.

" 'Peasants from all parts of the island, from all parts of the *mezzogiorno,* the south, are rioting. They're starving to death, they are watching their babies starve to death, and yet we—*they*—are surrounded by nothing but land. Fallow land. Rich fallow land from which more food could be grown than the peasants have ever dreamt of. Yet hunger is historical on this island, Tosca. Centuries of hunger were sometimes interrupted only by famine. And the so-called fortunate ones, the sharecroppers—like my sharecroppers—are hardly thriving. *Mezzadria* is a medieval scourge. More slaves they are than farmers, the sharecropping peasants are rarely allowed the half which, by its very meaning, *mezzadria* promises. Most landowners, most *latifondisti,* permit their peasants only enough to keep themselves upright. Only enough to keep themselves productive. The nobles feast, the peasants provide. I want the end of that. At least on my own land. My wife says I'm a zealot. I think Cosimo agrees with her.'

"I am surprised by this familiarity he uses in speaking of Simona. Not saying that she's waiting in the chapel or that she will be late to table but something the two of them have discussed privately.

" 'I am not calling for the decline of the gentry but for the decline of my *own* exploitation—albeit unwittingly—of my *own* peasants. What other of my dispassionate class choose to do or not do, that will belong to them. If absolutism and repression suit them, so be it.'

"He repeats, *so be it.* Over and over.

" '*Tosca, tu ricordi quel ragazzo che suonava il mandolino durante la festa vicino al fiume?* Do you recall that boy who played the mandolin during the party by the river?'

" 'Yes, I remember both of them,' I tell him, thinking of their purloined tuxedo trousers.

" 'The one called Filiberto, do you know who I mean?'

" 'Yes,' I repeat more emphatically.

" 'Well, a while back, I don't know, perhaps two or three weeks ago, someone—I don't know who—was walking about the *borghetto,* talking to several of the men. The boys. He was recruiting. He was looking for those who seemed the most desperate among the peasants. These recruiters know the signs. He settled on Filiberto. Filiberto, whose parents are both ill, whose brothers and sisters—all five of them—are always hungry. Yes, the recruiter settled on him. Desperation makes good desperadoes, you see. The recruiter offered food and medicine to Filiberto—food and medicine that I should have been providing, food and medicine that the boy was too proud to ask of me, to beg of me—in exchange for a simple deed. A few moments of work. But first he invited Filiberto to join him and his friends at a place somewhere in the hills, sat him down at his table where, together, they ate and drank and laughed and smoked cigars. Theirs was a complete seduction of the desperate Filiberto. He was being asked to be part of a *club;* he was being asked to *belong.* He would be doing men's work. This felt good, felt right. After all, he'd be working for his family, wouldn't he?

" 'I can hear them, Tosca. I know just what they said. *Lie quietly under the olive tree whose trunk is split in two,* they told him, *and when the man with the green shirt passes by, aim for his face. Yes, to destroy the face of a man is the greatest disrespect. Aim for the face. The moon will be bright, Filiberto. You'll see the target clearly. You'll be positioned directly in his path. Aim for his face. You do know how to shoot, Filiberto? Every good peasant can shoot. Here, this is your* lupara, *your shotgun. When the man in the green shirt crosses over the path that leads to the woods, that's the moment. Pull the trigger. Wait five seconds. Listen. Pull it once again. Slip into the woods. Run home. Sleep. Tomorrow the sacks will be outside your door. Beans, rice, potatoes, sugar, coffee. Cigarettes. The medicine in a white box. Before dawn.'* "

"He'd risen from his chair to pace. He'd been shouting when he hadn't been whispering. When he looks my way, he sees that I sit with my head down. He thinks that I'm weeping. I am weeping. Almost quietly swallowing the sobs.

" 'Tosca, forgive me. I didn't mean to tell you all of this. I'd only wanted to talk with you about, about you. About you and the *borghetto.*'

" 'It's okay that you told me.' I sob without restraint now. 'But Filiberto, what's happened to him?'

" 'He'll be buried tomorrow. There were no sacks outside his door yesterday before dawn, and when he went to try and find his way back to the place in the hills, someone shot him. Thrust him down at his mother's door. A grotesque, faceless heap.' And now the prince is weeping.

" 'Lord help me, why have I told you? No one from the palace knows or no one knows yet or perhaps they do, but this business belongs to the *borghetto*. They'll deal with it alone, want nothing of me, of us. The pain is too great. The tragedy belongs to them alone.'

" 'Why?'

" 'Are you asking for a reason, a motive? It could be the ease with which Filiberto was convinced to carry out this act, it could be that these men thought him weak. That he could be bought for rice and cigarettes, yes, they might have thought him weak. And so used him and discarded him. Not the right material.'

" 'But if these men are killers, why didn't they kill the man with the green shirt themselves? Why did they have to find someone like Filiberto to do it for them?'

" 'Theirs was an expression of their *Sicilianness*. They place themselves outside of and hence are indifferent to any form of reason or law but their own. There is no State in Sicily. The feckless governing that is meted out of Rome has never breeched the narrow chasm of sea that separates Sicily from the peninsula. Rural Sicilians have been living a brigand's life for as long as they've been hungry. There is no State to protect Sicilians. Men have made their own State. Perhaps it is the Scylla herself who holds the heads of State underwater while she sings her siren song. Thrashes them against the rocks for her pleasure. Yes, perhaps it's the Scylla who has kept the State from its arrival in Sicily. The men who killed *Filiberto*—and it may very well not have been the same ones with whom he made his pact—determined that he was in some way troublesome. No cunning. No courage. It's possible that the person who ordered Filiberto's death thought he wasn't *good.* You see these clans, these bandits, believe in their own goodness, their right-eousness.' He walks to my chair, places his hands on my face. 'I and my pitiful little revolution are too late. I'm too late, aren't I, Tosca?'

" 'No. Not even a prince could have changed Filiberto's destiny. And I don't think you can change mine, either. If you think that be-cause of this, this *happening,* that I will no longer want to live down there, think again. It makes me want to go all the more.'

" 'Yes. *Sempre di più.* Always more. Even now, the effects of the *festa* are still at work on your sense of romance. Oddly enough, even after all that's happened, they are at work in me, as well. But, as the story of Filiberto has screamingly brought home to us, the *festa* was not a view on the everyday life of the *borghetto.* Not since my father was alive has there been any such event.

" 'Rather than leaving them to piece together the means for some austere form of celebration that would be highlighted by my sending down some token sweet or whatever else I might convince the cooks to furnish, this time I sent a driver to take fresh sardines from Tra-pani. Cosimo and I went to the markets in Enna and brought back every beautiful vegetable and fruit we could find. I cracked barrels from the palace cellar, had firewood brought in. I did what I should have been doing for all these fifteen or twenty years since my father's been gone. But I did not take his example. His generous, affectionate example. I opted to follow the culture of the haves and the have-nots. Accepted it as a societal truth, telling the hungry people who worked for me to eat from that proverbial cake. I sat indulging my passions in my saddle or my reading chair or at table and, once in a while, I wandered down to the *borghetto* to feign commiseration or to pay fleeting respects to the sacrament of a baptism or a wedding. To lay a flower on a coffin. And yes, sometimes I'd wander down to drink wine with the father of a freshly blossomed girl, to view her as I would a horse I'd like to buy, and, often as not, I'd ride away with an appointment for another *jus primae noctis,* right to the first night. I'm not telling you that I am evil or even that I am without sympathy. I am telling you that I have been ignoble, and to admit ignobility may be the greatest form of a man's own damnation of himself. I have been smug and full of pretense and triviality. I have been corrupt in my passivity. It wanted a war, Tosca, to wake me. There are things I saw in the *borghetto* during these past years, things Cosimo and I witnessed, that I can never forget. Though I may not have been the direct cause of that suffering, I am not without blame for it. Of what happened to Filiberto, I *am* the cause. And I shall have to live with that in the best way I can.'

" 'Filiberto made his choice.' "

" 'Filiberto made a *desperate* choice.' "

" 'Perhaps. But mine is not a desperate choice. It's not the *festa* that brought me to my desire to live in the *borghetto.* It's the people, sir. The peasants themselves. I'm one of them and I want to be among my own people.'

"He is quiet for what seems a long time. As though the green and black pen absorbs him entirely. 'That's an interesting conclusion. What you're saying is that you want to go home. That's it, isn't it?'

" 'I didn't think of it precisely that way, but, yes. Now that you say it, it's my way back home. The *borghetto* is home.' I say this slowly, testing the words. wondering if they're true.

" 'Don't you think that, given the chance, any one of the young women your age or younger or older, almost anyone from the *borghetto*, wouldn't trade places with you?'

" 'Perhaps any one of them would. At least for a while. Until the pull of kinship takes over. The need to be among one's own tribe. What you can't live without is very different from what we can't live without. My little sister understood that before I did.'

" 'But you understand it now? I see. Once again, you are being romantic. But let's go forward. You know that the peasants don't dance and sing every day. Good. And you must know that they work far longer than they rest. You know that, don't you? But did you know that often there is not enough food on their tables? My own farmers are hungry, Tosca, while we sit up here already sated, waiting to be served some quivering, towering pastry that we nibble as though it was made of poisoned jelly.'

" 'But I know that the cooks send down baskets and boxes full of food to the *borghetto*.'

" 'Yes, the leavings on our table are given to the peasants. Feeding the animals. Parting with what one doesn't want is not giving. I can do better than that. I shall do better than that, Tosca. I shall never again keep anything worth giving away. I am not so romantic to think I can compensate these people for their own suffering or for the historical poverty that is their legacy. *Was.* Was their legacy. But I can help them now. The misuse can end with me. Will you help me?'

" 'Does helping you mean I won't be able to live down there? Is my helping you meant to keep me from that desire? Please don't treat me as a child. I'm not a child, sir. I don't think I ever was. Besides, what could I do to help you?'

" 'I will tell you what you can do. In time, I will tell you, but first please try to understand that my not wanting you to live in the *borghetto* is for your sake. More than for mine. If you were to go, all you've gained by studying and reading would become part of your past. The free reign of your curiosity would end. No time to read, Tosca. Can you imagine a life with no time to read? If the *borghetto* is where you want to be, you can be there, but without closing up your life here. You can have both.'

" 'Sir, I don't want both. I want to go home. And since that's not possible, I think I can *find* a home down there.'

" 'Perhaps you could. Sanguine as you are, you might do it, Tosca, but I refuse to be part of it.'

" 'Are you saying that you won't allow me to live in the *borghetto*?'

"He looks at me and, just above a whisper, says, 'No. Of course I'm not saying that.' He laughs then. 'You are not my prisoner.'

" 'Then who am I? Who am I *to you*?'

"Leo remains quiet. Picks up the green and black pen, caresses it with the flat of his thumb. I want to be caressed.

" 'I think you are an extraordinary young woman of whom I've grown very fond. I would like very much to always have you near.'

"He says the last words slowly.

"Why doesn't he ask me who he is to me? Because he knows? He stays quiet, absorbed in the green and black pen. He continues, 'Even if I weren't so selfish in wanting to keep you with me, I would still warn you against going to live down there. Though you imagine yourself to be of the peasants' tribe—as you put it—they do not recognize you as one of them. You are perceived as another daughter of mine by most of them. By some others you are marked in another way. *Una bella puttanina*. A beautiful little whore. I know you've heard the whisperers in the drawing room. They've wanted you to hear them. And me as well. They would like nothing more than for me to deny or, better, to confess, but I speak only of harvesting machines and the price of coal, titillating them with reserve. But there are whisperers everywhere. In the *borghetto,* there would be whisperers. As my daughter, as my lover, either way, the peasants will shun even the suggestion of intimacy with you. And yet, if you were to be placed—if I were to place you—that is, *if it would please you to be placed* in some authoritative position, the peasants would welcome you. You would be sufficiently set apart for their comfort. They would be free to interact with you within the boundaries of your position.'

" 'But what *position?*'

" 'As the teacher of their children. Their *maestra.* Everyone knows that you have been rigorously educated. Everyone knows that you are a superior student. Where you would not be accepted as an equal, you would be very much embraced as someone of a higher rank who'd come to teach their children.'

" 'And what would happen to my status as *la bella puttanina?* Are you saying that if I become *la maestra,* the whisperers will stay quiet?'

" 'No. The truth is that you shall remain sport for the whisperers no matter what you do. And, I think, no matter where you go. My long-ago taking of you as my ward secured that. Despite my intentions and my subsequent actions, I secured that.'

" 'So I'm marked. Stained. In the palace as well as in the *borghetto.*'

" 'Marked, yes. Stained, no. But this is much too much for you to hear all at once. What has taken me months to decide, I've set down before you in an afternoon. Let's stop now. We'll speak a little each day. About the ideas. About all of it.'

"For the first time since he began talking, he smiles. It's nearly dark in the library and he rises to switch on two of the abat-jours, but even the quiet luster they make seems rude. An unexpected ending. He must feel it, too, as he quickly turns off the lamps, lights a candle and a cigarette with a single match. Apologizes for not offering a cigarette to me.

" 'You know I don't smoke,' I tell him, liking that we're speaking of something as adult as a cigarette.

" 'You might want to begin when I tell you what we're going to do.'

"He says this as he sits back down in his chair, stretches his arms out straight on the library table, the cigarette held between his lips. More than his pipe, I like seeing him smoke cigarettes. He was smoking a cigarette that evening. He'd held it between his lips then, too. I saw it when I threw open his door. He took it from between his lips and tossed it into the fire. Walked quickly, nearly ran toward me. *Tosca, what is it?* I saw his naked torso above his riding pants. His voice breaks through my thoughts now. He's talking about the ride he took with Cosimo a while back. He'd like us all to take the same trail someday. Perhaps on Sunday. A long ride, he's saying. To the hunting lodge. A fine old place, he's telling me. Cousins are staying there now. Wild birds. Wild hare. *Potremo pranzare là con loro.* We can lunch there with them. Let's see what Sunday brings, he's saying. The chapel bells ring. Fifteen minutes until vespers.

" 'It's true, you know, Tosca.'

"I've said *a dopo,* later. I've curtsied, turned to leave. I look back at him to learn *what* it is that's true.

" 'My wanting very much to always have you near.' "

CHAPTER VII

"A FEW DAYS LATER, LEO AND COSIMO AND I DRIVE TOGETHER to the *borghetto*. I have never ridden in an automobile since that first day when these two came to fetch me at my father's place, to bring me to the palace. Gangly, sweaty little-girl thighs showing beneath an outgrown dress, sticking to the leather seat. My young woman's legs so long now, I fit myself, half supine, into the child-sized back seat, among the folds of my pale pink dress. Cosimo was driving on that long-ago day as he does now, Leo in the passenger seat. *Is this the same automobile?* I trust him to understand the question. He does. Tells me it *is* the same. He shakes his head in some kind of wonder, smiles. We've already arrived.

"In the almost seven years that I'd lived in the palace, I'd seen little beyond the courtyard of the *borghetto*. Beyond where the goats, chickens, geese wander about, where the shoemaker sets up shop sometimes, where the rabbit hutch stands in the shade of a small stand of poplars. Nothing much beyond that but now, in company with a group of men who Leo introduces as contractors, we three walk through or look into every building in the little community. Single-story structures built of stones and some *pasticcio* of bricks and wood; there is no sign of comfort. There is dignity. The intention of harmony. The *mensa,* dining hall, smells of sunlight and of tomatoes cooked in a pot where tomatoes have been cooking since forever. And at the long tables dressed in every color of oilcloth and on the bare benches beside them is where I think I'd like to sit. There is a dormitory where some of the unmarried men sleep. A bakehouse, a cheese-making hut, a smokehouse, and a chapel. A schoolroom. The remaining structures are divided into small, low-ceilinged, dirt-floored sleeping quarters where families and often the animals sleep together. There is a long, wide trough from which the animals drink, the same source of water where the clothes are washed, scrubbed on flat stones. There are neither bathing nor sanitary facilities. I think of my own childhood home and its relative splendor. I think of Leo's telling me that I am romantic.

"There are few people about—only those too young or too old to be in the fields or those otherwise occupied in the bakehouse or the kitchen. I stay a while to watch these women at work. With none of the haughty joy they spilt at the *festa,* they move about their tasks nearly in silence. Not the press of daily business, theirs is the work of survival. I go to sit near an old man—it's the same old man who played the mouth harp at the *festa,* or at least I think it is. Upon his skinny knees, he holds a black-eyed baby who screams, half in delight, half in want of swifter delivery of the pap the old man spoons into its tiny maw. I want to stay with the old man and the baby. I would give them both a good washing, put them down to sleep while I cooked for them. Leo calls me closer to the group.

"They speak of cutting windows in the exterior walls, of finishing interior walls, of roof tiles and chimneys and separate barns for the animals; a bath house, a *lavandería,* a latrine. There would be real beds built into the sleeping quarters. There would be a coal-fed stove with ten burners in the kitchen. I try to follow the discussion but, more, I follow Cosimo with my eyes as he walks about the place, opening and closing doors he'd already opened and closed before, as though trying to comprehend the misery. I leave the other men and join him.

" 'It will want a year or maybe two, Tosca, but Leo will transform this place. Make it a model, an example other landowners will follow. Either that or they'll make an example of *him*. Shoot him dead for interrupting the way of things.'

"I know the priest is joking when he says *shoot him dead*. Yet the phrase seems crass said here, where Filiberto had lain only days earlier. The priest disturbs me. Perhaps this was his intent. I will not let him know of his success.

" 'You mean other *latifondisti*.'

"He looks at me, holds my gaze, then smiles. 'Yes, other *latifondisti*.'

" 'What will you do to help in all this?' I ask Cosimo, wondering if Leo has spoken with him about the idea of my becoming the schoolmistress.

" 'Mostly I'll rescue Leo when he falters. He will falter. What's to be done here is the smaller part of the plan. It's the work to prepare the fallow land for planting, the work to encourage the peasants to use new equipment and accept new methods of farming that will daunt him. But even those are not the major parts of the plan. You see, Leo swears that, in his lifetime, he will parcel off the land to the peasants and to their children, make them independent farmers who will work to feed themselves, sell their surplus, begin to know the grim joys of handling cash. That will be his magnum opus. His great imprudence, perhaps. I am not convinced that the peasants who rise above their station find happiness. Rather, they find another kind of poverty. Discard their humanity or trade it for more bread. People should be what they were born to be, Tosca. Born to work the land. Born to own the land.'

"Shocked by his own gaffe, the priest cuts off his soliloquy, puts a hand to my shoulder, and says, 'You are so much a part of the prince's family that I find myself forgetting that—I mean to say, it's as though you've always been here, Tosca.'

" '*Va bene, Don Cosimo. Capisco.* It's okay. I understand,' I tell him.

"Once again, he looks at me as though I'm new or different somehow. I *am* different. Not just that my usual heavy taffeta skirt and starched blouse have been surrendered to this silky dress that stops above my ankles, nor that my braids are coiled above my forehead rather than in two fat buns about my ears; not just these make me different, and Cosimo is improbably quiet now, as though trying to connect this Tosca who is almost sixteen to that other one who had been nine. The budding *maestra* to the horse-stealing savage. Surely Leo has not spoken with him about me. Cosimo has begun talking again.

" 'As I was saying, some are born to work the land. Some to own the land. Tightening up the vast and historical distances between their tables, their beds, their birthing and dying—the reforms Leo has in mind to establish are just. But I wish he'd leave it at that. There is no need to parcel off the land. His is a wild scheme, my dear. Wild in the perilous sense. If only he could understand that the peasants would be happy enough just to sleep apart from their pigs.'

"Why does he talk to me of these things? *Wild in the perilous sense.* Does he think I have some sway over Leo? Of course he doesn't think that. But why then . . . He has taken up his story.

" 'The prince is a complicated man, Tosca. So complicated that his ideas can seem simple. Especially to himself. He says there are no villains, no heroes. He says all of us are base and all of us are kind, if not in equal proportions. He's Christ-like. Sometimes. When he's not being Tolstoy. But he is always *Candide*. He persists that what he's doing here does not make him a liberal, a progressive. Calls himself a patrician with a patrician's detachment to things not his own, says he's not trying to change things anywhere else but right here. In other words, Leo's world is small. His land. His peasants. Men and women whom he does not idealize, by the way. But for whom he feels responsible. He wants them to ennoble themselves, work with all their might, have the security of a laden table and a decent bed. He wants to take care of the whole lot of them as though they were his children.'

"Cosimo can hardly expect me to understand this business of reforms and sleeping apart from pigs and patrician detachment any more than Leo could have expected me to take in all he'd said that day in the library. And yet, I did understand Leo. And I think I do understand the priest. Mostly I understand that Leo is good.

"I walk, look about the *borghetto* with Cosimo, but all I hear is Leo's voice. *It's true, Tosca. My wanting very much to always have you near.* Words of love. Were they not words of love? Paternal love? Romantic love? I speak with Cosimo hardly knowing what I say. Less what he says. To my *graceful biding of time* with the palace regimes, I will now add Leo's revelations. Those which I understood and those which he left in the half-light of that candle on the library table. What I know for certain is that it will be me who rescues Leo when he falters.

CHAPTER VIII

"THE GREAT WORK IN THE *BORGHETTO* BEGAN THAT SUMMER OF 1946. The peasants went about their usual days in the fields while truckloads of day workers—many of them freshly discharged soldiers—began the tasks of restructuring the buildings. The peasants moved their pallets and personal belongings into the kitchen or arranged them along the walls of the dining hall and sometimes out into the open air while the men worked so the cottages—as Leo took to calling the sleeping quarters—would be readied by late autumn. Each day's progress brought cheers of delight from the peasants as they returned home from the fields to see another row of windows, yet another portion of the roof laid in terra-cotta tiles. Perhaps even more than the bath house and the laundry and the barns for the animals, it was the stoves in the kitchen that caused the greatest hallelujah. The stoves and the abundance they promised.

My excitement at being able to observe the work was akin to that which I'd felt when Leo first took over the pace and the content of my studies. I would ride down with Leo and Cosimo each morning and then, forgoing the ritual tea parties with the princesses and Simona and the teachers, I would go there again in the late afternoons. I thought of little else but how beautifully the village was being restored. Even the schoolroom. When there was no one to catch me at it, I would stand at its doorway and imagine myself walking among the tables and desks, reading to the children as Suor Diana had read to me, and Leo tramping in to hear them recite the Greek alphabet, to tell them the story of his beloved Demeter. It was the day of my seventeenth birthday when the schoolroom was finished. Without his saying so, I knew it was Leo's gift to me."

"His once faithful presiding over palace life gave way to his frequent absences. He would lunch in the fields with the peasants. Bread and oil and tomatoes and wine. Like an errant boy, he could be seen on a Sunday morning disheveled, breathless, taking the stairs two at a time on his way to a bath before Mass. And at those times when he was present among the palace household, he seemed always to be looking somewhere beyond. Beyond the great blue and white tureen from which he no longer served the soup. Beyond Simona's bobbed hair set in tight waves and beyond the points of her red cheeks. Beyond the princesses and beyond me, too. Impassioned by this work with and for the peasants, the prince was a man living a great love.

"Delicate as lace, the spaces between Leo and Simona were worked slowly and with the same *politesse* as the perfunctory, obligatory arrangement of their union had always been worked so that, in their eventual estrangement, the pattern of their lives, on its face, hardly changed. Refined adjustments. Tacit concessions. A year, perhaps more, passed with no more than these to imply that the artfully played farce of their marriage had been revised.

"Simona began to operate the household as if Leo no longer lived in his own palace. Stepping up the pace of her already legendary entertaining, she took on the triple role of grand dame, martyr, and femme fatale, one affectation more frenzied than another and all of them meant to gather about her those who would champion her in ridicule of Leo's purportedly crazed behavior. Panderers to her wishes she found in lush numbers. *The moment we step down to them is the moment they will step over us.* The nobles' creed, Simona would say it in her martyr's voice and, softly, gutturally, whatever bejeweled troupe over which she held court that evening repeated it.

"And to what hell did she assign me during that time? Her perfect pawn, she was kinder than ever to me, the nubile evidence of her bountiful sufferance. I paid small attention to her dramas for, like Leo, I was living a love. I had officially become *la maestra* in the *borghetto*."

"With neither credentials nor certification but with guidance from teachers from a school in Enna whom Leo and Cosimo had consulted, I went to work. A single rudimentary curriculum was offered to children ages five through twelve. Beyond the age of twelve, it would, for the time being, still be necessary for children to work alongside their parents. *Per ora, per ora.* For now, Leo would say again and again.

"Nine students composed my class. Three five-year-olds, one who was six, four who ranged from seven to nine, and one lovely thirteen-year-old girl called Cosettina.'

I break the pact to refrain from questions.

"Was she *that* Cosettina? The one who . . . ?"

"She was that Cosettina. Sixty-one when she died."

I'm sorry for my interruption, since now Tosca stays quiet. I ask her if she will please go on.

"Cosimo would join me in the schoolroom at eight each morning, greet the children with me. *Buongiorno, monsignore. Buongiorno, professoressa*—as much threat as greeting in their singsong shouted reply. Some days Cosimo would say the rosary with them or read from *The Lives of the Saints*. Always he would bless them. Kiss the top of each of their heads as they stood in a row before him, then stand still for their strangling hugs and wishes for his good day. And then we began. Quite literally. The alphabet. The saying and the writing of the characters. Quickly this proved too stringent. Who could sit still for so long, who could be indoors for so long, who could not laugh and say bad words for so long? Journeys to the latrine. Cosettina gone to herd escapees. Tragic screams over the rights to the stub of a pencil. Was it true that I carried *cioccolatini* and bread and cheese in my purse for them? They were hungry, and I knew how that hunger felt. I could call it up like my father's face. Their faces. Even as they shout and run and screech for me to watch them at some feat performed among the hot stones, the burning sand, the haunted starveling faces of them show through their deception. They are only in the disguise of children.

" 'But they're holding pencils and touching paper and listening—even if only for a minute or two at a time—to what you are trying to tell them. Patience. It's a beginning,' Leo would say.

"Sometimes the children would take my hands, pull me out into the courtyard, ask me to come to the *mensa* with them, fight over who should sit next to me if I ever did come. I never did, though, until one of the women, Cosettina's mother, invited me. I remembered months before when I'd first seen the *mensa* and how I'd longed to sit there. Be part of them. I knew now that Leo had been right. The only way to be part of them was to keep my distance. Be of service but be separate. The peach-skinned girl was there. They called her Olga.

" '*Olga, vieni più vicino.* Olga, come closer,' the men beckoned her. A red and green kerchief, bright red and green as though it was Russian, she'd tied like a turban about her head and from it fugitive curls lay flat upon damp cheeks.

" '*Pazienza, pazienza, c'è abbastanza.* Patience, there's enough,' says the peach-skinned girl.

"Carrying a great flat basket heaped with tiny spring onions, dirt still clinging to the gossamer fringe of their just-dug roots, Olga flits up and down the oilclothed tables, handing them out, those onions, like jewels. Two to a person. One for a child. On my plate, she places three, bends her head 'round to kiss my forehead. Says, *Benvenuta.* Welcome.

"Cosettina is spooning *maccheroni e ceci,* someone else piles bread in front of me, another fills my cup, half and half, from the jugs of water and wine. They whack the onions on the side of the table to dislodge the dirt, drag each one through the tin can of coarse gray salt that sits on every table. As close as these mountain people have ever come to the sea. Bite the crunchy, salty white bulb, let it burn the mouth. A spoonful of pasta, a bite of onion. Pique the hungers. Gratify the hungers. The poor are masterful at both. I did what they did. I did what I used to do. I did what, for such a long time, I'd wanted to do."

CHAPTER IX

"THE REVITALIZING OF THE FALLOW FIELDS, THE CARVING OUT of rudimentary roads was accomplished in a single spring and summer. It was 1948. A year after the reconstruction of the *borghetto* itself. Once again, workers were imported from many parts of the island so the peasants might keep to their routines. Keep to the business of feeding themselves. Leo took less and less from the peasants' harvests of fruits and vegetables. Less and less of the capricious bounty from the olive trees and the vines. To supplement the needs of the palace, Leo brought the oldest of the peasant men up to transform great swathes of the formal gardens into *orti*, vegetable and herb gardens. Pumpkins and artichokes flourished where once there were beds of roses. Leo adored this allegory. The old men, too, were transformed. They were doing something for the prince, especially for him. A bent and wrinkled band of cherubim, they dug and planted and weeded, tenderly bathing the seedlings, huddling about the pristine rows, willing the buds to swell and the leaves to flare. And they did.

As did the first crops in the newly planted fields. Wheat and corn and barley and fava beans swelled under the meek sun of winter and, sown again in spring, these same crops roasted under the great flames of the summer sun. As did, mysteriously, *la novara*—tomatoes and watermelons. These last asked no rain, no water fed to them from the new blue pipes laid like arteries under the flesh of the earth. Like succulents in the desert, *la novara* bloomed from the parched earth. Under the glittering beams of Demeter's smile, the peasants said. It was she and San Isidoro and Santa Rosalia and Zeus himself who were variously invoked and presented with, each peasant according to his own fondness, some small sacrifice. A loaf of bread. A wreath of wild poppies. A great fire tended through the night of the full moon.

"Significant changes had already softened their lives, and this first harvest augured well. Women swept and scrubbed their sleeping quarters and over every new windowsill there was lain, each morning, a new mattress to air and take the sun. From bolts of heavy canvas and thick fustian cotton, the women fashioned curtains for their doors and put jars of wildflowers on their single front steps. They were at home. Crisscrossing lines of lurid-colored clothing and linens flapped like buccaneer flags across the courtyard, and the bakehouse did two shifts a day. The children queued every second Saturday morning outside the tiny whitewashed room designated as an infirmary for compulsory visits with an itinerant doctor. A birthing room was arranged adjacent to it and the resident midwife in the *borghetto* fussed over its furnishings and counted out the new white towels, folding and refolding them every chance she got, and the mood in the *borghetto* was jubilant that summer of 1948. A temperate Sicilian jubilance. *Don't let the gods know how well things go lest they be tempted to send down some scherzo, if only to keep things interesting. S-h-h-h.*"

CHAPTER X

" 'But they have stolen from *themselves*. It's unthinkable.'

" 'Nothing is unthinkable if you will only refrain from limiting yourself to the boundaries of intellect. You insist on rational thinking in an irrational situation, Leo.'

"Leo and Cosimo are alone in the breakfast room when the princesses and I approach the door. We hear this exchange. Look at one another, wondering whether we should enter. No one else seems to be at table with the two men. Yolande steps in first, and Charlotte and I follow her. The two men are sitting at the far end of the table. They do not acknowledge us. We sit, and Yolande rings the bell. The maids bring coffee and milk and bread and biscuits, but only Yolande begins to eat and drink.

" 'Papà?' Charlotte calls out.

" '*Sì. Buongiorno, ragazze. Tutto bene?*' He hardly looks our way, rises, waits for Cosimo to rise, and they quit the room without another word.

" 'Don't you know?' Yolande asks me.

"Yolande is nearing seventeen, yet her face and body linger in some thwarted pubescence. Pinches of cornstarch paste she wears here and there about her cheeks and chin to mask the damage she's done overnight to her blemished skin. She is awkwardly plump and, when she speaks, it is too often with infantile petulance, jutting forth her broad, square jaw. Leo's same broad, square jaw. She has Leo's eyes, as well, though. Blessing enough for anyone. Like the violets under the lemon trees. I look at her.

" 'Don't I know what?'

" 'About the trouble in the *borghetto*. I went down to the kitchen to ask the cook to fix *frittelle* this morning and I heard them saying, *Qualcuno ha rubato tutto*. Someone stole everything.'

" 'Perhaps you misunderstood. Don't be concerned . . .' I tell her.

" 'I am only concerned that no one has brought the *frittelle*,' she assures me.

"Charlotte sits holding her carefully buttered bread. Casts her fawn's eyes back and forth between her sister and me.

" 'Don't worry, Tosca. Papà will take care of them.'

"An exquisite *infanta* in her full white dress and blond braids, Charlotte is the dainty issue of her parents' cold alliance. Suffusion of their coalesced charms. I think of my sister, who is one year younger than Charlotte. Wonder for the tenth time already that morning about The Tiny Mafalda. Charlotte and I have been chums in a closer way of late. Different from the initial and perfunctory rapport that proximity forced upon we three girls. I rarely speak more than a few words to Yolande in a day. But Charlotte, when she can, comes to visit me in my rooms in the evening. This sometime ritual began years ago—she was perhaps nine or ten—when she appeared late one night and, uninvited and without a word, tucked herself next to me in my bed.

" 'Is it true that you are Papà's *puttanina*?'

" 'Do you know what that word means, Charlotte?'

" 'Yes, I think it means *very good friend.* Or *little doll,* like *puppetta.* It sounds just like *puppetta.* Mamà said, Oh, Leo why don't you go to visit your *puttanina.* I know she meant you, Tosca, because it was you about whom they were speaking. So what I want to know is how I can become Papà's little doll just like you are. I don't think Papà likes me very much. But I like him so very much, Tosca.'

"I'd told Leo of my conversation with his younger daughter and he laughed until tears fell. Then another kind of tears came.

" 'I've been trying all these years to be with my children, especially with Charlotte, but Simona will not have it, he said. Someday I shall explain this to you.'

"I come back from my reverie to see Yolande, in her exasperation with the cook, busying herself with the bell. I blow Charlotte a surreptitious kiss. Rise to gather my things. Late for school. From the door, I whisper, 'I know he will. I know your papà will take care of them.'

"But there is no school that day. Nor has anyone gone to work in the fields.

"Everyone is in the courtyard of the *borghetto.* The peasants are gathered 'round Leo, who stands in their midst, chickens scurrying about his high polished boots. Children huddle their mothers' legs or sleep in their arms. The sun is pallid in a sky the color of stone.

"No one speaks. Moving only her hand, Cosettina beckons me to stand near her.

" 'I am not angry and I do not seek any sort of retribution. But I must know who it was among you who *did this.* Who, just as we are beginning to live the results of our work, has seen fit to thieve us. To thieve himself. Because I am convinced that whoever took the stores was one of us. One of us who was in collaboration with outsiders. There are signs and proof that this is the case. All I ask is that you make yourself known to me. There will be no punishment, per se. I want to understand what it was that could turn a member of this family against the rest of us.'

"There is silence. The thick, inexorable silence of *omertà* is broken only by the scratching of the chickens and murmurings of fidgeting babies.

" 'I will be in my office until vespers. I will wait for you,' Leo says, as if addressing a single person. And then he's gone.

"Leo had assigned the building of a new storeroom. Brick and stone, it had a proper roof of new red tiles and its cement floor was painted a metallic gray, like the hull of a warship. He stocked it with drums of olive oil, demijohns of wine, sacks and sacks of legumes. At one end of the place, he'd put in worktables and a small stove. It was to be a *laboratorio,* a workroom where some of the women would prepare conserves and marmalades with the oranges and lemons from the *agrumeti* and the sacks of dried pears and apples and almonds Leo had brought in. These would have been an unimagined luxury. Even the stove is gone. The still shiny gray floor is empty, save two demijohns of wine and the cauldron in which the jam would have been cooked.

"I go to Leo's office. The door is open and he is reading in a black leather armchair.

" 'It wasn't so much, Tosca. A token of my patronage. A small covenant, I suppose.'

" 'How could it have been taken with no one knowing?'

" 'Someone knows. Perhaps most of them do. They're Sicilians. It wouldn't have been difficult to port the whole lot away in the flatbed of a single truck. Three, maybe four, strong men would have needed less than an hour. The goods have already been reordered. I know that no one will come to see me before vespers.'

" 'I have. I've come to tell you that you'll feel much better if you will think of the peasants rather than of yourself. At this moment. *Loro sono vergognati.* They are ashamed. You are wounded, as a father would be. You gave your children gifts and one of those children wanted not the gifts, but what the gifts could buy. Think of how the other children suffer for the deed of that one.'

"He looks at me. Begins to rise from his chair but I don't wait. I fall into a curtsy, if less deeply than usual, and walk out the door."

"There is a trail that splits the lower pastures where the sheep graze in summer, and Leo and Cosimo and I have been riding it these past mornings, greeting the peasants on their way to the fields. This morning two men lie to the side of our path, nearly concealed in the high grass and the plumes of the wild carrots. Leo dismounts, then Cosimo does. Both tell me to stay astride. But not to ride off. I look at the men and they appear to be sleeping. Whole, save the wide black-red gashes in their throats. In a low-growing scrub of wild marjoram, the old man with the mouth harp sits against a purplish rock. When I look at him, he takes up the little iron thing and begins to blow."

"Cosimo has ridden on ahead. To get to the church, I think, and Leo and I ride, slowly and without speaking, until we are nearly at the stables. He says then, 'They neither desired nor needed me as arbitrator. Just as it was when Filiberto was murdered and they wanted me to keep my noble distance. *Cose nostra.* Our things. This was another of *their* things. They took care of it. I'm certain that none of them was conflicted over what was necessary to do. And it was done. Deft, inflexible, despising.' "

CHAPTER XI

" 'MY GRANDFATHER WOULD STAND AT THE EDGE OF THE FIELDS when the peasants were sowing or harvesting and recite hymns to Demeter.'

" 'Is that what you're going to do?'

"It's Sunday morning in the late September of 1948 and Leo and I, having raced over the wide, just-harvested field of a neighboring landowner, have stopped to wait for the other riders to come into view. More than a year has passed since he first spoke of the hunting lodge to me, but today we are a party of twelve bound for that very place, awaited there by cousins, Leo's bird-shooting companions, a contingent from the palace staff who'd gone ahead to help the lodge caretaker—a man who Leo calls *Lullo*—to prepare a feast of *colombacci*, wild doves, for our Sunday lunch. The week before, the birds had been left to swing from the eaves of the barn, to hang into putrescence, Leo says, promising that the rotting innards of them will have been pummeled into suave pâtés with grappa and wild herbs, a lush paste to smear over slabs of wood-baked bread. *A leccarda, in salmì,* roasted with lard and juniper; he recites a litany of dishes and I tell him, spoiling his hunter's glee, that all I shall eat is soup.

"From the high palisade above the field where we wait, shards of shale and small stones fall. Sheep graze up there and perhaps one has strayed to the verge, disturbing the fragile rock, or is it not a sheep who's strayed? A hawk, unseen, thrums it wings, and I think it's only he who knows what moved the stones as, side by side, we sit in our saddles, horses bending to crop the wheat stubbles. It is my eighteenth birthday. Leo has yet to make his good wishes to me. Nor has anyone else. Tradition has it that, on one's birthday, a small gift waits beside one's breakfast plate. The household comes in to join the family to sing *tanti auguri.* This morning, nothing. I shall be eighteen without them. I dismount and, without asking, tie my reins to the pommel of his saddle. I walk away a bit from Leo and his fiendish talk of corrupted birds. He follows me.

" 'I've been thinking that I would. I mean, that I would like to do what my grandfather did. To recite the old hymns during the harvest. The idea came from the *ortolani* who tend the palace vegetable gardens. Whenever I can, I go to sit nearby them as they work, open a book to read but instead listen to them speaking of Demeter and San Isidoro as though they'd grown up with them, which, I suppose, they did. Over the years I have passed far too little time with the peasants out in the fields or anywhere else about the farms, and so it was a revelation to me to hear these old men going on about Greek history, telling one another, in their rustic way, stories about Demeter and Persephone and Hades and Zeus and The Son of Kronos, embellishing the tales here and there, waving their arms and raising their fists, shouting sometimes or speaking softly, as though they were acting out the dramas. Which, of course, they are.'

"He says this last as though it were yet another revelation.

" 'That history is as much theirs as is the history of their own families. As much as the story of Jesus and Mary. They are descendants of the ancients who, with Demeter leading them, grew the first wheat from barren fields. That's how it all began, Tosca. With Demeter and with their ancestors, and I envy them their easy alliance with the past. I sit and read about it but they live it. I sit with my books while they, who can't read, carry it forth. Pass it on. As much as they can. If they could, I think many of them would be content to go back to the georgics, to Homeric chants and scythes and plow horses and passing 'round the saint. You think that I've forgotten what day it is, don't you?'

"I overlook the question. Pretend to. 'Passing 'round which saint?'

" 'The sainted wine skin. Better, a jug. Seven times between sunrise and sunset, women and maidens would walk the ranks of the harvesters with bursting wine skins or jugs of it on their heads. And the men would drink. Years ago, when all the work was done by hand, the sowing and the harvesting were as ritualistic as folk dances. Every move was choreographed. There were pipers who beat out music so the peasants could move their scythes in rhythm.'

" 'Like this?' I stride the shorn field, twisting my wrist as though it held a scythe, swinging my body as though it were cutting wheat. As though it were dancing.

" 'Yes. Somewhat like that,' he says.

"I run back to him. 'One field. Let's just harvest a single field in the old way. For good luck. As a prayer. The other fields would be cut with the machines. Will you do it?'

" 'Is that what you'd like as a birthday gift? A ceremonial harvest? I can't put all the pieces together by tomorrow when we begin, but I can try to be ready for the last field. Five, maybe six days from now. Is that it? Is that the gift you'd like?'

"I look at Leo, watch him pull a sack of fried sugared bread from his saddlebag. He feeds the horses and I wonder, for what must be the ten thousandth time, *who am I to you?* Yes, I answer to myself, I would like this ceremonial harvest as my gift but, as much, I would like to understand: *Who am I to you?*

"Since that afternoon in the library when Leo first began to tell me about his plans for the *borghetto,* for the peasants—that day just after Filiberto had been murdered—we two have been working in a kind of partnership. It has become the natural, the waited-for event when we meet once or twice each day to speak of his progresses, to speak of mine.

" *'The farthest northern field has been planted. The machinery broke down and broke down again but, somehow, the last rows were finished before sunset. I drove the tractor.'*

"*Cosettina read magnificently today and the children were so quiet. Enchanted by the story. Enchanted by her, intrigued that one of them, one of their own, had mastered all those jumbled letters that actually form words. They raised their hands, asked questions. It was wonderful.*

" *'Will you spend some time in the infirmary tomorrow morning? The doctor will instruct you on what to look for. The children are fearful of him. And timid in my presence. They trust you.'*

"As a couple might, as a father and daughter might, we collaborate. Much of the time, this suffices. It contents. The household and the peasants have come to look upon this collaboration with a benign neutrality. It is only the whisperers whom we fatigued, the famished music-hall audience come to see the lusty tale of the prince and the *puttanina.* Only a bucolic poem read by the hero and his muse did they get for their money. But Simona had strutted in the wings, poised to deliver a lascivious intermezzo. She brought lovers to stay at the palace. Sometimes introduced them into the family circle as distant cousins or sons of old friends. They sat at table with us, at Mass with us. They lounged in the salons. Gave orders to the staff. Leo was gracious. The princesses were mortified; other guests, visiting family, were outraged. The tables turned. Whisperers always know the right thing to say.

"*I, for one, have always taken Leo's part. By birth, by comportment, it's he who is the noble. Simona is nothing more than rich.*

" *'Her character has always been, shall we say, hysterical.'*

" *'Frenzied.'*

" *'Despotic.'*

" *'Poor dear princesses.'*

" *'Poor dear Leo.'*

" *'And that lovely Tosca. Where does she fit into this grand imbroglio?'*

"They want to know. I want to know."

"We walk our horses up the long pebbled road to the lodge, hand them over to the stablemen as the cousins and the hunting mates come out to greet us. All I see is this place Leo calls the lodge. A castle, it is. A turreted tower—no, two towers—with bowed iron balconies wrapped about the mullioned windows like the bones of a hooped skirt. Like those at the palace, the great marble portals are ornamented with the crests of the illustrious Anjou. Below, vaulted loggias are sustained by red marble columns, the carved capital of each one the face of a goddess. A saint. I am beginning to understand. The roof, steep and peaked in a way I'd never seen, is covered in small ovals of what look to be porcelain. As though the gods, sated from feasting, hurled their plates down upon the castle and, liking the felicitous pattern in which they fell, fixed the pieces of them in gold light.

"And what good ghost was it who long ago flung fistfuls of seeds from the towers? Everywhere 'round the place there are accidental gardens, blown tarnished roses gorging on the sun, climbing where they will, oleander tall as old trees and, here and there, soaring rusty mountain pines. The dappled trunk of a lone magnolia is cleaved to form a bed. There is no sign of a mortal hand.

" *'Gianpiero Sultano, ti presento Tosca Brozzi.'*

"Leo introduces me to his guests and I smile, say *molto lieto,* but I see only the gardens. I am not yet present among the embracing and greeting. I am in the tower flinging hollyhock seeds. Sleeping inside the heart of the magnolia.

"While we still mill about, small cups of cool almond milk are passed to us by a beautiful red-haired boy. The caretaker's son. In short leather pants and a fine white shirt, his feet brown and bare, he is called Valentino. He may be seven, and I think he must be the official host of the day, as he tells the other women riders and me of the ewers of lemon water and towels he'd set out for us on a table under a pergola.

" *'Venite, Venite,'* he says, leading us inside the shade with the same joy as if the path led to the baby in the manger.

"A long stone table has been laid under the loggia on the side of the house that looks to sheepfolds and an olive grove. Baskets and buckets of wildflowers and weeds and thick ochre candles in black iron holders ornament the table. *Everyone* is seated. The maids and the stablemen who've come from the palace. Lullo, the caretaker, and Valentino, his son. At the palace, the maids and the stablemen do not sit at the prince's table. Now each person takes the hand of the person next to him and Cosimo says grace. I am seated between Leo and Valentino. It is the first time I hold Leo's hand.

"Terra-cotta pitchers of wine and plates and platters of the glorified doves are passed from person to person rather than being served by a steward. A composite of the way things are done at the palace and the way things are done in the *borghetto*. The best of each has come together here. I take a thick trencher of bread spread with the black paste and bite it directly from my hand as the others do. As Leo does. It's splendid, and I take another. Lullo holds forth.

" 'Roast the grappa-washed innards in a copper pan over a good fire with rosemary, salvia, black olives, garlic, the dried peel of an orange, and red wine. As the wine is consumed, add more. Never let the pan parch. Never let the innards drown. When the mess is black as old blood and the perfumes cause madness, scrape it into a mortar and pound it to butter. Let it rest in the mortar under a clean white cloth for two days.'

"*Amen,* we say as one."

"Bottles of marsala and *moscato* and small silver cups. Plums on their leafed branches in bowls of water. Biscuits crusted in sesame seeds. Almond paste formed and colored to look like India figs set on a tray among the real fruit. *'Guess which is which,'* Valentino challenges, placing the tray before us. It's nearly five and only Leo, Cosimo, and I still sit at table, most others having made for the darkness of their bedrooms. A blessed rest.

"We will return to the palace in the automobile that one of the staff had driven earlier to the lodge. Our horses will be fetched and transported back tomorrow. We will start out at dusk, stopping halfway at a *locanda* of which Leo is fond. A stone house, or the ruins of it, set in a pine woods. There'll be cheese and wine. A walk to stretch our legs.

" 'I will stay the night here,' says Cosimo. 'Go on to Enna in the morning and be back at the palace by dinner. The Curia is not pleased with me.'

"Leo laughs. 'That must mean that God is *dearly* pleased with you, my friend.'

"The two men rise, shake hands. Embrace.

" '*A domani,* Cosimo.'

" '*A domani, principe. A domani,* Tosca.' The priest takes my hand, brings it to his lips without touching them to my skin. '*Tanti auguri,*' he says. "*Tanti auguri, cara* Tosca.' He takes his leave.

"The all-morning ride, the sun, the wine. The great dreamy work of flinging the seeds from the towers. The innards of a dove. I would like to sleep. More, I want to stay with him. Is it my birthday that makes me bold?

" 'You brought me to the palace all those years ago with the intent of making love to me, didn't you?'

"Leo has been feeding bits of almond paste to the hunting dog that sits at his feet. He looks at me now while still running his hand across the dog's muzzle. He nods, as though he has been expecting my question.

" 'The *intent,* as you call it, was not defined as such. You were a child. And I knew any number of delightful women with whom I might amuse myself. Certainly when I first saw you, the potential of your beauty struck me. Intrigued me. But I did not pace the upper floors, waiting for you to ripen.'

"It's I who am caught off guard with his parry. His openness. I like it, and yet it frightens me. A rite of passage.

" 'You know it was your father who *offered* you to me. He found you incorrigible even at nine. He called you a scowling vixen. Said your sister was as meek as your mother was. When he came to me to propose your becoming my ward, I could barely hear him out. I've always found it painful to listen to one father or another—more, to a mother—who has decided to surrender a child. Whatever the reason. Often they are babies, newborn bastards whom the nuns have refused because all the cribs in the convents are full. Since the rich don't seem to breed as easily as the poor hereabouts, sometimes the bastards are sold to a barren couple who will often pass off the child as its own miracle. And, in my position, there are always the children of one's own succumbed peasants. Influenza, consumption, a tired heart that explodes one afternoon in the fields. A slip, a fall, a cry for help unheard over the noise of the thresher. Often there is neither sufficient space nor food among the other families to permit any one of them to take in another little soul. Said little soul is then bathed and dressed and combed and brought to the servants' entry. With apologies. With gratitude. From time to time my parents had as many as ten or twelve of these orphans in our home.'

" 'Has it happened to you? Did people leave babies in your care?'

" 'Of course it's happened. But Simona is not a woman like my mother was. I pushed fat white envelopes through the Catherine wheel of one convent or another. Waited by the gate for some shrouded nun to take the swaddled bundle from my arms. I have always done this myself. Thinking that somehow my personal passing over of the baby would assure care and safety. Even affection. I have a book that records each child's placement. And the yearly envelopes that I continue to send in their names. Still I am plagued. The *giumpe* is often not sacred.' Elbows on the table, head in his hands, Leo is quiet. After a while, 'But what your father did was rare, at least in my experience or my memory. I'd never before been faced by a young, able-bodied man who enjoyed what was, for those times, a relatively thriving business and yet who sought to 'turn over' to me his perfectly healthy, perfectly bright, perfectly lovely nine-year-old daughter.'

" 'I've never thought about what your first encounter with my father must have been like. I mean, how the two of you arrived at your *agreement*. I'm certain my father made no such thing as a sentimental appeal. A straight-forward business discussion it must have been, for I was neither a bastard nor an orphan. I was chattel. An excess of goods that could be turned into cash. Or was it horses? Rather than my father beseeching you to take me because he couldn't care for me, he sold me to you, didn't he? I knew it back then as I know it now.' I am shocked at my own words.

"The spilling of bitterness was not deliberate and yet I have launched it. Leo comes to where I sit, bends to take me in his arms. A paternal embrace. I push him away. I stand up before him in a coquettish pose.

" 'Look at me. Am I a pitiful creature? Am I broken, cowering because my father didn't want me? I think not. I won't tell you that I have never felt sadness because of his treatment, his eventual liquidation of me. I won't tell you that. But whatever pain there was had begun to dissolve before you came to fetch me. You didn't save me, sir. I saved myself.'

"How ungrateful I am. What devil do I channel? I sit back down. Leo sits next to me. Without looking at him, I dare to touch the back of his hand that rests on his thigh. I touch his hand with the tips of my fingers. Penitence.

" 'Tell me about your father. Some of what you remember about him,' Leo says, shifting my hand to lie inside his.

" 'Early on even my instinctual love for my father began to feel wrong to me. At first, when my mother died, I would reach out to him. Mimic her, I suppose. After all it was my turn to be *Mamà,* wasn't it? I'd put an extra biscuit beside his coffee in the morning, which, because they were all counted out and had to last for a certain number of days, he must have known meant one less for me. He always ate the biscuit but he never said *thank you.* He hardly spoke to me at all.

" 'He never came home until late in the evening. I would put The Tiny Mafalda to bed, tell her the story of the princess who had three beautiful dresses and who bathed in warm milk and ate cakes with violet icing every morning at eleven and whose mother promised she would never, ever die. I would kiss her, hold her hand until she fell asleep, and would go then to sit on the step outside our house, the cat in my lap, to wait for my father. Sometimes I would fall asleep like that, awakening only when the cat started at my father's approach.

" '*Papà, I was waiting for you. Are you hungry? I left an egg for you and some bread.*

" 'He'd sit and eat the egg, tear at the bread with his teeth the way Mama told us only animals did. I'd stand beside the table babbling on about how long it took for The Tiny Mafalda to fall asleep, or about how her arm still hurt and her shoulder in the place where she'd fallen on it last week. And if there wasn't any, I'd always invent some good news for him. Mama used to do that, too. About the hay looking as though it would last another week or about the mushrooms I'd found under the big pine that morning on the way to school and that I'd already set to dry on the roof. I'd stand there talking and talking, not daring to stop for fear of the silence I'd hear instead of his voice responding to me. I didn't like the silence between him and me. He'd open the spigot on the barrel and hold his glass under it, all the while looking at me. Drink down the wine in one or two long swallows. Unbuckle his belt, step out of his pants, and lie down on his bed, which I'd made up with the sheets that Anna Lavanderia had left all clean and folded that afternoon or, if it wasn't her day, the ones I'd smoothed and tucked tight under the mattress just the way he liked them.'

" 'Who was Anna Lavanderia?'

"Does it really matter who Anna Lavanderia was? I ask myself. I understand that my story makes Leo feel sad, that he searches for an excuse to distract me from it, and I oblige.

" 'Anna Lavanderia. That was what everyone called *la lavandaia,* the washerwoman, who went from house to house—each one on a certain day—to do the washing and the hanging out to dry in the sun. She'd come back in the afternoon after her rest for the folding and the ironing. Mostly rich people used her, but since The Tiny Mafalda and I were just too small to handle the weight of the sheets, my father began bartering with Anna when my mother died. A sack of tomatoes and two cabbages one week. Artichokes or rice or sometimes things from the *dispensa* that I'd thought I'd hidden from him. Like sugar and real butter to make a cake for Mafalda.'

I return to my story.

" 'So, still saying nothing, my father would lie down on his bed, fold his arms under his head, and stare at me. I never could tell whether he was waiting for me to bend to kiss him the way Mama had taught us to do. But I never did. I never once bent to kiss him after Mama died. I'd take up the cat, climb the ladder with the fat beast in my arms, and settle us both down beside The Tiny Mafalda. I'd stay awake for a while, at least until I heard the even rumbling of his sleeping breath. I was the *vigilessa,* the guardian. The cat and I. Together we would keep The Tiny Mafalda safe.

" 'But it wasn't long before I stopped being the next mama and started being just plain Tosca. It wasn't right that I try to be mama. It felt like I had to go to confession every time I'd flash him my big, sweet mama smile and tell him I'd saved an egg for him. The mama smile felt like a lie. It felt better when I just went about my business, not even considering what might or might not make him happy. I began to think only about The Tiny Mafalada and me. And about my friends and my teacher and the people who were so happy to see Mafalda and me in the market every morning.

" 'I'd put my mother's brown purse across my proud flat chest, and even though it hung down below my knees, I thought it made me look fancy. How I loved that purse! How I loved brushing my sister's hair, braiding it tight and neat, using my own spit to smooth it 'round the parts and tying the ends with red ribbons, sometimes pink, buckling her sandals, taking her by the hand. *Sei pronta?* She was always ready, as though we were going to a fair or a *festa.* The market was like having relatives to visit. Like it must be having a grandmother. Anyway, I loved that it was my sister and me off to buy the cabbage or the potatoes or two hundred grams of *maccheroncini* or whatever it was I'd cook that day for our supper. Every merchant gave us something extra. Sometimes a fistful of parsley or an apple cut in two, a handful of golden *zíbbíbi* that we'd never eat on the spot but that I'd put in my bag so The Tiny Mafalda and I could have a tea party later. One of the shepherds almost always took his knife from his belt and chiseled out a nice, big crumble of his oldest pecorino. One part into the bag, the other divided into two pieces. With the same reverence I'd show for a communion wafer, I'd tell Mafalda to stick out her tongue and I would place it directly into the tiny open waiting mouth. A hungry little bird. The other into mine. *Now don't chew,* I'd tell her. *Let it melt. Let it fill your mouth, your nostrils,* I'd say, and I knew that she loved that burst of big, harsh flavor the way I loved it. Even when it didn't, we would tell each other that the flavor lasted all the way back home.

" 'I was supposed to go to school and leave my sister with her doll and the bread that was her lunch, and sometimes I would. Sometimes I would take her with me, let her sit on my knees or in the back of the schoolroom, where she could play with the other children who were left in the care of their older siblings. But often I didn't go to school at all in those months right after Mama died. As soon as we came home from the market, I'd start right in cooking the supper. As though I had ten children and six starving shepherds to feed, I would chop and boil and fret over the cabbage or the potatoes, set the table, make things look nice. I found that I could be perfectly happy even without my father's love. You see, I'd figured it out. With the help of Francesco Brasini.'

" 'What did you figure out? And who was Francesco Brasini?'

"This time Leo is not trying to distract me but is genuinely rapt and wanting to follow my story.

" 'It doesn't matter who he was. It only matters what he did. If you'll listen, you'll understand. I figured it out like this: My father was never kind to my mother, and so why in the world would he be kind to me? And why would I expect him to be kind to me? I figured out that he wasn't kind because he *couldn't* be kind. *He wasn't a kind man.*

Like he wasn't a *tall* man or a *blond* man or a man with big feet. Understanding that made me feel better. Some people are born empty, sir. All manner of good deeds and patience and loving kindness can't even begin to fill them up. My father didn't smile at me or talk to me not because *I* wasn't a good person or a worthy person but because smiling and talking and being kind were not things he had the capacity to do. He couldn't grow blond hair and he couldn't smile. That's how my eight-year-old mind began to comprehend things. And once I'd got all that clear and straight in my mind, I was able to get other things clear and straight. Like how one part of a puzzle put in place helps you to see where the other pieces fit. What I learned about my father helped me to be ready for Signor Brasini.'

" 'Tosca, who in hell is this *Brasini?*'

" 'Your interruptions force me to repeat myself. My father didn't smile at my mother or talk nicely to her or hold her face in his hands and kiss her lips the way I'd seen Signor Brasini do to his wife one day in the market. I never forgot that. The way Signor Brasini just stopped and turned to his wife, put his big farmer's hands out and caressed her face, pulled her close to him and kissed her just like in the films. He kissed her for a long time and then he looked at her and smiled. I watched Signor Brasini and his wife. I watched them putting onions in a sack from the pile in the back of lo Mastro's truck. They even smiled while they were choosing onions, sir. And when I saw all that, I knew that their way would be my way. Their way, not my father's and my mother's way—their way was how I wanted my life to be. I knew that someday I would be loved by a man like Brasini. Or was it that I knew that I couldn't love a man if he wasn't like Brasini? All of which led me to the truth that there are two types of men in the world. Those like Brasini and those who are not like

Brasini. Those who would take your face in their hands and kiss you like in the films and those who would never in ten million years take your face in their hands and kiss you like in the films. But the sort of man who wouldn't do it, well, it wasn't his fault. He just *couldn't* do it. Just like my father couldn't be kind. Some men were never going to grow blond hair and were never going to hold a woman's face in their hands and smile at her as though she was an angel. And no matter what that woman did or said or looked like or was, she couldn't make him take her face in his hands and kiss her like in the films. Now, as I said, I was about eight that morning in the market when this epiphany struck me. I might have been seven. But that's what helped me to not feel hurt even knowing that my father didn't want me. And it also helped me to recognize you. You are definitely a Brasini, sir. I knew that by the time I was ten, maybe eleven. But what I'm trying to say is that once I'd understood the Brasini theory, I slipped myself off the hook about my father not wanting me. The emptiness, the conflict, the guilt that I might have carried 'round my neck for my whole life, I just put down right where I stood. I threw it all down and walked away from it. *I understood how things worked and how they didn't work.* And if it's not true, if this is not the way things work and don't work for everyone else, well, then let me just say it's how things work for me.'

"'I find it improbable that a child of eight—even a *Tosca* of eight—could find her way through such an emotional forest.'

"'It's not improbable at all. That children don't always say what they know doesn't mean they don't know it. Sometimes it's enough for them to just stay quiet with what they know and what they feel. Sometimes they suffer for what they know, or, as in my case, they are liberated by it. But either way, they don't necessarily talk about it. I thank Signor Brasini for showing me, in the full light of day, how other people went about their lives. Without him, I might have thought that men were all like my father. And, while I'm at it, I thank my father, too. And not only because it was you to whom he sent me. I thank him for being so constant in his impassivity. It wouldn't have been much longer before I'd have run off from him anyway. I would have taken The Tiny Mafalda with me, though. And don't think for a minute that I couldn't have arranged a life for us.'

" 'You would have made a good job of it. I know that.' Leo pours a few drops of *moscato* into two of the silver cups and offers one to me. Holding his cup high, he says, *'Tanti auguri, Tosca.'*

"We sip the wine, stay quiet. He has once again taken my hand in his.

" 'Who am I to you, sir? Do you think of me as your daughter?'

" 'No. Not my daughter. Though I feel, have always felt, duty-bound to you, ready to defend you—though the gods know you hardly need a cavalier. You invoked a curious affection in me almost immediately. You made me laugh with all your boldness, your fight. I admired you and I think I was envious of you. Folding your arms and sticking out your chin, refusing everything you didn't want and taking an extra portion of all you fancied. And I don't mean only at the table. You were a hellion, my sweet. More than half savage when you arrived. But what my sentiment has become for you, I cannot tell you. Surely it's changing. It's changing as we speak. Suffice now to say what I've said before. I am happier when you're near. And that, for a very long time now, I've felt a grand inclination to hold your face in my hands.'

" 'And to kiss me like in the films?'

" 'Perhaps that, as well.' Letting go of my hand, he rises and walks about for a bit. He comes back to where I still sit and looks down at me, his fatherly face restored. 'But you should rest now, Tosca. I'll ask Valentino to show you the way to the *mansarda*. The rooms up there are quiet, and there might even be a breeze on the loggia. Valentino will bring cool water and whatever else you might want. He'll come to wake you when it's time to leave. I think at eight or so.'

"He is already off to find Valentino and I pick up my little silver cup, thrust the tip of my tongue into its hollow, and lick the last sun-dried drop of *moscato*."

"I stop counting after five flights of narrow stone stairs, each one of which seems to veer off in a different direction. Valentino leads the way to a double wooden door, unlocks it, leaves the key in the hole, places water and a glass and two small linen towels on a table in the *salone* where we enter, wishes me a *buon riposo,* and quickly retreats. Even by palace standards, the room is large, its ceiling a high silver-gray vault, its walls covered in tufted watered silk the color of coffee beans. A man's *salone,* I think, running my hands along the top of a faded brown velvet settee where Leo might have rested his head. My boots make a hollow sound on the bare stone floors as I walk from room to room, opening and closing doors. I find several where all the furnishings are covered with sheets and thick canvas throws and one empty room where rolled carpets line the walls. On one side of a long corridor I notice the faint outline of a flush door with no knob. A single push of my hip opens it to reveal yet more rooms with long un-washed windows flanked by tatters of drapes. Behind another door there is a bedroom decorated much like the first *salone*. A bed draped in layers of brown silk seems almost small, adrift on the great sea of the stone floor. A chandelier with tiny bronze brocade shades on each candle-shaped light swings low over the bed. There is a single chair, a dresser with no mirror, and a small chest of drawers. On one wall doors are open to the loggia, from which the wide view of the land stops only at the horizon, at the place where the nearly colorless honeydew sky bends into the wheat. The loggia is empty save a four-postered daybed laid with fresh white sheets and pillows and surrounded by opalescent curtains, thin as a spiderweb and weighted with a wide border of heavy rose-colored satin. I will rest here, I decide. But I've forgotten to take the water and so must first traverse the whole apartment to retrieve it. On my way back to the loggia, I stop again in the bedroom. I slide open each drawer of the little chest. What am I looking for? Is it these? Two thin silk white night-dresses, perfectly ironed and folded. A bottle of perfume with a beveled glass stopper. Chanel No. 5. I unseal the stopper, begin dabbing myself with the perfume, which is not Simona's scent. If no one will ravish me, I will ravish myself, I think, quickly unfastening the buttons on my shirt, throwing off my *canottiera*. I throw down the stopper, too, pour the perfume over my chest, rub it into my arms, my neck. Pulling the pins from my braids, I pour what's left of it in my hair. I walk out onto the loggia, kick off my boots, and wearing only my riding pants, I part the thin curtains of the daybed and lie down. The curtains sway to a rogue breeze and I wonder about the woman who is not Simona and who wears Chanel No. 5 and thin white silk nightdresses. I hold my perfumed arms across my face, and from behind them, I sing. *Tanti auguri a me. Tanti auguri, cara Tosca.* Happy Birthday to me. Happy Birthday, dear Tosca. There is wind now, and it whips the scent of reaped wheat roasting in the late sun and mixes it with the smell of the rain rumbling its way west across a darkening sky. Proclaiming itself. The rain will fall before sunset. Will Leo come to lie with me before the rain? I submit to the wind, let it play across my body as the sky turns almost to night and the curtains sway faster. I hear something then, someone in the adjoining room. I rise to my knees, instinctively holding my hands over my bare breasts. Leo walks out onto the loggia, walks slowly to the daybed. He carries my shirt and my *canottiera* in his hands. I am still kneeling, still covering my breasts. Without parting the curtain, Leo takes my face in his hands, kisses my lips through the spiderweb. Still without parting the curtain, he gently pulls my hands away from my breasts and places his own hands where mine were. He caresses my breasts. He throws off his clothes then and parts the curtains, pulls me down onto the bed. It's Leo who is on his knees now, unfastening my riding pants, sliding them down and off. He pushes his open hands hard over the length of my limbs, molds the flesh with his fingers, pummels it over and over again. All of me. Leo is a sculptor who will shape a woman from a girl. The light returns, red and gold now, and the wind rages and the heavy satin border of the curtain slaps hard and constant against the bed like the flounce of a Spanish dancer's skirt."

"As we drive back to the palace I understand that everything that happened in my life before this afternoon was preparation for it. I understand that all that is yet to come will be because of it. Because of this afternoon. I understand there will be rapture and there will be grief and that I will be safe from neither of these. I lay my head on the prince's shoulder."

CHAPTER XII

"LEO KEPT HIS PROMISE. ON THE SIXTH DAY OF THAT FIRST harvesting of the newly planted fields, he was ready. He'd resurrected old scythes from some half-forgotten place and taken them to be sharpened by the man in the *borghetto* who kept the axes and hunting and kitchen knives in good form. Then he sought instruction on how to use one from the most veteran of the peasants. Umberto, he was called. Well, the other men came 'round, wanting to learn, too, which is what Leo had hoped for. And so they did. One evening after Leo and I had taken supper with the peasants and all of us were sitting out in the courtyard on the steps or on stones or wherever we could find a place to be still and wait for a breeze to rip the windlessness of the night, I remember one of the peasants shouting the suggestion that they should practice their reaping dance right there. They cleared away brooms and shovels and buckets, the things that passed for children's toys, shooed the animals back, and with Leo and Umberto in the lead, made their formation. Under a rising waxing moon and in the light of the single torch still lit near the *mensa,* they strutted and swung to the prince's rhythm, to the rhythm of Umberto's proud, brittle gait, and all of us were quiet as we were when the peach-skinned girl twirled under another moon. How beautiful they were moving through that powdered light. All those men with all those dreams."

"It is perhaps two hours before dawn on the day of the ceremonial harvest, the day when the last field is to be cut by hand. The road leading from the *borghetto* to the field is already trafficked with trucks and wagons porting the peasants. Leo, Cosimo, and I are among them, as are a father and son from Enna—pipers both—whom Leo has located and commissioned for this day. Several of the smaller boys from the *borghetto* stand near them, each one wearing a drum— primitive, handmade—tied about his waist or hung from some string or strip of fabric about his neck. Valentino, the little red-haired boy who lives at the hunting lodge, stands there, too. Also with a drum. He has been imported, no doubt, to fill out the ranks of the corps, and every once in a while, one of them taps out a sharp roll. As though to test the instrument. To test himself.

"We all speak barely beyond a whisper, as though someone sleeps nearby. As though the enemy crouches in the tall, still wheat. At the far end of the field, sheets are spread on the ground and baskets of bread and cheese are laid upon them. Jugs of wine lined up. The oldest women and the youngest girls who will pass these to the reapers stand at the ready. I hadn't noticed before, but all the men are barefoot. And now—the habitual *coppola* cast aside—they tie kerchiefs low on their brows. Slapping the handles firmly into their waiting hands, Leo distributes the scythes to the first team and they position themselves at the starting place. The second and third relays line up behind them. In suspense, thick as the blue-black air, we await the sun god. I barely breathe for the haunting beauty of the scene, a fragment of our collective existence, or is this moment all of existence, distilled? The darkness shatters, breaks into lilac dust, and the smudged lines of night take on the form of day. People look at one another, say good morning, pat one another on the back. The women kiss one another on both cheeks and, with no more prelude, Apollo torches the purple gloom with a great rubescent flash, staining the sky in all the reds of the world, and the pipes screech and the boys beat the drums and the reapers bless themselves, bellow *hallelujah* to their goddess, and the fierce slashing begins. Just as it was under the moon in the courtyard, the prince and Umberto lead out, plunging themselves into the deep, high-grown rows, swinging the scythes high and wide and in perfect rhythm as though both were born to it, and it makes me wonder if both were. The relays follow one after another, each one completing a row and passing his scythe on to the next man in line. For every four reapers there is a gatherer, a man who follows in their tracks, collects the cut stalks in the crotch of a forked branch. The gatherer then ties the stalks into a great sheaf with a length of dried hempweed, and heaves the sheaf, finally, into the pile to be threshed. After two or perhaps it was three or four turns with the scythe, Leo goes to stand at the top of the field, triumphant, not for himself but for them. Sweat and tears staining his chaff-whitened face, the prince recites Demeter's hymn. In his great, croaking *basso,* he chants:

> *I begin to sing of rich-haired Demeter, awful goddess.*
> *Of her and her trim-ankled daughter whom Hades rapt away,*
> *given to him by all-seeing Zeus, the thunderer.*
> *Apart from Demeter, lady of the golden sword and glorious*
> *fruits, she was playing with the deep-bosomed daughters of*

Oceanus and gathering flowers over a soft meadow,
roses, crocuses, and beautiful violets, irises also and hyacinths and
the narcissus, which Earth made grow at the will of Zeus, and to
please the Host of Many, and to be a snare for the bloomlike girl—
a marvelous, radiant flower.

"The pipes moan and the drummer boys beat their sticks upon the hide drums and the "saints" are passed, not seven times between sunrise and sunset but each time the bells ring the hour, and the men drink the wine and eat the bread and they finish the field in the early evening just as the light begins to leave. Leo gives the call to halt work and the peasants fall where they stand, lie back upon the stiff gold stubble and look up at the sky, breathing hard and laughing and yelping. Olympians not for glory but for food. They help one another to their feet and, in a line, pass by Leo, who waits to shake their hands. The older men kiss Leo's hand rather than shake it, resuming the ritual they'd seen their fathers and their grandfathers perform after the harvests when they were young. As the peasants kiss his hand, he takes *their* hand. Leo kisses the peasants' hands in return. A gesture that no one has ever seen—the noble returning his peasant's kiss. A sparrow flutters its wings inside my heart. Cosimo makes the sign of the cross. *The moment we step down to them is the moment they will step over us.*

" 'Scemo. Scemo beato, blessed fool.' Cosimo's whisper is angry. He looks at me. Repeats the phrase."

CHAPTER XIII

"LEO REMAINS INEXHAUSTIBLE IN HIS WORK FOR AND WITH HIS peasants, though once the first great leaps are accomplished, the shape his work takes on is less conspicuous and, hence, less irritating to Simona's sensibilities. A stiff cordiality once again reigns at the palace. Simona seemed to have passed through her salacious phase. Or perhaps it was that she continued to live it but with greater reserve. I don't know. What she did expose the household to was the epoch of her Grand Tours—recurring and extended journeys to the Continent. Whirling about in extravagant traveling costumes and veiled hats, trilling out orders to the servants about how to handle her trunks, when to expect cousins from Rome or Milan and where they should sleep, what they should be served, she would take the princesses—by then eighteen and nineteen years old—roughly by their shoulders, hold their heads to her sable-trimmed breast, and pucker rouged lips repeatedly in the direction of their cheeks. They would curtsy. '*Buon viaggio, Mamà.*' She, sniffling into a tiny lace handkerchief, would glide away. Marie Antoinette on her way to the Tower. Down the steps, into the waiting automobile. Polychrome postcards and brown paper–wrapped packages, exotically stamped and illegibly cancelled, arrived regularly for the daughters, yet their detachment to these was such that stacks of the unopened boxes, silver trays piled with the high-colored, unread cards, languished on hall tables.

"I will tell you that I sometimes envied Simona her freedoms. I would try to imagine myself stepping into the backseat of the long, green Bugatti, boarding the ferry at Messina, settling into the overnight train for Venice. Though Leo was often present in those fantasies, there were those in which I remained alone.

"Once, after another of Simona's departures, I ask Leo if we two might speak to Yolande and Charlotte. Propose our own sojourns together with them. Reticently, he agrees. At supper that evening, he begins breezily enough.

" 'What would you say, my mountain-bred daughters, to the idea that we four have a holiday together? Perhaps to ride the train from Enna to Palermo, stay in a fine hotel on the water, go to dine in fish restaurants whose terraces are built on stilts pounded into the floor of the sea?' he asks, his voice falling more timidly with every word until it settles back into his usual indifference as he finishes the sentence. They have hardly raised their glossy, braided heads from their soup.

"Since I'd never been farther away from the palace than the destinations of our morning rides, I am hard put to take on the job of tantalizing the princesses. I can only suggest what I would like to do. I take a turn.

" 'Have you ever thought about camping in the mountains, roasting sausages over a fire, sleeping under the stars?'

"Repelled, Yolande says, 'No, I have never thought of any of those things.'

"I refuse to surrender.

" 'Would you like to walk in a big city?'

"Noise. Confusion.

" 'To swim in the sea?'

" 'We don't swim.'

"Leo begins to speak about their studies while I am still launching one-line propositions. What else can I present to girls whose armoires bulge with French silks, who live in a palace furnished in sixteenth-century antiques and adorned with Renaissance sculpture and paintings? Surely not the prospect of shops and museums and galleries. I have never been to visit a museum. At least I shall make them laugh.

" *'How about a castle in Spain?'*

"All three pelt silence at me. Their truth is round, perhaps inviolate. They prefer their rituals to the placing of a single white kid–shod foot into the outside world. The morning hairdos; the dressing, intricate as a matador's; the endless buttering of hard toast, the endless passing of silver trays, the endless presentations of towering, many-colored cakes. Dispassionate, blunted discourse when there must be discourse at all. The bells to rise, the bells to dine, the bells to study, the bells to pray, the bells to sleep. *Ave Maria.*"

" 'It's because of me,' I say to Leo later.

" 'But it's not. It's because of they, themselves.'

" 'They are still in their childhood.'

" 'Yolande is one year less than you. Charlotte is two years less than you. But perhaps you're right. It is not uncommon for women of our class to remain forever in childhood. Aged girls they become. But their disinterestedness in me is as old as they are. Since the days of their births, I have tried to know them, to impose my presence on their lives in even the most perfunctory ways. Daily curtsies. Christmas kisses. There have never been greater expressions of filial affection than these. I was dismissed, excluded, first by their mother and then by them. Beyond my place at table and at Mass, I represent nuisance, obstacle to the otherwise consecrated order of their lives. You have long been witness to this fact.'

"He is angry at the private pain that my meddling has uncovered. Angry that there *is* pain. I go to stand beside the chair where he sits in the library.

" 'I'm sorry. It's only that I thought, by now, we might begin to be together with them in a different way. If we keep trying, perhaps . . .'

" 'No amount of trying will change a thing. We shall all go on endlessly being ourselves. They are not you, Tosca. They are not me. They are of another race. They are of Simona's race.'

" 'And now who is dismissing? Excluding?'

" 'Does not your Brasini theory apply to women? *Some people are born empty, sir. All manner of good deeds and patience and loving kindness can't even begin to fill them up.* Isn't that what you told me you'd learned by the time you were eight years old?'

"A quiet, neat throttling are his words.

" 'Why did you marry her, anyway?'

" 'I shall tell you that story. One day soon, I will tell you more of that story.' "

"From every quarter there is unspoken acceptance of Leo and me. Of our shared life. Of our romance, decorously, tactfully avowed. All know it is not I who caused the schism between Leo and Simona.

Most especially does Simona know that. Neither interloper nor third in a *ménage,* I am a woman who loves and is loved by another woman's husband. I live in the house where they live. All know that theirs is an *arrangement* rather than a marriage. And as well, all know that the sacrament of matrimony is insoluble. Inexorable in the eyes of Mother Church. Leo will always be married to Simona. *Until death do them part.* Most of the household is better acquainted than I with the early circumstances of their pact. But I understand that—in this time, in this place—betrothals such as theirs are legion. They are legion in every part of the world among the wealthy. Sentimentally, these betrothals are without significance. There are times when the burden of these truths, of these purported truths, falls like a bludgeon. Though I know that I could no longer live without Leo, I sometimes pretend to plot my departure, fantasize my going away from all of them, my slashing a path out of their labyrinth. He is not mine. His home is not mine. Even the labyrinth is not mine."

"I sit reading in the garden one afternoon, waiting for Leo to return with Cosimo from their weekly appointments in Enna, when I hear the delicate crunch of her shoes on the stones, look up to see Simona moving toward me, her path encumbered by the luxuriant reach of artichoke fronds. She kicks, swipes, mutters at them.

" 'I shall never quite adjust to this invasion of *vegetables* among my roses.'

"She doesn't say, *nor to this invasion of you among my roses,* though I think it is even more true. I nod to her, smile. Her smile is false.

"She is already seated when she asks, 'May I join you?'

"Still I say nothing. Still I smile. She takes my book, reads the title aloud in English.

" '*Great Expectations.* Apt,' she says, her smile less false. 'It's so unusual to see each other without the multitudes about us,' she says as to a dear friend.

"For a moment I think she must be talking to someone else before I hear her saying, 'Yes, without the multitudes.'

"Now I am stunned, fixed into my silence, but she seems to neither notice nor be distressed by this. As though it were the most natural thing in the world, she speaks of her latest journey, the insuperable differences between Sicilian and Viennese pastries, pinches the stuff of my yellow crepe dress, says she found one very much like it for herself in a little shop in Milan, and with no further patter, says, 'And so what are your plans, Tosca? You'll soon be twenty. I suspect you'll soon be thinking about your marriage.'

"Once again, I hear what she omits. *You'll soon be thinking about your marriage rather than my marriage.* But I am mistaken. Simona proceeds.

" 'What I want to say is that I hope you'll not be too hasty. The post-war climate out there in the world is anarchic at best. I know life is confining for you here but, bit by bit, we'll help you to *expand your horizons,* shall we say. Great expectations. Lovely to contemplate.'

"My silence is immutable, and now I doubt my ability to hear. To discern her words. She has spoken like some loving aunt, has used the *we,* referring to hers and Leo's joint concern over me. She has more to say.

" 'Mountains on an island are doubly remote, my dear. Twice removed. But also twice as predictable. Almost everything that happens, happens over and over again. You know—perhaps Leo has told you—that my mother and father lived much as he and I do. Together, yet not at all together. It's quite common here where the protection, the maintenance, and the passing-on of the patrimony takes precedence over all other matters. Certainly over something as evanescent as love. Stones and earth and buildings,' she raises a thin, white, sapphire-braceleted wrist to take in the palace behind her, 'these are the lasting things. These are what count.'

"I look at Simona and she fidgets with the sapphires, with her rings, her hair. She meets my gaze then and we stay that way for a while. Comfortably, I think, and saying more in those few moments with our eyes than we've said to each other for all these eleven years.

" 'I hope that you know, that you understand, I feel no *rancor* toward you. Though I did. Rancor, or was it pure envy, jealousy? At first, I thought you quite adorable, actually. An unbroken colt with those long, spindly legs. We were all quite enamored with your spirit. Mostly you were just another face 'round the table until I noticed other people noticing you. Leo, of course. But everyone else, too. Though I didn't want Leo for myself, I didn't want you to want him. Strangely, I didn't see *it*—your romance—as Leo's betrayal. He'd had so many women before you. I saw it as yours. I felt that you'd betrayed me. You see, unconsciously, I'd begun to think of you as one of my daughters. Indeed, it was as though a daughter had betrayed me. I'd been doing for you all, nearly all, that I did for the princesses. I chose your clothes, saw to your medical care, discussed your education with the teachers. I insisted upon your catechism instruction, that you take your first Holy Communion with Yolande and Charlotte. Your Confirmation into the Church. Knowing her sensitivity, her bent toward tenderness, I arranged for Agata to watch over you. I am not a motherly woman, Tosca, though I've tried to be. But as motherly as I've ever been, I have been to you. Not much, was it? Is that what you're thinking?'

"I shake my head. A frail denial. I close my eyes, see my mother's face. My sister's face so like hers.

" 'Ah, Tosca,' she sighs, and I think it is a sigh of ending, though I can hardly fathom what was the beginning of her soliloquy or why I still cannot speak to her. She is quiet but she does not rise to go, and I wonder if she has dismissed me with that sigh, if it is I who should rise to go.

" 'Of course my envy of your beauty was a normal response. You turned fifteen in the year when I turned forty. You, at the beginning; I, passing the first milestone on the way down. I'd never before paid much attention to the seven years of difference between Leo's age and mine. Suddenly my forty years to his thirty-three seemed some horrid breach that widened at a furious pace until I staved off time, yes, until I dammed the rushing waters with all those bodies. My new friends. The men and the boys. My paid paramours. I am loath to re-call those days, but recall them I do. While you and Leo were finding your way to each other—do you know that I anticipated your *coupling,* shall we call it, almost to the day? And did you know that I could see the change in you even as you sipped your coffee?—while you and Leo were finding your way to each other, my impulse was to despair. I'd been fine during all those years of his dalliances in which the women were as insignificant to him as I was. Life was balanced. You *disarranged* that balance. You see, I am not at all certain that I'd ever witnessed love. Before you and him. It's rare enough, you know. Cer-tainly I'd never felt it—or even mistaken it—for myself. Even the thought of happiness terrifies me. Fragile as a blown rose. Why would anyone choose happiness over the long-enduring qualities of fear and pain? I've often wondered if fear and pain would die, too, if I'd only let them. If I would stop caring for them, fussing over them. I suppose I'll never know. I'll never know what you know, Tosca. I've thought about this rather a great deal over these past two or three years. I do truly wish you well. I've sensed lately a bit of skittishness in you that I've never seen before, and that's why I wanted to speak with you. You're restless. Perhaps dwelling upon the complexities. There will always be complexities, my dear. Don't go away, Tosca. Stay here. Love him, if you do. If you dare. Love him a little for me.'

"All the words said, she wept. I had been weeping for a while by then and, through the tears, she seemed a gauzy spectre, an eloquent ghost in blue-spotted chiffon. *How her bobbed hair was set in tight waves and the points of her cheeks went red, and how she was almost pretty at that time of day.* A woman come to soothe me. To tell me that the labyrinth is, indeed, my labyrinth."

"As life at the *borghetto* continues to improve and as Leo sees, senses, a growing serenity among the peasants, he, too, takes on a greater tranquility. We wander off on our first jaunts away from the palace. We pack one of the trucks with firewood and baskets of provisions and some sort of Army-issue cots and feather quilts and candle lanterns and drive through the mountains to a high plateau where we sleep in a field of wild marjoram and hyssop and mint. Leo crushes handfuls of the herbs on a stone, brews a *tisana* with them over the fire, serves it to me in a mother-of-pearl cup, tells me it was with this elixir that the Eleusinians—when she rested in their camps—comforted a mourning Demeter.

"We drive to the sea, and when I finally look upon it, I run from the car. Tearing at my skirt, my shirt, pulling my camisole over my head, loosening my plait, I race into the surf. Splashing, screaming, diving, swallowing the good briny juices of it, I am sluiced and lustrous, a long brown fish prancing in the curling steel-blue waves on the edges of my island. But then I miss the mountains. Wherever it is on the island that Leo takes me, I find beauty and feel joy. But always I miss the mountains. I miss the horses. I miss my everyday life. Yolande and Charlotte are wiser than I.

"As we had done for years by now, Leo and I continue to ride each morning. We no longer set out with palace guests or with Cosimo to trot upon the conventional trails of the social rider, but rather we take to the less-traveled mountain or woodland paths or head for open meadows on the high plateau where we can race. Where we can feel free. Though we might easily arrange our days and nights to include a rendezvous within the palace, these pre-dawn journeys become our courting hours. I think it is the private joy of rising, dressing, and meeting in the dark kitchen where Leo—yellow curls sleep-matted to his temples—would be pouring out two tiny cups of espresso. We run then, shivering, across the gardens to the stables, thieves in the thick quiet of the night. Even the horses seem conspiratorial, patient as meek children as we saddle them, ready ourselves then with sweaters and tweeds that we keep there in the barn. When there is no moon, we take the open trails, and when there is, we ride twisting paths in and out of silent, spookish woods.

"One morning, as the dark is fading, we dismount and lead the horses up to a clearing, step warily along a palisade and into the new pearly light. We stay still, stroking the horses' necks, waiting for the sun. A hot, violent wind swarms among the dry yellow leaves of the oaks behind us and the soughing of them sounds like a woman crying.

Shivering even under the weight of Leo's old suede jacket, how cold I am, trembling and trying to hear the woman whose cries are softer than the raucous hissing of the leaves. The wind sweetens then and the light roars up behind the mountains, firing the stone and the sky in long yellow flames. And the crying ceases and we walk, less warily I think, along the rim of the cliff, and when we reach the plateau and remount, we ride hard, ride to breathlessness, find shade, walk the horses to cool them. Settle ourselves to rest. In the delicious trembling light under the branches of old poplars, we are lovers.

"Most mornings we ride to the half-ruined *locanda* in the pine woods, the place where we'd stopped to drink wine and walk a bit on the night of my eighteenth birthday. We stay a while there in a small salon, the pale-green paint of its high walls bruised, peeling, the red-tiled floor worn to undulations, the ivory satin skin of the chairs and sofas in tatters. A dark wood Bechstein grand sits at the far end of the room and sometimes I sit to play *Saint-Saëns*. To play *Le Cygne*. Leo stands, eyes closed, arms folded upon his chest, to listen. I play only a few measures before he interrupts.

'It's a swan, Tosca. The music was composed to give the impression of a swan. There is no indication that an elephant approaches. *Piano. Piano, amore mio.*'

"There is always tea, still tepid, in a porcelain jug. Bread, marmalade, some sort of biscuit. A melon, artfully carved. A few wild berries in a mended pink dish, the leaves and stems of the tiny things still dusty from the woods. Flowers and blossoms on branches stand in a blue and white ginger jar on the wide stone mantle. We neither hear nor see a soul though our benefactors live in a far wing of the house. Soft, tree-filtered light pours through the wavy glass of the long, many-paned windows and onto us, over us, reclined upon a plush, fringed carpet embossed in great yellow roses. We lie there on the yellow roses before the fire and pretend we are at home. We talk and fight and laugh and eat and drink. We sleep and dream upon the dark red carpet with the yellow roses as though its length and width mark the confines of the world. I run my fingers through the silky fringe of the carpet as I listen to Leo speak. Arms raised over my head, sometimes I clutch at the fringe, hold it in my fists. In the ice-green light, the thin, shimmering underwater light of those mornings, the dark red carpet with the yellow roses does mark the confines of the world. And when the clock in the hall outside the door chimes eight, we gather ourselves to leave. We must be back at the palace, back at the *borghetto* to begin our day's work."

"The letter is handwritten on thick, vanilla-colored paper, sealed with red wax in the old-fashioned way. It is delivered to Leo at the breakfast table by one of the servants.

" 'A gentleman is waiting in the hall, sir. For your response,' says the servant, smartly restraining a smirk. This is all eighteenth-century behavior and Leo is perplexed. We stay quiet as he slits the seal, opens the note.

" 'I hope it's an invitation to a masked ball,' says Charlotte.

"We laugh, keeping our attention upon the prince as he reads.

" 'Ah, yes. Yes, please tell the gentleman that I accept. And thank him, Mimmo,' Leo says to the servant, who rushes off, shaking his head almost imperceptibly.

"Leo hands the letter to Cosimo, pours more coffee, letting it spill from his already full cup into the iridescent white saucer painted with small blue flowers. He smiles in our direction. Cosimo reads it, hands it back to Leo, and they both rise, saying *buongiorno*. Leo's nod to me says that he'll see me a bit later."

"Leo has been invited to a dinner hosted by the nobleman whose lands are separated from his by a small village. The letter informs him that upon this occasion other guests will be present, both local and from as far away as Palermo. Though Leo presumes it to be a social gathering, the letter is worded more as a summons than an invitation. It is the very first such approach—social or otherwise—that Leo has received from this 'neighbor.' The dinner is to be that very evening. It is early in December 1950.

"Though he says he would like me to sit with him in the library and, later, in his office, Leo hardly speaks to me throughout the day. I ask why he so readily accepted the invitation if it does not please him to attend. He tells me, 'It's a matter of duty.'

"I stay with him even while he dresses, ties the formal black shoes he wears only to weddings and funerals. From a cobalt glass vial he pours neroli oil out into his palm, runs it through his yellow hair, still damp from the bath, and strokes two heavy silver brushes through the short, thick curls, and I think that my prince wears fewer than his thirty-eight years. He asks if I will spend some time after supper with Cosimo. He desires that Cosimo and I wait for him in the small salon near the chapel. He says he won't be late. But the priest, also dressed in his most formal clothes, awaits him in the hall, the main door open, the automobile purring at the foot of the palace steps.

" 'Since I was fresh out of sealing wax, I sent live word to your host via Mimmo. I told him to say that, as the *sacerdote* of his very own parish, I would be most willing to put aside the business of the church this evening in order to bless his gathering. I didn't ask Mimmo to wait for an answer,' Cosimo tells him.

"They laugh and embrace and laugh again. Don Quixote and Sancho Panza in the front seat of the faithful gray Chrysler."

"Among the local landowners with whom both Leo and Cosimo are acquainted, their host presents two men they have never met. These are introduced as *politicos* from Palermo. The others present seem to already know the two *Palermitani*. In fact, save Leo and Cosimo, the group—twelve in all—demonstrate an almost fraternal camaraderie. The subject upon their collective lips is agrarian reform. They speak of the soon-to-be-signed into law State decree that will demand that Sicilian landowners sell, at token prices to their peasants, all abandoned or unproductive tracts suitable for agriculture. Soon it is clear that Leo is the evening's quarry.

"When the gentlemen are settled at table, the murmuring, headshaking discourse of the cocktail hour becomes pointed. As though by rehearsal, each man 'round the table tells of one of Leo's follies: his restructuring of the *borghetto* buildings; the medical care; the instruction in hygiene; the birthing rooms; the *borghetto* school and the mandatory attendance of the peasants' children up to twelve years of age—*at least five years after the children should have been working in the fields,* says one of the men. Another tells of the well-stocked storerooms, the well-laden tables, the distribution of clothes and bedding, the evening Mass celebrated in their chapel. Decorum is soon surrendered to shouting, so eager are they to boast of another and another of the prince's indiscretions.

" 'And have you heard, gentlemen, that good Prince Leo's peasants need no longer relieve themselves in the sainted peace of the woods? *A white-tiled latrine,* gentlemen, only a white-tiled latrine is good enough for Prince Leo's peasants.'

"The laughing is bawdy now. It is threatening. As though only a gunshot could quiet it and yet, with a single clink of his silver knife against a glass, a hush falls. It is one of the *Palermitani* who commands the floor.

" 'Prince Leo, we do not deny the need for reform. The time has come. But the time has only recently come. Let the changes take due course. If you set about righting a thousand years of wrongs too abruptly, the reforms won't last. These people need authority far more than they need an evening Mass or curtains on their windows.'

" 'Or a shiny new latrine,' shouts another.

"The laughter starts up again but is short-lived as Leo begins to speak.

" 'I have no doubt of the peasants' need for leadership any more than I had doubt of their need for more bread and a clean, dry place to sleep. The changes I've made—and those I shall make—I make in my own name and in no one else's. I hardly consider myself a social reformer. I do not look at you and urge you to follow me, nor can I concern myself whether you do or you don't follow me. I will not parcel my land because the government demands it of me. I will parcel it because I know that it's the right thing to do. You, kind sirs, must do what you must do. But so must I.'

"There is a long silence scratched, now and then, by a match run against a pocket flint, the loosening of a tie grown too tight. The repeated clearing of a throat.

" 'Is it true, Prince Leo, that you kiss the hands of your peasants?'

"It is the other *Palermitano,* the one called Mattia, who asks the question. He has spoken so softly and without moving from his slouched position at the table that Leo does not know from whom the voice has come.

" 'Now why would that be of interest to you?' he asks, looking at each one 'round the table.

"This other *Palermitano,* this Mattia, then stands, walks to the place where Leo sits, lays his short, blue serge-covered arms upon Leo's shoulders, bends his head to Leo's ear, says gently, 'If you don't bully them, they'll despise you, Leo. You've heard that before. I tell you it's true.'

"Mattia raises his head, crushes his voice to a cracked, exhausted whisper. 'When, someday, we hear you've suffered a misfortune, we'll understand the source of it. The loss of respect, I mean. Yes, we'll understand that you invited your misfortune with a kiss.' "

"When Leo had returned that evening, he had not come to my rooms. This non-observance of our nightly ritual—our spending an hour or so being quiet together, in reviewing the day—signified his distress and caused mine. The next day, with apparent pain and in great detail, it is Cosimo who recounts the events of last evening to me. As he describes the gathering, the atmosphere of palpable bitterness, flagrant distaste, my worry gives way to a choking fear.

" 'But who are these men, these two from Palermo?' I ask Cosimo.

" 'They are of the clan,' he says with maddening simplicity.

" 'What is this clan? In whispers and asides, I've been hearing this word since I was a little girl. Are they a family, a group of bandits, renegades? Is this the same *clan* who murdered Filiberto?

" 'I would say that the answer is 'yes' to all parts of your question. They are a family—related by choice rather than by blood, which is often the stronger of the two attachments. They are a group of bandits. Bandits among whom you would find the illustrious, the high-ranking, the many-starred members of our society. You would find priests in as many numbers as you would find politicians, nobles, and merchants. Well represented, too, would be the State and local and military and financial police. And finally, you would find hungry men who are willing to carry out their orders, no matter how gruesome.'

"As he speaks, Cosimo looks anxiously at the door to the *salone* where we sit, expecting Leo to enter, I think. But then he turns his back to the door, ceasing to care if Leo should hear what he says to me and be displeased by his candor.

" 'Where there is no State, someone steps forward, for better, for worse, to take on the role of the State. The clan is Sicily's State. *La Mafia.* Interesting, don't you think, that its name derives from the Arab? From *mahjas.* Sanctuary. Refuge. Place of succor. That's what the medieval bandits had in mind to provide for themselves and for their families when they began their missions. Twelfth-century Robin Hoods, they were. Who could fault them? Swashbuckling brigands out to thieve those who had more bread than they could eat in a day. Does that sound familiar to you, my dear? Were you not a swashbuckling *brigantessa* yourself? Stashing bread and cheese and cakes in your pockets so you might feed your sister? You can understand how this all began but can you, can anyone, understand or defend its evolution? The clan no longer steals sheep or butchers cows

by the light of a clandestine fire, drags the bloody parts of them back
to their villages. Like lions taking their kill back to the lair. They leave
that sort of activity to the unenlightened. They want more now. Now,
they want everything. Now they want to crush the poor as they were
once crushed. Memory does not always arrive whole from its journeys across the generations. Over seven or eight or nine centuries
and, more recently, under the strategic guidance of the victors of the
Great War, the clans have reached far beyond their humble, rural
roots. Like Etna, the Mafia spits violence at will. It spits at the State
when, every once in a while, it stirs from its langourousness. It spits
at the Church, which has always been prone to its own form of sanc-
tified violence. It spits at anyone daft enough to stand in the way of
its eruption. And so where are the defenders of the poor? Where are
the hussars who will ride over the mountains to save them from the
wolves? I shall tell you where they are. Sitting at table with the clan.
Feasting and plotting their glories. Just as they were last evening. All
the tribes are in league. They are as one. Mafia, Church, and State.
Father, Son, and Holy Ghost. Leo has yet to—how shall I say this?—
Leo has yet to hold this truth in reverence.'

" 'And he won't,' I say. 'He never will.'

" 'You puzzle me, Tosca. The sage in you puzzles me. And so is
there nothing to do?'

" 'It's you who say there is nothing to do. *All the tribes are in league.*
Leo is his own tribe and if there is something to do, he will do it. Not
you. Not me. I remember years ago your telling me that it would be
you who would catch Leo when he faltered. You said, *And he will falter.*
I promised myself then that it would be me rather than you who
would be close enough to catch him. We were both wrong, both pre-
sumptuous, weren't we? I know now that *falter,* Leo shall never do.

But you, Don Cosimo, have you faltered? Where is your place in all this hierarchy? ' My unusual use of the formal address causes him to look sharply at me.

" 'I have no place save as the prince's confessor. Through my own crises of faith and through the behavior and refusals of behavior that have resulted from those crises, I have forfeited most all other duties and rights associated with my ordination. The Curia has yet to defrock me only because of Leo. Because of his full and indisputable knowledge of certain events and practices within the Curia. And because of his generous support to the parish. To the Dioceses. Funds and favors—and perhaps even silences—that they know he would withdraw should I be further stripped. You see, dear Tosca, Mother Church is the only true whore in Sicily. You know well enough that I think Leo to be foolhardy, imprudent, and yet my allegiance is to him. My allegiance will always be to *Candide*.' "

CHAPTER XIV

"Leo kept often apart from me after his meeting with the clan. And when we were together, I felt the distance between us even more than when he'd go off by himself to ride or when, having locked its door, he stayed hours alone in the library. When he did talk, it was about his fear. Not ostensibly of course, since he couched the fear behind fake practicalities. *We must discontinue our morning rides because there is so much more to do at the* borghetto, he would tell me when the evident truth was that, with the new systems in place and in operation, the peasants had always less need for us. For instance, efficiency and yield had increased at an almost incalculable rate in the fields. The peasants were better housed, better fed, better clothed, better cared for than most of them had been in all their lives. These fundamentals intact, the two programs that next concerned Leo—the school and the infirmary—also flourished.

"Cosettina had so progressed in her studies and had expressed such longing to take on the post of *maestra* that, for her seventeenth birthday, Leo gifted her a small, thin briefcase covered in red ostrich skin and engraved with her initials. Inside it was a note of congratulations to the new *maestra* of the *borghetto* school. I, myself, had been advanced to the post of Saturday-morning Story Lady.

"Even my weekly presence in the infirmary had become redundant, since the doctor's visits had been increased to thrice weekly and the State had begun to send 'round nurses and social workers to assist him and, I suspected, to gather intelligence. Talk of Prince Leo's *borghetto* and his new programs had quietly traveled across the straits and up the peninsula.

"Countering Leo's insistence on the peasants' greater need for us, I would remind him that it was the development of their independence that was his ultimate goal. He would acquiesce. Until he'd spun another veil. *I need more rest, Tosca. And you,* amore mio, *you must return to your studies of the classics. I've been neglecting my business affairs and must be more diligent with attorneys and accountants and agricultural consultants. I have a 'farm' to run, after all,* he would tell me, fixing his gaze somewhere just above and to the left of mine.

"I understood that he feared, not for himself, but for me. Together in the early quiet of the woods, I would make as accommodating a target as would he. And so our morning rides were abruptly suspended, as were my solo jaunts. My own fear thrived, undisclosed. Little by little, Leo clipped and pinched at our already reserved lives. A boy dragging a stick through the sand, he drew the boundaries of his unassailable realm. As though the clan could not scale the walls, we were to live inside the palace. The gardens, the lemon groves, the *borghetto,* and some of the closer fields were as far away as we would venture. But this would pass, I told myself. He is suffering the first cut of horrific fear. He will take up his peace again in the spring, I told myself. He would take up his peace again in the spring after that. For nearly three years, he at best mustered only a figment of it. And even then, it came and went, his peace. Slits of light from behind the shade. Yet in all that passage of time, no more red-sealed invitations written on thick vanilla-colored paper were delivered to him at breakfast. Neither summonses nor admonitions interrupted his days. Nary a snake in the grass where he deigned to walk. Though we never again, *would never again,* ride together nor go out upon our little journeys to the sea, we adapted. In truth, the way we lived during that time was not so different from how we'd lived when I was younger. Once again we followed the rituals. It was the only life that the princesses had ever lived and the one that, when she was present, Simona fell into with comfort. If we wanted new clothes, merchants or their representatives ported trunks and wheeled wardrobes into the small *salone.* If we wanted music for an evening, concertists were invited to sing and play. If we wanted to have supper in the *borghetto,* laden with baskets of sweets and fruits, we walked over the meadow to join our neighbors. We often worked mornings in the fields, side by side with the peasants or with the *ortolani* in the palace gardens. I wanted to learn to cook, and so stayed with the palace brigade among the roasting pans and the simmering pots and the heaps of flour lined up on the scrubbed wooden table where the pasta and the bread were made. And there were always guests. More even than in my earlier days. Generations of cousins and widowed aunts and longer-widowed great aunts and brothers-in-law and friends of friends arrived and departed and arrived again. As if it were true. As if there really was safety in numbers. And if there were whisperers in their ranks, I never heard them. Somehow and at some point, I had become one of them."

"It was Ascension Day, the day when fresh water is said to become holy and when the peasants go to bathe themselves in the healing waters of the ascending Christ. And then to rest in the sun, to eat their bread and ham, and to drink their wine. Though we'd always gone with the peasants on this holy day, Leo had preferred, this time, to remain quietly at the palace. But the day had not been quiet.

"It's just after sunset now and Leo and I and Cosimo stand in the road beside the *borghetto* to wait for the procession of old carts that carry the women home. We see the lights from a long way off across the spring-shorn fields, the scintillas of the candle lanterns swinging from the axles of the wagons. As they come nearer, I can hear the carts creak and groan under the weight of the women who sit upon unsteady chairs, lace shawls over their braids and about their shoulders. I know that they are holding hands and I strain to hear them singing plainsong under the rising May moon. I wish that I were with them in their tilting chairs, swaying in rhythm to the slapping of the horses' flanks, the heavy clumping of their hooves over the ancient stones.

"We've come to the *borghetto* not to welcome home the peasants as much as to prepare them for what they will find. For what is no longer here. Surely they will smell the smoke, see the black smudges swirling about the twilight. There has been a fire. Skillfully set and left to rage while the peasants were away. The *borghetto* left to burn. From the palace veranda where we went to sit with our coffee this morning, Leo and I saw the flames leaping from the buildings. Men from the palace household had seen them before we did, were already on their way, Cosimo among them. We'd telephoned several of the villages. More help arrived. Onto the bed of a truck we'd thrown garden tools. We'd joined the line, hurtled shovels of earth, relayed water from the well in feed buckets. Chaste weapons to stay the beast. Even as it tired. Even in its last throes. The sleeping quarters are least damaged. The *mensa,* the kitchens, the chapel are all stone shells heaped with smouldering ash. We know, perhaps everyone knows, this fire is a calling card. The clan is a persevering suitor. Inventive, unpredictable, compelling.

"Yet the next day officials, summoned by Leo from Enna, investigate the site with the thoroughness of archaeologists. The fire was not set. No indication of arson is established. The fire was not the work of the clan but of simple distraction. The bakers' distraction. Once the oven was hot enough to shovel in the risen loaves, the bakers—as they do always—swept the oven floor clean of the piles of white-hot embers, heaved pailsful of the live ash behind the bakehouse. But this morning, in their rush to join the departing wagons on their way to the river, they were careless. The undampened embers fell upon dry grasses. Too close to the woodpile. The dry grasses were like tinder, the embers caught the wood. The fire seethed, spread. When it reached the containers of cooking gas in the *mensa,* it exploded. Rather than giving himself over to relief that the fire was accidental, Leo resists believing the authorities. *Might not someone have instructed them to call it 'spontaneous'? Who can be certain? After all, have we Sicilians not cultivated secrecy to a fine art? Every last one of us?* Far more than what had become his usual expressions of quixotic terror, it was this incident of the fire and Leo's refusal to accept its innocent source that showed me the force of his ravings. And against those ravings, logic is feeble as the trickle of water that could not stop the blaze.' "

" 'One evening during this long epoch of our siege, Leo came to my rooms. Agata opened the door to his knock. Seated at the pianoforte, a silvery-brown tea gown puffed up about me on the little bench, I was trying to play *Saint-Saëns*. Still trying. Still working on *Le Cygne*. Leo arranged himself on the *divanetto*.

"I began to silently mouth the words even before he could say them aloud.

" 'It's a swan, Tosca. The music was composed to give the impression of a swan. There is no indication that an elephant approaches. *Piano. Piano, amore mio.*'

" 'But I'm so big and these keys are so small. What do I do with all my strength?'

" 'Strange, but it's precisely your strength about which I'd like to speak this evening.'

"I rise from the bench, go to him to receive his demure double kiss, and he pulls me down to perch on the edge of the small hassock in front of where he sits. Without overture, he says, 'Essentially I have no heir. I am the last one, the last to be born of this noble, ignoble lineage of mine. I have no sons. Only those two twittering, rustling reflections of their mother, save their souls. Simona has raised them as her personal pets. I have given them only my name. It's as though she somehow separated and replaced even the blood in them that was mine, though God knows, it was my very blood for which she married me. But I'll get to that. I tell you once again, I have no heir. I am concerned not at all for Simona's material comforts since she owns more land and more grand edifices than she's had time or will to look upon. Our marriage was motivated not only by my father's debts but by her father's wiliness. Her father offered no dowry, you see. An unheard-of display of arrogance. He wanted his daughter's wealth to stay with her, not to be drunk or whored or gamed by some blackguard. Certainly a husband would have the peripheral benefits of her wealth, but he would have access to only that part which Simona, herself, deemed worthy to share. Had Simona been lovely or talented or simply kind, simply tender, she might have attracted suitors even under those hostile conditions. That she was none of these had its effect. By the time my father presented the idea of my marriage to her, she was dangerously near to twenty-five—the official age when a never-married woman becomes *la zitella,* a spinster—and her father had softened, if only slightly. The two men had been lifelong friends. My father, Laurent, needed help. And if only to save face, Federico's daughter needed a husband. It was all accomplished with grace. Dutiful and correct in my liaison with Simona, I also kept certain elements of my former life uninterrupted. I was eighteen years old, Tosca. Not much more than a boy. A boy sent off to do his duty for his family. Not unlike being sent off to war. *From the rich* zitella's *bed, you will provide salvation for us all, my son.* The compromise worked for everyone. Or so I'd believed until I fell in love with you. All this is to tell you that you are my family, Tosca. You and Cosimo and the peasants. And all I have will be yours. Cosimo and I are seeing to that.'

"I have been listening to him as to a fable. Yes, as to a strange, sad fable. And so when he said, 'To seal the pact, I want you to have this,' I was startled. Even though I'd already known, if not in such cold detail, much of what he'd been telling me, hearing it all in a piece like that caused grief in me and something akin to anger.

" 'Your father was as cruel as mine,' I tell him.

"He shakes his head in defense of his father. He fumbles trying to unbutton the vest pocket of his rumpled suede riding coat, which, though he hasn't mounted a horse in three years, he wears almost exclusively. His long, thick fingers tremble as he tries to grasp something tucked away there. He pulls out a small purse shaped like an envelope. Made of quilted silk in a burnt brown color. Leo opens its clasp and takes out a necklace. A square-cut emerald hangs from a short braided chain of rose-gold. In his open palm, he holds it out to me. Says, 'I have always imagined that this, hanging from my mother's neck above my crib as she sang to me, must have been the first object I saw. It's not likely true, but it hardly matters. Until the night she died, I don't recall ever having seen my mother without this. If we were to have been married, this would have been my wedding gift to you.'

"I don't take the necklace; I hardly look at it, but rather at him. Trying to tell him that it's not an emerald that I want or need. Not even his mother's emerald. I try to say that I would have loved to have been his bride but that I am content being who I am to him. Even though, until now, I've never been certain of who that might be. Surely I don't want to be his heir. I say all of this, I say more than this, and he hears me. Puts the necklace back in its burnt-brown purse.

" 'My mother was called Isotta. I don't know if I've ever told you that.'

" 'You have,' I tell him.

" 'Have I ever told you how she died?'

" 'No.'

" 'May I tell you that story, the end of her story, right now?"

" 'Of course.' "

" *Signora Isotta, you cannot do this,'* the nurses told her.

" *'Try and stop me and I'll have you smothered in your beds. Send Leo to me at once.'*

" 'The two nurses had entered her room thinking to prepare her for sleep. My mother had a different idea about how she would spend her evening. I'd been waiting nearby. Waiting for Isotta to send a nurse to fetch me or for one of them to come tell me that she had died. I'd been pacing and sleeping and smoking in the little parlor down the hall from her room for days and nights by then. Permitted to sit by her bed, to stroke her fine old head for a few moments whenever the nurses deemed her peaceful enough to bear such excitement as my silent presence would cause. But now, there she was, standing by the bed. A broad smile upon her wonderful face.'

" *'Ah, Leo, how I love you. Surely I've told you hundreds of times, but I'll tell you once again how honored I am to be your mother.'*

" 'She walked toward me, reached out to hold my cheek in her hand, then rushed past me and to the window, thrusting it open, inviting the cold February afternoon in upon the death-smelling room. It was her first breath of good air since she'd been rushed, dying, to the hospital nearly a week earlier. The curtains, limp and gray, went wild, flapping in what seemed like joy. She called for pillows, demanded pillows.'

" *'Two, no four.'*

" 'Divesting them of their white slips, she unfolded her own lovelier ones pulled from her case along with her nightgown, a matching satin jacket with deep cuffs of lace. She sprayed the room with neroli. She sprayed more in her hair, gathering it up then, fastening it on top of her head in a wild pastiche and pulling out wisps, which fell in ringlets down her cheeks. Her hair had been blond like mine and most of it was still. She was beautiful. She announced she was going to bathe and so she did. Over her arm she held the satin gown and the satin jacket, a towel big as a sheet and monogrammed in gold thread with her single bold *I*. In her hand, she held soap in a flowered tin. She came back then, her hair arranged even more artfully, and, as though dinner guests were expected momentarily, she lit candles, poured whiskey out into two good glasses.

" '*I packed for myself for this particular journey,* she'd said, her laugh tinkling like a thin silver spoon bouncing along a marble floor.'

" 'She settled herself in bed, made a long work of it, wished me good health and, if I had the stout heart she thought I had, she wished me great love. We sat there then, among the scent of the neroli and the candles and that clean February night, and I kept saying that I should close the window, that it was so cold, that she would catch her death, and then we both laughed and we both wept.'

" '*I left it open so he wouldn't have to knock,*' she said.

" 'It was then that she asked me to take this purse from the inside pocket of her case. I did, passed it to her, but she folded her long fingers over my hand.'

" '*It's for you, Leo. To give to the woman you love. I trust that you understand I do not intend it for that fool* grisette *you married. I do not care a whit how you divide the rest of my treasures but I ask that you keep this one. Just in case you ever fall in love.*'

" 'She looked away then, staying quiet, twisting her wedding ring one way and then the other about her finger. As though trying to recall the numbers on a lock.'

" '*I remain uncertain whether to wish you love or to wish that love never finds you. The pain is severe in either case. The emerald belonged to my mother and to her mother. I cannot tell you that it brings fortune or health or any such elusive gift. I can only say it has been my companion for all my days since I was fifteen years old. The weight of it 'round my neck has always been a comfort, a kind of ballast, I think. Will you keep the emerald safe for me, Leo? Keep it safe until you find her. She'll understand what it's meant to me. I know that she will. There is one more thing I want to*

tell you, Leo. You already know that I was and have remained contrary to your fa-
ther's misuse of your generosity. He asked too much of you when he asked you to marry
into that gang of arrivistes. Federico had been your father's gaming partner at the
spas. He might very well have contributed to your father's financial destruction; I
have never known the whole truth. His asking you to save him, to pay his debts, to free
our properties and our lands from the filthy clutches of the vultures who beat their
wings about us for all those years, his asking you to do all that was what killed him. It
was no accident that he died only weeks after all of it had been put into place. In the
end, he asked you to save the patrimony for yourself. He was not a bad man, your fa-
ther. But he was a weak man. A weak man whom I loved far too much.'

" 'She laughed the silver laugh again. Laughed it quietly, like bells
clinking in a fog. She pulled me to her, kissed my eyes, told me to
leave her. She said that she would never leave me. In her own good
time, in her own good way, she died that night. She died two days shy
of a month before I'd come to take you to the palace and more than
once I have thought that it was she who sent you to me. It's only right
that this be given to you. You are her son's bride. It's your wedding
necklace, Tosca. I truly wish that you might have the wedding to go
with it. You have a devoted husband in me. But you can have no wedding. If only I could change that truth! I am tormented sometimes
that it's only this half-life that I can offer you.'

"Leo rises from the *divanetto,* pulls at his hair, paces the room.

" 'I must find a way for us to be together in peace somewhere.
Away from the threats, away from the pretense. And if I cannot, you
must leave, Tosca. Yes, you must leave here, save yourself from all of
us. From all of them.'

" 'That's the strangest dictum a husband ever gave his new wife.
Telling her that she must leave and save herself. Don't you under-

stand, Leo? I'm already part of the *pretense*. I am already part of the *us*. And, maybe, after Isotta, I am the heroine of your story. Why would you want me to run away?'

"He continues the pacing, and I say, 'I'm not so fond of this part of you. When you play the tragic baroque prince I want to strike you or laugh at you. Don't you have enough, Leo? Why must you always want more? With all her tendencies to unpleasantness, Simona has behaved admirably under the extraordinary circumstances that we've created in this household.'

"He says, 'Not for a moment has she ever considered me to be hers. It's not as though she has, for the sake of gallantry, surrendered me to you. A wedding was what she wanted from me. That and legitimate children sired by noble stock. I've never been anything more than a legal and willing breeder. And since Charlotte's birth, when Simona was warned by her doctors against further childbirth, she has never once responded to my, however insincerely proffered, advances. Certainly she has proffered none of her own. I find little to admire in Simona save the revival of her civility, her aesthete's aloofness.'

" 'I'm not suggesting that we venerate her, Leo. No matter what the circumstances of your marriage or its subsequent events, you are husband and wife living together in this palace with your children. And with your ward, who has become your lover. Isn't that enough compromise and complication without trying to scheme for more? It's when we want more from a person or even from an idea or from a thing, it's then that we get into trouble. It's that little bit more that, in the end, foils all the rest. Maybe it's because I began with so much less than you that I can be so content with this life, grateful for it despite its curious or painful moments.'

"He takes his former place on the *divanetto,* half reclines, closes his eyes.

" 'I suppose it is enough. I suppose it is, Tosca. Perhaps all will remain as it is for a long time. But perhaps it won't. And now I am speaking not of Simona, you understand.'

"He lifts me from the hassock, settles me against him, along the length of the little sofa, my breast to his. He speaks in a whisper, his chin resting on the top of my head.

" 'If, for any reason at all, I am no longer here you must promise me that you will leave the palace. Promise me that you will leave without delay. Don't think that you can continue to live here midst this cloisteral serenity if I'm not here to insure it.'

"I pull away from Leo.

" 'What do you mean when you say *if I'm no longer here?* Are you going to tell me that you have lands to partition and disperse somewhere in France or Spain? There was a branch of your family somewhere in Andalusia, wasn't there?'

"As I did on the first day I knew Leo and as I will do always, I act out fear with sarcasm. Now it's I who pace. Close by a scream, I ask, 'And where am I supposed to go if this mythical event of your disappearance should occur? Have you decided that, too?'

" 'You're no longer a child. Or as you've told me often enough, you've never been a child, though in many ways you have been protected as one. But you're strong, Tosca. You can arrange your life to suit you, most especially if you are not without funds. The remainder of your wedding gifts are in Cosimo's care. I've left him instructions, provisions. Wherever you decide to go, you must keep him informed. Should the time come, he'll help you to find your way.'

"In a quieter voice I say, 'I understand nothing of this. You're running in circles. Are you talking about the eventuality of your death?'

" 'No. Yes, but not just that.'

" 'Is *the eventuality of your death* part of the reason why you are proceeding with your intentions to parcel the land here? Is it part of the reason why you talk about sending the children to village schools, dismantling the infirmary and trucking the children into Enna for checkups, arranging for the older peasants to be transferred to nursing homes? Just when things seemed to be going so well, you propose yet more change. Do you think you're going to die? Is that it? And like the land to the peasants, now you're parceling off jewels and money to me. That's it, isn't it? You're preparing for some sort of departure, aren't you? But I don't think it's your death. You're going to run away. Is that it? The clan, your wife, your daughters, your peasants, your lover, your ideals, history, propriety, passion, beauty, treachery. I know the maze, Leo. I have known it longer and I may know it better than you.'

" 'I don't doubt that. And I am not preparing for escape.'

" 'Are you preparing for suicide? For the love of God, explain all of this to me.'

" 'I can't explain it to you because I don't yet understand it myself. I just want you to be *expectant. Vigilant,* as I am trying to be. That's the first thing I'd wanted to tell you. And the second is that, even considering your fine attitude about how fortunate we are, how we should be content, I don't believe that I can—at least not for all the rest of my life—continue to live only moments at a time in freedom. I am a strange one to speak of morals and yet I shall do just that. I find it *immoral* for us to continue as we are. I never counted on falling in love with little Tosca. And it's because I love you so purely that I am trying to prepare you for a life without me. You may well know some things better than I do, yet I believe I am an expert in my understanding of the nature of our race. I know that if we take a *fiutino*—a little flight—and go away together, if we do that, sooner or later there will come a time when you will be crushed with guilt. That the guilt would be unfounded won't make it less painful. You will feel responsible for taking me away from my life, however meaningless it had been before you and would be without you. And without our work together. You will feel the villainess. The freedom we will gain by running off, we will lose in the imposed separateness from society that we'd be forced to keep. Out in the world, we would live in yet another kind of estrangement. Out in the world we would be judged and reminded, even if subtly, of our indiscretions. If, in the past, you have been distressed by the whisperers, you would be crushed by what you would hear should we ever go away from here together.'

"He reclines again. Closes his eyes, and in the lamplight he is white as marble. Finally, 'You're right, I am speaking in circles. I don't want things to remain as they are and yet I can't see a way to begin again. Who knows what might befall us or Simona or . . . I don't know.'

"Abruptly he sits upright and says, 'I have considered suicide. It would be the gallant way to save you. From them and from me. You would be forced into a life of your own. The idea of suicide can even begin to take root for an hour or so until I remember one more thing I'd like to tell you or show you, or until the sun rises and I imagine you waking, your plaits all undone, your eyes the color of a shallow green sea. I know the eight long strides you take to the door of your bath and the song you sing as the water gushes into the tub and I know the shorter, quicker strides you take—your body still wet, the ends of your hair dripping—back into bed to dry yourself against me. I know too much of you to be able to leave you forever, Tosca. But apart from you, thoughts of Yolande and Charlotte keep me from the self-indulgence of killing myself. Though I feel little paternal love, I feel great paternal responsibility and so I will not bequeath any of this macabre business to them. Nor will I bequeath it to you.'

"Neither of us speaks then. For a long time, we sit like that, silent, distant from one another, until I say, 'Isotta was right. About being uncertain whether to wish you love or to wish that love never finds you. The pain is, indeed, severe in either case. Were you not in pain before this love of ours, and are you not in pain now because of it?'

" 'Yes.'

" 'So does it all divine down to choosing which pain we prefer? Like which poison? Is that a fair distillation of life's propositions?'

" 'Perhaps it is.'

" 'And so you will you always be unhappy in your happiness? This is what I am beginning to believe about you, Leo. And that frightens me far more than *they* do. You see, I've taken on your habit of excluding even their name. Well, let me say it aloud. You and your obsessions frighten me more than the clan frightens me. The worst they could do is to kill me. Kill you. But the menace of you may be far greater. You insist that we sit—prettily, I admit—like prey in a hole to wait for the wolves. This listening for them as we walk across the meadows, this looking for them even among the lemon trees—you've reduced our existence to some sort of vagrancy.'

" 'Cosimo is right. You are remorselessly lucid.'

" 'I think that I am more *lucid,* as you say, than you are at this moment. Let's return to the question of beauty. How much beauty do you think is enough for a life? And how is it that one *measures* beauty? And how must it be wrapped, and how shall it be doled out? The truth is that we've likely lived more than our share of beauty. More than most get to live, I mean. But our portion may not be used up. Let's risk it, Leo. Let's ride tomorrow morning. Let's ride to the *locanda* and I'll play *Le Cygne* for you and we'll drink our tepid tea by the fire and sleep on the dark red rug with the yellow roses.'

" 'I'll go to fetch the damn rug from the *locanda* and we can sleep on it right here.'

" 'You know that's not the same thing. It's time to stop being afraid of them, Leo. If they want you or they want me, if they want us, they'll have us. Stop practicing for death. The only way out of the maze is to take back our life.' "

CHAPTER XV

"BUT WE DO NOT TAKE BACK OUR LIFE. AS THOUGH IT WERE A stone tied upon his back, I try to take the fear from Leo. *Let me help you, I can handle this, I can help you to put this down,* I tell him. But the fear sullies me, too. So diabolic has it become that now it is nameless. It is not the clan. It is not vendetta. I cannot even call it death. Like phantoms, Leo and I move in ever-narrowing arabesques, one so close by the other who can know which of us leads, which of us follows.

" 'Anything would be better than this,' I tell him.

"It is a late afternoon in the month of August 1954, and Leo has come to my rooms. Though he has not left the palace for nearly two months, he announces, feigning nonchalance, that he will go with Cosimo to Enna. Some final business about the deeds. The sham diffidence thrown down, he holds me then. Tight against his chest I stay while he strokes my hair and whispers over my head. Whispers so softly that I understand only his tone. His old tenderness. His heart is a frightened bird. He speaks in the slurred, sweet words of dialect.

" 'I must go,' he says, rather than *I will go.* In Sicilian there is no future tense. 'I must go,' he says again. The chapel bells ring. Fifteen minutes until vespers.

" 'I'll wait for you,' I say, but he's already at the door. He's already gone. Why are the bells still ringing? Strange. Something amiss with the clocks. I feel free. Yes, that's it. The bells are freedom bells. I am free. Leo will be gone for a few hours and I am free. I'll go and ask cook if I can prepare a supper to take up here to my rooms. No, better to set up on the veranda. Agata and I will set the table out there. I'll wear the silvery-brown dress. Weave magnolias among my braids the way he likes them. This is wonderful. Even after such a brief time away, Leo will return refreshed. And refreshed I shall be to await him. We must begin to think only of us for a while. It will seem pretense at first, but if we sustain it, the pretense will become natural. Yes, *only of us.*

"Agata and I are arranging the table, and it's been so long since we did anything at all apart from the strictest routines that even she and I must resort to pretense. She is cautious against my prattle, takes away the magnolia that I tuck behind her ear, places it near Leo's plate. With Leo's dialect still in my ear, I speak in Sicilian with her, a reach toward intimacy.

" '*Ma io non ricordo più. In dialetto, quale é la parola 'piacere'?* I no longer remember. In dialect, what is the word for 'pleasure'?'

" '*Non esiste.* It doesn't exist.' "

"I've brought out a small bottle of *moscato* and the two glasses that Leo keeps on the table beside his bed. A welcome-home drink. It had been chilled, but now the icy beads on the thin amber bottle have dried. I pull my shawl tight against the breeze. Where can they be? Mimmo has already taken in the table settings, the little pots of jellied broth. He appears every once in a while to urge me inside. This time, he's brought a *tisana* of chamomile.

" 'I'll stay just a little longer, Mimmo,' I say as I see Cosimo mounting the stone steps.

" 'You see? Here they are. I'll be fine, Mimmo. You get some rest.'

"Mimmo seems old to me this evening. I don't recall ever noticing how old he's become. Cosimo is beside me now and, for some reason, he carries Leo's suede jacket. At least that's what it looks like all crumpled there in the clutch of his left hand. What foolish thing has Leo got to, I wonder.

"I get up, take the jacket from Cosimo. My relief at their return I conceal in giddiness.

" 'When did you take on the duties of the prince's valet, Don Cosimo?'

"I shake out the jacket, smooth the wrinkles as best I can. Shake it out again. I notice the tremor in my hands. I find that I can't look at Cosimo. I find that I can't speak.

" 'He's gone, Tosca.'

"I look at him then. Hold the jacket against me. Against what I know the priest is telling me.

" 'We were stopped on the Enna road. Two autos converged in our path. Without lights, we didn't see them until they were upon us. Two men got out from the autos, the motors still running. I don't know if there were other men who stayed inside the autos. I think there were. The two took Leo from the passenger seat. Blindfolded him. Took off his jacket and threw it down. Manacled his hands. Pushed him into one of the autos. They were gone. No one had spoken. I sat in our auto for a long time.'

" 'He'll be back. He'll be back anytime now. Another threat.

They would have taken you, too. I mean, if they were going to hurt him, why would they have left you a witness?'

" 'I was witness to nothing except two dark autos, two swift-moving, dark-clad figures. I never saw a face or heard a word. I was witness only to the disappearance of the prince. I know that he is not coming back, Tosca.'

" 'How do you know that?'

" 'I know it.'

" '*I* don't know it at all. Tonight was just the second part of the torture. Don't you see that? They are nothing if not skillful, these men. Whispers and silences. With only these, they've done the work of knives and axes. But Leo is not gone. I assure you, Cosimo, Leo is not gone.' My voice is thin and pitched close to hysteria. I, too, know that Leo is gone.

"I know that I am sitting here on the veranda, I know that Cosimo continues to speak to me, that he tells me he's already been to see Simona. That, when he'd returned, he'd entered the palace through the back way, gone straight to Simona. *It was the proper thing to do,* he keeps repeating. Yes, Simona is the wife. The widow. It was the proper thing to do. He says that Simona is with the princesses now, that I should go to join them. That we will keep the vigil all together. Candles. Incense. The household will keep the vigil together. He tells me that he is going to the *borghetto.* I must go inside now, he says. I must not be alone. Doesn't he know that by going inside I will not be less alone? I have entered into some vaporous province, into a heavy, confused mist where there are no borders. I'll fall away if I try to walk. I must stay here. I think of Mafalda, who wanted to stay at home so she might be there to welcome us when we returned. I must stay right here where Leo can see me. I take the magnolias from my hair. My heart thuds in a quickened grace note. One two. One two. One two. I hear his voice in my heartbeats. He's calling me. I open my mouth to answer him but there comes no sound. I try again and again and then from far off I hear a woman's soft wailing. The wail is mine. A jackal howls then from that same far-off place. The howl, too, is mine."

"It is morning, and strands of opal light fall from the high windows of the palace chapel. Birdsong and someone's hoarse whispering over the beads make the only sounds. Charlotte holds my hand, as she has through the night. Yolande sits apart from us with Mademoiselle Clothilde. Alone, Simona sits in the center of the front pew. Though, with the dawn, the vigil has ended, Simona has made no move to leave. We must await the widow's departure and follow her from the chapel. Mimmo enters now. He walks to Simona, hands her the thick vanilla-colored paper sealed with red wax. Her back is to me yet I know that she has opened the letter. I know from whom it came. The first note of condolence is from the man named Mattia. Leo is not coming back."

"Every place in my mind is empty. I do not weep or speak or feel pain. I feel nothing at all. I listen. I observe. I sit in the *salone* with my book. People begin to arrive and I begrudge even their quietest moving through the rooms. I begrudge the dancing light that stabs through the drawn curtains. I go to walk in the garden but find I have no strength for it. I sit on a stone and let the sun pour fire on my face.

Sometimes a breeze whirls the dry leaves of the poplars and I think of the rustling our dresses made as we three girls used to walk down the long hall to supper. Rooks chatter above me and in their noise I hear the long-ago voices of the princesses. Perhaps I hear even my own. I go back into the palace, sit in my same place in the *salone*. I see the long boxes of mourning clothes that are delivered by men in white gloves. Simona and Agata open them. A slim black dress, a large-brimmed hat with layers and layers of black tulle to hide the widow. For the princesses, black faille skirts and jackets and lace mantillas that fall to their ankles. Simona comes to where I sit and places a dress on the cushion next to me. And a silk cap with a short thick veil. She bends to kiss my cheek."

"Newly rebuilt after the Ascension Day fire, Leo's funeral Mass is said in the *borghetto* chapel. Simona has arranged everything. And not according to her own sensibilities but to Leo's. She will lay to rest the prince she wed with great benevolence. Truckloads of formal flowers fill the courtyard. Goats and chickens and a few geese wander among the sprays of yellow chrysanthemums, the beribboned pillows of red roses. The animals gently peck, nibble at the flowers, but no one shoos them away. The chapel is small; the crowds are endless. People stand on the stones of the old white road, in the meadow that leads to the palace, along the edges of the wheat fields. Under the bestial sun, they stand motionless.

The altar is piled high with sheaves of wheat tied 'round with hempweed. On the table where Cosimo prepares Holy Communion, there are white candles set among branches of olive—the fruit still in small, tight buds—and lengths of the oldest vines heavy with sun-

broken grapes. There is no body. There is no casket. There are no
ashes. The man called Mattia stands among the mourners on the left
side wall of the chapel, perhaps three meters from the place where I
sit at the edge of my pew. I know it is he from the way Cosimo keeps
looking at him from the altar. And from the way he stares at me. I
would have known him anyway. How did you do it, Signor Mattia?
Did you shoot him? Did you choke the life from him with your bare
hands and then go on with your plans for the evening? Or didn't you
soil your hands at all? Did you order his death with a gesture, a half-
lidded glance? The least you might have done, Signor Mattia, is to
have let us bury him.

"Is it true, Prince Leo, that you kiss the hands of your peasants?"

"Now why would that be of interest to you?"

*"It's just that if someday we hear you've suffered some misfortune, we'll under-
stand the source of it. The loss of respect, I mean. Yes, we'll understand that you invited your misfortune with a kiss."*

"The father and son from Enna who played the pipes each year
for the ceremonial harvest wait outside the chapel. As Simona rises
from her pew, followed by the princesses and me and all those who'd
been inside, the pipers begin to play. The drummer boys from the
borghetto are there, too, and it is they who lead the procession along
the white road to the mausoleum that sits beyond the palace lemon
groves. The drummer boys, the mourners, the pipers. Simona and
the princesses each place something onto the threshold of the long,
dark space where Leo's casket would have been. Flowers, letters,
books. Simona makes way for me to approach the space but, not

knowing of this ritual, if it is indeed a ritual, I have nothing to leave. I take off the silk cap with the short thick veil and lay it inside. A mason and his apprentice step up, and set the sealing stone in place. The apprentice backs away, bows his head. I know that Cosimo prays but I hear only the mason's small hammer ringing."

CHAPTER XVI

"IT WAS PERHAPS FOR TWO WEEKS OR MORE AFTER THE FUNERAL that Simona kept to her rooms. She was not, I think, so much in mourning as she was in a state of flux. She had given leave to Mademoiselle Clothilde, the only teacher who'd still remained part of the household. Though Cosimo visited nearly each day, he'd gone to live in the parish house that had always been provided for him at San Rocco. He once again took up the observances, the submissions of a rural priest. Without the shield of Leo's influence with the Curia, there had already been talk of his transference to what was termed 'a more challenging post.' With no one else in residence, there was only Simona, Yolande, Charlotte, and I.

"The princesses dosed themselves with valerian and fell onto their beds or assembled themselves in some remote *salottino* to scratch petulant homages to Bach across their violoncellos. When Simona did appear, she was cheerful enough, more indulgent with her daughters than usual, though they, too, seemed past any suffering. She would speak of her plans with me. Plans for herself and the princesses. The apartment in Geneva might be opened. The girls should spend a year or so in Paris. The loss of Leo had released her from the once-in-a-while tributes she'd had to pay to the strictures of their marriage. Though she was sorry for his death, in her brilliant oblique language, she would refer to it as *another of his choices*. Now that she no longer had to act out her minimalist role in the palace theater, she was quite prepared to take on the part of the merry widow.

" 'And you, Tosca? Has Cosimo brought out all the documents that concern your inheritance? It's quite substantial, I would imagine. Substantial enough.'

" 'Yes,' is all I say.

" 'It's not that I wouldn't want you to stay on with us. In fact, not so many years ago I recall imploring you to stay. To not be so foolish as to run off. But Tosca, I fear for you now. I fear that you will believe as we all believe that we can keep breaking into our store of time without counting. Our lives seem infinite until we reach in one day to find how little of them is left. That's how I feel, Tosca. That so little remains. I'll soon be fifty. You are not quite half my age. Apart from the wealth that Leo has bequeathed to you, you are still rich in time. Don't use up these next years by living here with only the spectre of your prince. He would have been the last one to have wanted that for you.'

" 'He'd told me. He'd told me more than once that if anything ever happened to him, I should go. Cosimo is telling me to go. I think he says this on Leo's behalf but also on his own. I will go. I want to go. I just don't know how to begin. Where to begin.'

" 'That's the part that hardly matters. Leo has left you the lodge, hasn't he?'

" 'Yes. But I don't want to live alone.'

" 'Of course you don't want to be alone. Yet here you shall be very much alone. Should you go to the lodge you would still be alone. Even if you go somewhere altogether new, the solitariness will go with you. For a while. It's only that, in another environment, more will be expected of you than is expected of you here. Here life proceeds according to the bells. The lodge is so immense that a similar troupe of help would be necessary to keep it going, and so, life *there* would also proceed according to the bells. But in another place, you could begin to invent a life. I think that's the right word, Tosca. Or is it reinvent that I want to say? Yes, to *reinvent* yourself. To study, to work, to make friends with people your own age, to *choose* how to spend your time rather than to be passive against what you shall come to notice is its ever-quickening pace. I do not suggest that you go to live in the lodge now. But it could serve as your security. Your own place, should you need it. Should you, someday, oh I don't know, should you someday have a family. Put your things there now, take what you might need from here, from your rooms, from Leo's rooms. Set up some sort of household for yourself there and then go. Far or near. The palace has been left in trust to me for my lifetime and reverts to Yolande and then to Charlotte. Though I can't say if any of us will be here or, if we are, for how long or how much of a staff I shall keep in the meanwhile, the palace will always be here if you want to come back.'

"'I'm thinking to go to live in the *borghetto*. I've always wanted to, you know. I mean, I'd wanted to years ago, and now it seems . . .'

"'I know very well of your earlier desire to live there. Leo had discussed it with me. Asked me to try and convince you to stay here. As it turned out, he was successful himself in turning you away from that plan. Valid as his reasons were then, they are more valid now. You cannot negate the years you've spent here, the privileges, the relationships of your life. Though they love you—though they loved you loving their prince and him loving you—you are not one of them,

Tosca. They would be too kind to deny you a place among them, but you would cause their discomfort. Leo himself would have caused their discomfort. Besides, I think that many of the families will eventually build homesteads on their own land. Over time, the *borghetto* itself will become obsolete.'

"She had noted my startled glance when she'd said that Leo had discussed my wishes with her. Surely there must have been a substance to their relationship that neither of them openly displayed. Or was it that it was not displayed to me? Or was it that I chose not to notice it? She is speaking now of my spending winter holidays with her and the princesses in Geneva, yet I still don't trust my legs to carry me up the stairs to my rooms. Simona knows I do not take in her words. She holds me in her arms, tells me, " 'Leo has died but it's you who is in limbo, Tosca. Find your own way home.' "

"It is sometime in late September when I begin to feel stronger—healed, I think, by spite. Should the clan still be inclined toward killing me, I will do all I can to help them. I begin to ride again. Leo's jodhpurs belted about my waist, his suede jacket buttoned over my bare breasts, my hair left loose, I ride the prince's stallion. In a swoon of sweet revenge, I ride him bareback. *If you want me, here I am, dear 'friends,'* I would shout into the wind. *Sono qui, Signor Mattia. Sono qui tutti, voi bastardi. Venite a prendermi.* I'm here, Signor Mattia. I'm here, all you bastards. Come and take me. Sometimes I would shout to Leo, too, dare him to watch me, tell him that this is what we should have been doing rather than cringing behind the walls. I make a target of myself riding hard over open spaces, through the woods, along the precipices of the rocky outcrops, even into the villages.

How easy it is to call up the little savage in me, the horse thief's daughter. How well she serves me. *We are all endlessly ourselves.*

"Often I would stay out most of the day, exhausting myself in the hope of a peaceful night. No hat against the blazing sun, I let my skin grow dark as a Turk's. I would eat only broth and bread, sometimes an egg. The suppers of my childhood. The right food for a Fury. I begin to smoke in earnest. Thirty or forty cigarettes a day. What flesh there'd been on my slender body falls away.

"I ride to the lodge, walk the vast space of it, go to lie on the daybed on the loggia in the *mansarda* where we'd first made love on that late afternoon of my birthday. I fondle the opalescent curtain with the wide satin flounce. If it's cool enough, I close my eyes, sleep sometimes, either there on the daybed or sprawled in the cleaved trunk of the magnolia. Yes, Chou, this magnolia. I begin to wonder what it would be like to live here. To set about revitalizing this fallow land as Leo had done his. To make a working farm of it. And how much there could be done in the gardens and in the house itself. It would be so beautiful. But who would live with me? If only my mother and Mafalda were here. My father, too. I would ask Agata to come and maybe Mimmo, and surely Lullo and Valentino would stay. Could Cosimo be convinced? Simona spoke to me of reinvention. Is that what I'm dreaming of? To reinvent the *borghetto* here? I think it's not that. Not really that. Nor is it to gather all the waifs of the world 'round me because it's a waif whom I think to be, myself. No, the dream is simply to live together and work together with good people. I want to give the way Leo gave. I suppose, in some ways, I want *to be* Leo. His pants, his jacket. His horse. His goodness. I suppose I do want to be Leo. To keep him alive.

. . .

"The virago wasted, a mincing coward takes over. I like her less. It is nearly December and, as Simona had predicted I would be, I am too much alone in the palace now that she and the princesses have gone, embarked upon the next phases of their lives. I will go, too. I know that I will go, but the constant thinking about to what place, about what it will be like, what I will see, whom I shall meet, the fainter grows my heart.

"One morning, from the back of an armoire where I'd placed it, I take an old black valise that looks like a doctor's bag. Inside it there are no medicines, though. It is filled with little plush envelopes and sacks. Inside these are Isotta's jewels. There is a long letter that Leo had written years ago. It is dated August 1948. He speaks of the jewels as my birthday gifts, as my coming-of-age gifts. There is another, shorter, note that speaks of certain of the envelopes and sacks as my wedding gifts. There are documents that insure and validate the worth of the jewels. These I crumple and push into a too-small compartment at the bottom of the case. The letter I place in my handbag. Propped against my pillows, I settle myself in bed and, one by one, I open the envelopes and the sacks. Among the bedclothes, I let the jewels fall 'round me. There are ropes and ropes of pearls in all sizes. There is a necklace of oval diamonds. A sack of rubies both polished and unpolished and a note in what must be Isotta's handwriting that says *tutti sangue di piccione,* all pigeon blood. There is another sack of rubies without further identification. Apart from the one that she always wore, Isotta must have been particularly partial to emeralds since there are two emerald rings, several pairs of emerald earrings.

There is a sack filled with rings set mostly with diamonds. There is much more. When I've put all of it back in its place, I begin to pack. Fingering these treasures, I feel crazed with yet another kind of fear. It is a terror caused by something far more horrifying than the clan. I imagine myself propped against these same pillows, settled in this same bed, these same glittering stones heaped 'round me among the bedclothes. Only in my imaginings, I am far, far older than I am today."

"Simona had left me a small wheeled trunk and two medium-sized suitcases. I decide that whatever I can fit into these three will comprise my worldly goods for the next part of my life. Whereas I had been languishing for the past month or so, now I am ruthlessly inspired to change things. I pack clothes, books. When I am finished, I have hardly filled the trunk, while the suitcases remain empty. In one of them, I place the medicine bag. The other I stow under my yellow and white bed. I bathe and dress, wait for Cosimo's late-afternoon visit. Before I finish telling him all that I've decided, he says, 'You'll have to wait a day or so. The appointment with the attorneys that you've been avoiding is necessary. They will explain to you the procedures and the regulations for the distribution of your income. There will be documents to sign. After that, you'll be free to go.'

" 'I see. Do you know where I mean to go? At least for a while?'

" 'I suspect it's Palermo.'

" 'Is the choice so obvious?'

" 'No. Not obvious but superior. I would think it to be the best place to begin. There are far more advantages and disadvantages in Palermo than there are almost anywhere else right now. I know of a *pensione.* In the historic center. I can arrange a stay there for you while you look about. Until you can find something more permanent. That is, should you wish to remain in the city. You'll find many of the *Palermitani* to be genteel. Particularly this family. Beyond this introduction, I won't be of much help.'

" 'I am not asking you for help.' My bravado is lofty. Almost rude.

" 'Let's get this meeting with the attorneys scheduled. If I can arrange it for a morning, you can depart for Palermo on the same day. I can drive you to Enna. To the train,' he says.

"As if from far off, I have listened to our terse exchange. To our voices, mine peeved, his woeful. Neither of us reaches for the line that drifts between us. I look at the priest, who is looking away as though mesmerized by the blood-red walls of the *salotto* where we sit. Cosimo is weary. Most of all, he is weary of me. Longing to quit the duty, I think, with which Leo bound him.

" 'Thank you,' I say but he is already walking away."

"And so at the age of twenty-five, I trade my status as *la puttanina* for one of heiress. Jewels stuffed in plush pouches. A numbered Swiss account. Safety deposit boxes. I know that if I begin to speak with Agata or Mimmo or anyone here of my will to leave the palace with this sort of immediacy, their affectionate counsel could confound my new resolve. The cut must be quick and clean. *Find your own way home.*

"Less than a week later Cosimo comes to fetch me in the old gray Chrysler, its shuddering, as it idles in the drive, as violent as my own. I take a last look about. I touch the emerald at my throat. I wear my mourning dress. A beaver coat that touches the tops of the high thick heels of my lace-up shoes. A black velvet toque I've tilted over the crown of my braids. Cosimo carries my trunk, I, the suitcase that holds the medicine bag. I am settled in the passenger seat where Leo always sat. I take a deep breath, and in it there is the still-lingering perfume of neroli oil. As Cosimo shifts the car and we begin to move, I turn to see Agata and Mimmo standing in the portico, chins high, hands at their sides. I place my splayed, gloved hand against the window."

PART III

Palermo
1955

CHAPTER I

THE NEXT AFTERNOON AT FIVE WHEN I GO TO MEET WITH
Tosca under the magnolia, I find her somehow changed, as though
her great, powerful presence has waned, given way to a winsomeness,
a fragility, even. She is older, and yet more a girl. Tosca continues her
story.

"A just-foaled, unlicked beast staggering against a sharp wind, I
hold my hat in place with one hand, the suitcase packed with the
medicine bag in the other, and hobble along the oil-slicked, burnt-
smelling trackway. I cannot keep pace with the young porter who
drags my trunk from the train. He turns every few meters to see that
I follow. Still I lose sight of the small, thick figure of him snaking in
and out of the billowing steam and among the crushing throngs.
Each time a whistle is pulled, I am startled, panicked, close to tears.
Once out onto the street, I stand there beside my bags and look
about as though I've not been transported one hundred kilometers
distant from the palace but catapulted into another universe by some
hell-born fiend. I nearly laugh at the essential truth of this. Curse
Mattia. I hear dialect spoken and, though its city form is different

enough from the mountain one, I stay still to listen to it, take comfort in it. My heart beats more slowly. I am still in Sicily.

"I wave my hand in the general direction of the bank of taxis across the way. This has little effect save from one of the drivers, who waves back and blows me a kiss. I watch what other people do. I do what they do. Step right up to the driver's window, lean in to tell him my destination. It works. My driver wears a red fez and some sort of military jacket, unfastened to reveal the stupendous girth of him. He rolls out of the car, stows my trunk in the boot, nods at me to get going. Get in. I slide into the seat, he slams shut the door and lurches into the frantic dusk of Arabia.

"The city looks freshly sacked. Buildings black and hollow, as though great fires have only just been spent in the bellies of them, sit cheek by jowl with sublime palaces that glitter, unembarrassed, I think, by the cruel obstinacy of their survival. Palermo is in conflict with itself. It's good that the traffic moves slowly. Good that the driver bounces in time to the merciless screech of his radio, the tassel on his fez swinging up to brush the roof of the taxi on every third beat. These past twenty or so minutes mark by far the longest stretch of time during which I have not thought of Leo. This, too, must be good. Before I would have wished him to, the driver stops abruptly in front of a narrow red-stuccoed palazzo with arched and colonnaded windows. He places my trunk on the narrow sidewalk while I gather together the fare. So rarely have I handled money that I thrust what are far too many coins into his roughened paw. Patiently, still bouncing to his music, he counts out the correct amount, pockets it, takes my hand, turns it palm up, and slaps down the remaining coins. Wishes me a good evening. I stand there watching the taxi until it's out of sight. I wave too late for the driver to see me, even had he been looking in his mirror. Maneuvering first the trunk and then the suitcase up the few steps to the entrance, I press the button under the small brass plaque. *Pensione d'Aiello.*"

Even though she and I have been sitting together for hours each day for the past week or so while she tells me another and then another part of this story, Tosca looks at me then almost in surprise. How did I come to be here with her in the darkening under the magnolia?

"What was it like? Your arrival in the *pensione*?" Banality meant to lead her back into the story. Rather she smiles, sits quietly.

"I hardly recall anything of that first evening. Those first days. I do recall what didn't happen. You see, I'd thought that the new place would make *me* new as well. That the journey would strip me clean. Eclipse the noises. I'd thought to outrun the ghosts, outwit them. I'd counted on Palermo, the refuge of *the new place,* the refuge of a train ride, the sympathy of a malodorous man in a red fez, to do for me what I hadn't been able to do for myself. But the man in the red fez and the train and the city were powerless against the ghosts. Leo, Cosimo, Mattia. All of them had gathered, awaiting me in the third-floor room in *pensione d'Aiello.* Over and over again, I heard Simona saying *find your own way home.*"

I'd grown used to the stylish tripping of Tosca's storytelling. Ebullient or wistful, the plummy tones of her voice never faltered.

She'd trace back and forth, picking up threads she'd dropped, but always, she'd had the next thing and the next thing after that to say. Now she is cautious.

"I don't think I can tell you about those years in Palermo without telling other people's stories along with my own. Stories that are not mine to tell. Life until I left the palace was largely about Leo and me. In Palermo it included, it grew to include, many others."

"Did you fall in love again? Is that what you mean?"

"Perhaps that, too. Not only that. During that time Palermo was a city even more explosive than it had been during the war. An ancient, exhausted city in the throes of yet another rising-up from the ashes. Only then it wasn't the Greeks or the Saracens or the Normans who'd invaded. It was the boys from the mountains. Hungry, desperate boys from these mountains. And a few boys from across the sea."

"What sea?"

"American soldiers. I'm talking about American soldiers—some of whom were island born, who had emigrated to and been naturalized in America—who landed back here in 1943. The American invasion of Sicily re-formed the clans from their historical careers as rural brigands—the boys who'd slit throats for a sack of flour—into another class of criminal. There were drugs to traffic, State funds to embezzle, protection fees to collect, a black market to exploit."

"What did all that have to do with you?"

"Think about the frescoes in the dining hall. About the fragments within the allegories that are empty. Those blank spaces. They are empty because there wasn't enough of the original design left for the restorer to re-create those portions with authenticity. The restoring artist would have had to paint his own figures and, hence, dishonor the intrinsic virtue of the work. It's quite the same with a life. There are blank spaces that I cannot fill."

"*Io capisco. Io capisco.* I understand," I tell her even as she picks up her brush.

"I was a Pirandello figure, Chou. A character in search of an author. In search of a story. So used to the prescribed life in the palace, so used to the bells and the rituals, even used to Simona selecting my clothes, to Agata taking care of them, of me. In fifteen years, I'd never chosen my own food, never thought about what something cost. I'd never drawn my own bath. I don't even know if, from the time I was fifteen and understood that I loved the prince, I don't know if I ever had a whole thought that didn't include him. As a six-year-old motherless child, I'd been far more skilful at the business of living than I was at twenty-five. I'd once believed that Leo had made a woman out of the girl in me and yet the greater truth might have been that he'd kept me, I think unwittingly, a child. He refined and inspired and educated and protected me so that without him to breathe the very life into me, I died, too. A character in search of an author.

"I chose one dress and I wore it every day. A dark brown dress with a pattern of white camellias and small green leaves. A long brown woollen shawl. Thick black stockings and black lace-up shoes. My hair I fixed in a single plait, let it fall down to the small of my back. I wore a white basque. Wanting nothing of the forced intimacy that would come of my sitting at table thrice daily in the *pensione,* I lied to my patrons. Told them I'd made other dining arrangements. Besieged by ghosts, I would be one, too.

"I would slip down three flights of carpeted stairs, leave quietly of a morning. Return then as quietly to rest. Back down again in the afternoon, the early evening. A final, stealthy turn of the long, flat key in the lock and I'd climb to my room for the night. Two exits, two entrances without speaking a word. An easy ghost I was."

"I began my exploration of the city by following people. Some days I would let myself be led to the waterfront, sometimes to the markets. In each place, I began to draw my own route. Make my own map. Where to sit to watch the boats. Mark the hours when the fleets came in, went out, came in again. The fishermen's wives who waited. Sun-browned faces slashed with lipsticked mouths, bosoms spilling out of tight cotton pinafores, fraying sweaters straining across thickened waists. Patched rubber boots over unmended stockings, they marched three or four abreast to the edge of the pier and I thought them a dazzling troupe. I waited for them as I might have for friends, forgetting that I was invisible to them. In the markets, I would always have two 100-lira coins ready in my hand. A sack of plums. Two scoops of pistachios, salted in the shell. Always a slice of pecorino *pepato* and a quarter loaf of sesame bread. Or two flats of Arab bread from the man everyone called Santo. Though I might go to the same merchants and even buy the same things for days on end, no one paid notice to the good ghost I'd become. Whatever change remained from my purchases I would drop in the upturned hand of the gypsy who smelled of night jasmine and old sweat and who crouched near a fishmonger who I think was her son. Recognizing her as a ghost, too, she was, for months, the only person in whose eyes I looked.

"Though everyone who had something to eat ate it on the street, I was embarrassed to do likewise. On a bench in the *Favorita,* my lookout place between the shacks and the oil drums on the pier, in one place or another, I would dine. Unwrapping my cheese from its thick white paper, I would sometimes think of the crumble of pecorino that the shepherds would chisel from their great, dark yellow rounds for Mafalda and me in the markets and how she would hold her mouth open for it, a famished little bird. Now I could buy as much cheese as I wished. As though I had children to feed, a husband on his way home to lunch, *di più, di più,* more, more, I would say to the merchant as he moved the great glistening blade of his cutter above a larger and yet larger wedge of the cheese. I would try to taste it with the old hunger. I'd close my eyes and wait for the burst of sharp, sour heat on my tongue but I felt nothing. I'd refold the thick white paper 'round the cheese and put it in my bag, walk along until I came upon a child bent on some mission or another or, less often, a group of children playing, and offer the cheese. Oh, the wonder, the ecstasy it never failed to cause, that slice of cheese, and that impulse would always make me think about the many emotions of which hunger is made."

"Everywhere I walked, I looked for him. Not a conscious, deliberate search, mine was the instinctive chase of the lover longing for the beloved. In the market, in the bar, in the street, along the pier, I am a constant huntress tracking her dead prince. The sighting of any man, tall and light-haired, visible above the crowd, would stop my heart. I would run, snake through the throngs, traverse screeching traffic to intercept him. *Leo. Leo.* I would call and people would make way for me, shouting oaths or cheering, applauding the classic scene of a woman in pursuit of a man, their eyes saying *get to him, kiss him, shoot him, do what you must. But get to him.* And so it was not at all startling to me when, one day, I saw my mother.

"Her same fragile beauty I think to see in a woman who stands among those waiting for an *autobus.* Tendrils of straw-colored hair fall from a kerchief tied behind her head. Just like my mother. A pale blue cotton dress with padded shoulders and black leather pumps with white cotton socks turned down at the ankles just like my mother's Sunday clothes. I stop on the edge of the group as though I, too, have come to wait for the *autobus.* I stare at the woman who I am certain is my mother. Unlike the times when I'd approached a man who I thought to be Leo and then saw it was decidedly not him, now I am sure. The still sane part of me knows it is the madness of grief that makes her appear now. But why doesn't she look at me? How can she not see me if I can see her? I walk closer to her, stare openly at her. I study her as though she is wax.

"*Mamà, it's me,* I tell her softly. *Mamà, can you see me? Tosca,* she whispers. *Che cosa ci fai qui?* What are you doing here?

"She is not Mama. She is Mafalda. Mafalda, who is now the same age, nearly the very same age, as my mother was when she died. As my mother was when I last saw her. In the almost thirteen years since I have seen my sister, she has grown to be the *sosia,* the twin image of Mama.

" '*Ciao, piccola,*' I say. She allows my embrace but does not return it.

" 'What brings you so far away from your palace, Tosca?' She pulls away from me, adjusts her kerchief, narrows her eyes so tears won't fall.

" 'I, I live here now.'

" 'Oh, does your prince also have a palace here?'

" 'Why didn't you let me know where you were? Why did you abandon me or hide from me or whatever it is that you did?'

"I pull Mafalda over to a bench that has just been vacated since the *autobus* has arrived but she pushes me away, reaches up the flat of her hand, and strikes my cheek. She strikes me three times before I have the presence to take hold of her arm. She screams, 'Me? *Why did I abandon you?* Are you sure you remember things as they really happened, Tosca? You left me and you left Papà and . . .'

" 'Mafalda, stop it. Stop it. You didn't know, you were too little to understand, but the truth is that Papà sold me to Leo. He traded me for a horse, Mafalda.'

" 'I know that. I know that was how it began. You love to say it, don't you, Tosca? You love to be the victim, the poor little orphan girl sold to a prince. Truth is, Papà did you a favor sending you to them. He didn't sell you into slavery after all, he set you down inside a fairy tale. But you could have returned. You weren't held captive, were you? I can understand why you would have stayed there for a while, a year or two if only for the relief, the change. You were still little, too, and your head was turned. But to stay? I never believed that you would stay with them. I waited for you. Papà waited for you, too.'

" 'You're lying. Papà forsook me and you know that. He wouldn't let me return. Have you forgotten that?'

" 'He was testing you. Even I could see that. He wanted you to prove to him that you preferred life with us over life with them. I believe that, Tosca. But you surrendered so easily to the temptations of the palace.'

" 'I was nine years old, Mafalda. I was frightened and angry and grieving and hungry and yes, at that time in my life I suppose I did choose Leo over Papà. But I stayed at the palace, in part, because I believed it was the best way to take care of you. You were too young to understand that, and perhaps I was too young to have carried through with my plans as fully as I might have. Yes, you're right, I had my head turned. But taking care of you was what I'd set out to do. And I did, didn't I? Didn't I come to see you whenever I could, bring you presents? But when you went away and then when Papà did, too, all I could do was wait. Remember, *you who knew where I was*. Leo and Cosimo worked for years at finding you, following the thinnest threads. They wrote letters to the communes and dioceses of the towns and villages where people with our name and Mamà's name were registered. More than once they traveled to talk to someone who knew, someone who remembered . . . but nothing. I've been angry with you, too, Mafalda.'

" 'You have no reason to be angry with me. You're angry with yourself because I'm different from you. Maybe you envy me a bit, Tosca. Envy me because I didn't sell out. The best way you could have helped me would have been to share bread and cheese with me and to stay close to me. We were fine, then, Tosca. We were just fine. I won't say that I didn't look forward to your gifts but you see I was already safe. I still knew what we used to know together. I knew that I would always *get by*. That no matter what, I would always be able to *arrange* things. Somewhere along the way I guess that turned out not to be enough for you. Getting by. Arranging. But it's always been enough for me. It's still enough for me, Tosca.'

"We are quiet, appraising each other, each one of us beginning to speak, both deferring. Silence. Until Mafalda says, 'And when Papà got sick—did you even know that he was sick?—he told me that I, too, would have to go to live with the prince's family. I cried and screamed and begged him not to bring me to Leo and that's when he made arrangements for me with *zia* Elena. He brought me there, promised to visit me soon, and that was the last time I saw him.'

"Mafalda sits on the bench then. Perches on the edge of it, her face pale, tortured. I look at her hands, which are red and dry, old for a woman of twenty-two. For the Bellini Madonna whom she so resembles. As though they are borrowed hands or hands fixed, by error, onto the slender white wrists of her. I sit next to her. Hold her hands in mine. She tells me, 'When Papà didn't come to see me, I got myself back to our place. It took me a week, but I got there. Too late. He was gone, everything was gone. I didn't want to go back to *zia* Elena. Things were not so good there. I never even considered knocking on the great doors of the palace. And so I have been on my own since a few months before I was twelve. Mostly it was easy to find work, since I would do almost anything to earn my food and a place to sleep.'

" 'But why, why didn't you come to me? Ask me for help? Why didn't you *allow* me to help you? *I didn't know. How could I know?* All this time, I didn't know.' I've pulled Mafalda to her feet and now I'm screaming and weeping and shaking her. Then holding her to me. *Why? Why, piccola?*

" 'Because I didn't want your gifts, your food, your clothes. I wanted *you*, Tosca. I wanted us to be a family.'

"Mafalda is quiet then. Wipes her face with a fresh handkerchief pulled from her purse. 'I will take the next *autobus*. It's due in a few minutes. I have an appointment that I intend to keep.'

" 'An appointment? You can't mean that you won't come with me now. We can sit somewhere and talk, I can take you back to my room. I don't even know why you're here or where you live; you can't just get on an *autobus* after thirteen years . . .'

" 'I'm still trying to find Papà. Whenever I've had money to spare, I've spent it in looking for him. I know what it's like to write pleading letters to strangers. I'm here in Palermo to see a woman who knew Papà. I think they were lovers. A long time ago, when Papà and I were still together, I found a letter, a note really, among his things. I kept it. I don't know why I kept it except that it was a sweet note, written on pretty paper. Signed *Loretta*. I liked the name. Long afterward when I began trying to find him, it was this Loretta, this Signora Capella, to whom I first wrote. I was living in Piazza Amerina then. She never wrote back to me and so I came here, went to the return address on the letter. Of course, she'd moved, or at least the *portiniera* said she had. I never thought about her again. I managed to discover some other remote leads, but I think he's long since died. Or so I thought until a few days ago, when I received a letter from this Signora Capella. I've kept in touch with the people for whom I worked in Piazza Amerina and they forwarded her letter to me. She asked me to telephone her, and when I did, we made an appointment for today. Nothing, not even you, Tosca, could keep me from going to her.'

" 'Meet me afterward. I'll be wherever you say.'

" 'Come with me, Tosca.'

" 'I don't care to come with you. I'll wait for you.'

"Mafalda rises, begins walking toward the bus, which has just lumbered up to the curb in front of us, the hiss of its opening doors muffling her parting word.

" 'Tomorrow,' she says.

"She mounts the steps, pays her fare, turns back toward me, and waves.

" '*Pensione d'Aiello*,' I shout. '*Pensione d'Aiello*.' "

. . .

"I go out early the next morning, buy bread and cheese from the *gastronomia* down the street, a sack of ripe brown pears, a liter jug of red wine, then head back to the *pensione* to wait for my sister. I ask Signora d'Aiello for glasses, plates, napkins. A knife. I tell her that I am expecting company. She says we are welcome at the family table for lunch or dinner. Offers to fix tea, to send for pastries, and seems disappointed when I respectfully refuse. I straighten up my already very orderly room, take up my book, and I wait. I can't read, though; I can't rest, I can't stay quiet. Alternately I pace and look out the window. By five I begin to reason with the fearful voice inside me. *But she didn't give a precise time, did she? And if she has a job, which she surely has, she's had to work all day. The only thing she said was 'tomorrow,' and that could mean any number of things. Not a visit but a call. Not a call but a letter.* At ten I eat the bread, drink some wine, undress, and go to bed.

"For three days, I trace the same template. By the fourth day I begin to wonder if I'd only imagined Mafalda. I try to find some evidence of our meeting, but of course, there is none. I'll take an *autobus* to her village, to Piana degli Albanesi. Thirty kilometers away, perhaps less. And it's not a place so big that it will be difficult to locate her. How many Bellini Madonnas can there be in Piana degli Albanesi? It's three in the afternoon on the fourth day and, my morning's shopping in a sack slung on my shoulder, I am on my way to the bus station. How I wish I had a horse. How much simpler it had been when we were little and I knew the way, knew where to find my sister. It occurs that she has stayed away these past few days so she might think upon what we said to each other. So that we both might think. I queue at the ticket desk, try not to look out of place. I have not ridden on a public bus since before my mother died. Mafalda taps me gently on the shoulder.

" 'Are you on your way to find me, Tosca? I'm sorry I didn't come to see you sooner. Papà is dead. *La signora* Capella didn't want to tell me on the telephone. He died in the spring, but she only learned about it a few weeks ago.'

"I take her arm and we begin to walk outside to the street.

" 'She couldn't tell me very much except that Papà had been living in Calabria. That he'd been sick, in varying degrees of gravity, for a long time. Though they continued to correspond, she herself hadn't been to visit him, nor he to her, for four years. When so much time passed without receiving an answer to her last letter, she called his landlady and it was she who told *Signora* Capella that Papà had died. That's when she wrote to me in Piazza Amerina. She and I will go to visit his grave, have Masses said for him. I hope you'll come with us. Now you know all that I know. I needed to be alone for a while before coming to see you. You understand, don't you?'

" 'Let's go to my room,' I say."

"Mafalda lies down on my bed and I sit in the chair that I have placed beside it. I want her to talk. I desire only to listen. She seems at ease and begins to tell me things as she recalls them, without order, without finishing one piece before launching into another and then returning to an earlier event, trusting me to follow her. I do. Prone in the soft curves of the feather bed, she is very beautiful. Her telling seeks neither pity nor wonder.

"She has worked in a fish-canning factory as a cook's helper on a deep-sea trawler; she has been an au pair to an English family living in

Taormina; she has moved about the island harvesting grapes and almonds and olives with itinerant farm workers. I understand about her hands now. She has lived in Piana degli Albanesi for almost two years and she thinks she will stay there. She works as a seamstress and a house model in a small, exclusive atelier owned by two French women. Sometimes a client will come to them for a wedding dress from as far away as Rome, she tells me. The two French women are wise, I think to myself, to have found this lovely creature to do justice to their skills. But now she is talking about a man. She loves a man called Giorgio. By day, he is a clerk in the city hall in Piana degli Albanesi and by night, a violinist in a chamber music orchestra. He is the eldest of the eight children—two boys and six girls—of a Slavic mother, a Sicilian father. She tells me about his eyes—gray and sharply slanted, gift of his mother. She says that he goes to her apartment and cooks for her in the afternoon after his day work is finished, leaves her supper warm in the oven, flowers on her table. A note. And then he's off to rest and later to play his violin. He comes to stay with her on the weekends, but only sometimes. As much as she likes to be with him does she like to be alone. Besides, she must study, since she is attending classes at the technical school that will prepare her to receive an accountant's license. I think that somehow the accountant, the house model, and the almond picker seem equally fine careers for this Madonna. She tells me that Giorgio has bought her a hope chest, that his mother and sisters have set about to fill it with embroidered linens and towels and nightdresses and even with baby clothes. Giorgio asks Mafalda to marry him every Sunday after Mass. She doesn't know yet if someday she will say yes. She has worked so hard, this little sister of mine. She has done what I have not yet done. She has found her own way home.

"When it's my turn to speak, I try an abridged reading of the events. When I tell her that Leo is dead and at whose hands he died, she weeps. She asks my pardon for her sarcasm regarding Leo when we met on the street. She says that she never considered the possibility of our falling in love. The age difference. The cultural differences. His wife and children. I tell her nothing about Leo's legacies to me, fearing that bank accounts and hunting lodges and emeralds would cause further estrangement between us. A greater divide. Mafalda asks why I stay in the *pensione,* which must cost far more than would a modest apartment. I lie, say I've just begun to look about. And as for finding work, well, she is an expert, she says. She will help me. She will share her earnings with me should I have need. And yet she is reluctant to promise that we will see each other often. Her life is already full, she tells me. She sits up, dangles her thin, little-girl legs, her thin, small feet in the ankle socks and the black pumps over the side of the bed, holds her arms lax upon her thighs. She looks at me, says, 'Tosca, it's too late for us to be a family. At least I think it is. And now that I know that Papà is gone, I think that, in a way, I am a family of one. I've made a good life. Someday I may choose to share it with Giorgio or even with you, if you might want that, but for right now, I want very much to keep to myself. It was a wild, hungry road I traveled from the horse farm to reach my little flat in Piana degli Albanesi. Much of the time the march was hard, I can tell you that. But I did it. *My being at home is so new.* I still wake up and can't believe that the bed on which I lie is *my own bed.* That I actually *live* somewhere. That I'm no longer passing through. That I can bathe whenever I want, that I have some pretty clothes, that I have two pots and an entire set of dishes with blue and silver rims 'round the edges. I can't begin to tell you how I marvel at everything. But you, your will, your character are so strong, Tosca. I think you could upset the balance, the delicious balance of this new life of mine. I can't let you in. I won't take the risk. I am not punishing you for your earlier decisions, but neither can I disregard the consequences of those decisions. I can't do that right now. We have led separate lives and I believe that's how we should proceed. If you let me know how you're faring, I'll do the same. We won't lose track of each other again, that much I will promise. I'll invite you to Sunday lunch one of these weeks, perhaps present you to Giorgio. Will you let me sleep here tonight? It's so late now and I'm so tired.'

"She washes, refuses a nightdress from me, pulls off her outer clothes, sets her black pumps on the windowsill like an icon, kneels by the bed to pray, then settles herself under the covers.

" 'Do you want me to tell you a story?' I ask, going to her, bending to her, lightly running the back of my hand over her face.

" 'I missed you for years, Tosca. How I longed for you, cried for you. I remember that sometimes I circumvented Jesus and *la Madonna* and even Santa Rosalia and I prayed directly to you. *Don't let me go, Tosca. Don't ever let me go.* I cried for you more than I did for Mama. I can barely remember her. I think that in my baby's mind, you really took her place. You became the mother. My mother. And then you went away, too. I don't want a story. We can't go back, Tosca. We can't. No one can. Papà is dead. Mama is dead. I'm happy there was this splendid love between you and Leo, but he is dead, too. And we two are no longer those little girls who held hands in the night. You should never have let go of me, Tosca. Not for anything.'

"I sit in the chair while she sleeps. I doze fitfully, as though I am on watch. Once, when I awaken, it's just before dawn and I see that she is gone. She has written a note on a flyleaf that she has torn from my book. She includes her address, the telephone number of the atelier. Tells me to use the number only in times of emergency. She asks me to write to her when I have a fixed address or if I am in need. She has enclosed 2,000 lira in the folded peach-colored paper."

"I saw Mafalda from time to time. She earned her accountant's license, she parted with Giorgio, offered the full hope chest to one of his sisters who was to be married. Slowly she took on the economic affairs of several small businesses. She moved into a larger flat, fell in and out of love in rapid, fevered succession, though no one won her heart. Surely I did not. Yet on a late afternoon in December perhaps six years after that day at the *autobus* stop, we were walking in the city, talking about her work as I recall, walking quickly so as to keep ourselves warm and, as though it were the most habitual gesture, she slipped her arm through mine, kissed my cheek, arranged her mouth in that elusive Bellini smile."

CHAPTER II

"Far less eventful than Mafalda's life was my own. There were days when I'd all but decided to return to the palace. Simple enough. A train going the other way. But when I looked again, I saw that, in those first months, the distance had grown, the space between the palace and me. Mines lay buried along the road back. *Not now, not yet,* the other ghosts would tell me.

"In the sun-baked stupor of high summer, I wandered less about the city. Rather I would sit for hours in the *caffès* under the scant succor of a Campari umbrella, smoking black-market cigarettes from a short silver holder I'd fished from among Isotta's jewels. My preferred drink was warm Coca-Cola sipped through a paper straw. If in one place people encroached upon the ghost of me, jostling familiarly upon my small private territory, I would secure lira under some glass or dish, move a few meters down the Via Maqueda to the next bar. I don't know when it was that I first began to arrange my time so that I would arrive at the last bar on the Maqueda, the one on the corner of Via del Bosco, at six every afternoon.

"Posed against white canvas drapes and under freshly washed black awnings, fancy ladies in silky dresses, their hats stuck with velvet roses, cluster in twos and threes over teacups and Brandy Alexanders and small sumptuous cakes tinted green and pink. I sit inside, though, under the whirring wings of the ceiling fans, in the dusky precinct of the bar. The smallest table, the one flush against the wall. It's always free. From there I can see them as they enter. The other ladies. Often as many as ten of them, though I think sometimes there are more. Eyes squinting at the smoke of the cigarettes they hold between their lips, metallic voices ripping through the hush, they push and tug tables and chairs together and sit in comfortable sisterhood. They wear silky dresses, too. Shorter, clingy ones and higher heels on their white sandals. Eyes fetchingly smudged with peacock or turquoise, hair rolled into wavy pomps. One night before going to bed, I'd tried to roll mine the way they did theirs. Just to see how I'd look. I thought I liked it, but surely it wasn't the right hairdo for a ghost. Perfect for them. Whoever they are. Who are they? A company of dancers? Laundry workers just ending their shift? Shopgirls on their way home? They are young. As young as I am. Younger than I am.

"Nearly all the afternoons of that summer I sit at my small table against the wall in the darkened bar on Via Maqueda. And as the merchants in the markets and the fishermen's wives on the pier had left me unheeded, so do the ladies with the wavy pomps. *La puttanina,* the whisperers in the palace had called me. Now, here I sit in quiet contemplation of real ones. Courtesans. *Les demi-mondaine* in the flesh. It wanted weeks before the signs fell into a limpid truth. How they'd primp into their tiny mirrors, pass lilac perfume and rouge 'round the table like bread, break into raucous screams at stage-whispered confessions, open their purses to one another. Coins, pills, handkerchiefs. How ravenously they would eat! As though they'd been half-starved. The way the barman touched them with his eyes. Slain lambs on hooks, his gaze slid from one to the other of them. Which haunch would he choose? Mostly what revealed the Maqueda ladies to me was the sadness showing under the rouge. Under the pomps. My own sadness deepened for theirs. And once I'd understood who they were, I began to wonder if, sitting here in the shadows, I'd been granted a Dickensian look at myself. As I might have been if not for Leo. Can it be true that I am, at last, recognizing that Leo saved me? That I might not have had the strength to save myself? That, at best, I might have died of the same febrile desolation that I have always believed took my mother? Can it be true that I am ready to loose the rapturous hold of my mostly unnamed hate? Of despair? Can I keep for longer than a moment the truth that hate and despair are two of the disguises that fear wears most often?

"Day after day, I sit in the shadows on the edges of the Maqueda ladies' tables, listening to them. From my purse I sometimes take out the thin green bank book stamped with dates and deposits and withdrawals and balances. At the beginning of each month when I'd go to the bank to sign for the next dose of funds, I would find that I'd spent not even a small portion of the previous month's stipend. Aware of the growing balance in the account, I never thought— beyond the next carton of cigarettes or the next bar bills or the next sack of pistachios or the two splendid banknotes that I would fold into a yellow envelope and slip under the door of Signora d'Aiello's office on the first Monday of every month—I never thought about the privilege of my position. And then there was the original stash of bills that had been stowed in the medicine bag with the jewels. I'd never even counted them. Now I watch a Maqueda lady counting out coins, stacking them in front of one of her colleagues. The receiving one keeps telling her, 'No, no. You can't always save me.'

"There are days when a man comes to sit inside the bar with the Maqueda ladies, the low-pitched drift of his dialect landing close to my table by the wall. They open their purses to him, too. Rolls of banknotes from some. A few coins from others. With the back of his hand, he throws a hard, quick blow onto the cheek of one of them. A random warning from which they all cringe. In his loping shiny-shoed wake, they are silent. Tears. Oaths. I make an oath. *I have been smug and full of pretense and triviality. I have been corrupt in my passivity,* Leo had said to me on the day he told me about the death of Filiberto. My oath is to come out from the shadows."

"It is September, early in the month, when I go one day to Piazza Venezia, to the Benedictine convent to buy the nuns' good cannoli for my lunch. I'd learned about the pastry-making nuns by listening to tales told about them in the *caffès.*

" *'The best cannoli in all of Palermo.'*

" *'Exquisite.'*

" *'The delicate shells fried to crispness while one waits. Barely cooled, they are filled with that morning's ricotta whipped with sugar—not too much—slivers of candied orange peel, scrapings of black chocolate.'*

" *'Rum.'*

"I stand in the stark vestibule with many others. I am next in line to approach the Catherine wheel. I say, *tre per piacere,* place my coins in the little box, push the wheel. A few minutes later, the wheel is spun back my way. I take the small paper box and turn to go. Two or three paces behind me stands one of the Maqueda ladies. I nod to her as I pass by but she does not acknowledge me. I go outside to the steps, find a splash of shade about halfway down, and sit there. I eat the cannoli, one after another. I realize that I am waiting for the Maqueda lady to exit. When she does, she carries a very large box. Brushing crumbs from my thighs, my lips, I stand, say, 'I see you often at the bar on the Maqueda. I just wanted to say, hello. My name is Tosca.'

"I hold out my hand, but perhaps for the large box or her own disinterest in the strange, tall woman in the old-fashioned dress, she does not offer me hers; she manages a smile, keeps to her path down the steps. I want to run after her and I think I might have had she not stopped then, turned, and called back to me, '*Ci vediamo, allora. Più tardi. Mi chiama Nuruzzu.* Well then, we'll see you. Later. My name is Nuruzzu.'

" '*Ciao,* Nuruzzu.' I wave to her. I notice that it is I who waves. Not the ghost."

"With that brief exchange on the steps of the convent, everything changed. Began to change, if very slowly. It was only Nurruzu among the Maqueda ladies who was prepared to befriend me. Some of the others believed I was looking for a way to join them, to be recruited into their ranks by the man who came to take their money. *Our designated territory is already too crowded. Too many girls. Not enough clients. Get away.* Others thought me a spy. An innocently dressed, bare-faced girl from a rival territory. Closer to the waterfront. They were the ladies who would pucker their mouths 'round their cigarettes and, with smoke fuming up from their nostrils, motion to the others with rolling eyes to beware of me. Nuruzzu tried to defend me, told them some of the abbreviated, selective biography I'd given her. I was new in Palermo. Had lived all my life in the mountains. I wanted neither to join them nor was I in any way connected to their métier.

" 'Besides, she's too damned tall and she has no breasts,' Nuruzzu said once when I was sitting with them and some of the ladies were speaking badly of me in the dialect that they thought I could not comprehend. They all laughed then and I laughed with them, thinking how Leo had so loved the long narrowness of me. My small, hard breasts.

"But no matter how I looked or what I told them, the Maqueda ladies remained aloof. Protective of themselves and their work. Only Nuruzzu risked a friendship with me.

"Like stealthy lovers, we would meet in places and at times when Nuruzzu knew we would be unseen by her sisters. And by the man who came to take their money. Our rendezvous were mostly in the mornings, in a small, unclean *caffè* behind the Vucciria. Without her uniform—the too-small dress, the too-high heels—her face unpainted, Nuruzzu looked no more than fifteen years old. Not recognizing her at all as she came toward me the first time in a white shirt and wide black pants, tiny feet shod in round-toed, beaded velvet slippers, just-washed hair slicked back in a ponytail, I was startled by her leaning down to kiss me on both cheeks.

" 'Nuruzzu.'

" 'Yes, the real Nuruzzu.'

"For months, we met like that. Twice a week. Sometimes only once. There were weeks when she didn't come at all. From that time, though, I never again went to the bar on the Maqueda where she met with her friends before their evening's work began. I was content to wait for Nuruzzu.

"She was a talker. I guess sitting with her, I was reminded of how Agata and I used to go on and on. Cosettina, too. In the schoolhouse in the *borghetto*. In any case, she told me that she lived in a *monolocale*, a one-room apartment in a *palazzo* near the train station. She lived alone. She was nineteen. She said that her dream was to leave her métier, to work in a shop or even to find a position as a maid. She'd once been a maid. Or a maid's helper. She'd worn a black dress and a white apron and a black crocheted net over her chignon and she'd spent her days polishing silver and tidying things that never seemed in the least untidy, passing small goblets of marsala to her mistress's afternoon guests. She said she'd saved most of her earnings, shared a fine bedroom with a woman called Assunta, dined, at 6:30 every evening, with all the servants at a table covered in white linen in a room papered with maroon and green stripes. She'd had Thursdays free. It was on a Thursday when she'd met Piero.

" 'Like all the villains in this business, he was seductive,' she said. 'At first, he was. They know how to court a girl. Tell her what she longs to hear. He'd said he would find me a better job. More money. Far more money. More time, so we could be together for more than just Thursdays. He said it was a very special sort of work that only beautiful girls like me could do. I was sixteen. A virgin. He took the net from my chignon, spread my hair over the pillow. He fed me cherries. It was a beautiful apartment. I thought it was his.'

" 'Your parents.' The words I did not form as a question.

" 'My father was killed in the war, or I might say that he used the chaos of the war in which to disappear. Many men did that. Women, too, I guess. My mother hadn't waited for the war before she ran away. I haven't seen her, except once when she came to ask my father for money, since I was nine.'

"Nuruzzu spoke of Piero's promises, his patient instruction in what was to be her new work. He brought her to the *caffè* in the Maqueda, introduced her to the others. They assumed her education, her grooming for the streets. They called her *picìò,* the littlest one. Nuruzzu insisted to the others that she and Piero were *fidanzati,* that they would be married as soon as he'd sorted out a few things. She didn't mind their laughing. She never saw Piero again. The Maqueda ladies said he'd just been passing through. That he, too, had gone on to better work.

"She says she's run away twice. Once to Trapani, another time to Messina. Found, beaten, brought back to Palermo on the bare floor of a van. Rocking on her stomach, arms and legs trussed behind her. She says sometimes it's difficult to say who is more brutal, the villains or the clients. They are men made of the same stuff. A cross is the shape of a man, she says. She says this over and over again.

" 'Until they're through with me, until they stop making money on me, I can't leave,' she'd said. 'I'm not a bad girl, Tosca. Most of us are not bad. I don't think any of us sat down one day and decided that this was the work we desired. Ours is the life we think we deserve. And if we didn't deserve it when we began, surely we've earned it by now. None of us has all her teeth, our bodies have been burned and beaten, our throats twisted. They let us keep only enough to live this side of starvation. That day you saw me buying all those pastries from the nuns, I'd stolen that money. It was my birthday. I made a party for myself. Do you know why we go to the bar on the Maqueda every day? We want to be together, but, as much, we go because we can eat and the villains will pay our bills. For most of us, it's the only food we have in a day.'

"At some point Nuruzzu had bent to kiss me good-bye, left me at the table in the *caffè* behind the Vucciria. I'd hardly noticed for the sound of Leo's voice. He pushes at me. *Most landowners permit their peasants only enough to keep themselves upright. Only enough to keep themselves productive. The nobles feast, the peasants provide. I want the end of that. At least on my own land.*

"But how, Leo? How do I help them? Do I save Nuruzzu? Do I take a room for her at Aiello and do we both live like ghosts, she hiding from the villains, me hiding from you? There are so many of them, Leo. So many like Nuruzzu. So many like me."

"It is a morning in November and rain purls against the windows of the *caffè* behind the Vucciria. The little room seems less shabby in the bluish light of the storm and, with the edge of my shawl, I rub the steam from the window next to my table. Nuruzzu is late. I crush pine-nut biscuits into my hot milk, eat them like soup. Rub the steam from the window again. A red-kerchiefed blur, she races past the window then. Snakes through the crowded area of the bar, settles herself across from me. She wears dark glasses and I do not wish to see the vileness they shroud.

" 'Tonight you will not go to work. Neither will you go tomorrow night. I've been trying to find a way to tell you. To beg you to let me help you.'

" 'You do help me, Tosca. More than you know. Besides, it's not so bad. Last night one of my clients invited me to supper and I went with him. I felt pretty. Two men were waiting for us as we came out of the *taverna*. My cavalier was beaten more fiercely than I.'

"If you had a place to live, I mean if you didn't have to worry about *how* you were going to live, would you leave your villains?'

"I might think I could. Until I remembered that they would never let me.'

"Falsely playful then, she removes the glasses, thrusts her face close to mine. 'Why?' she laughs. 'Are you going to take me home with you, Tosca? Introduce me to your brother? Is that what you have in mind? It hurts to think of freedom even for a moment. Don't make me think of freedom, Tosca.' From slits of blackened swollen flesh, two tears cling.

" 'I'm going to find a place to live. For me. And for you. Maybe a place with rooms for others, too. I want to buy an apartment.'

"The glasses in place once again, she laughs another kind of laugh. 'You want to *buy* an apartment?'

" 'Truth is, I want to buy a whole *palazzo*,' I tell her.

"She appraises the shoes I'd bought in the market for 75 lira. Leo's suede riding jacket under my shawl. I do not convince her of my power to acquire.

" 'You're not anyone's paid girl, are you? I've never asked you about your living arrangements. I thought you would have told me if you'd wished me to know,' she says.

" 'I'm on my own, Nuruzzu. I was married once, but my husband died. I'm a widow,' I tell her.

" 'I see. You're so young. The war?' she asks softly.

" 'One of the wars, yes. I have enough to take care of both of us,' I say.

" 'But you're serious, aren't you?' she asks.

" 'Very serious.'

" 'And very mad. They'll throttle you, leave you to the dogs. I belong to them. Should you be fool enough to *intercede,* you wouldn't be able to hide from them any more than I would.'

" 'I've already been through that.'

" 'What do you mean?'

" 'I mean that I'm not afraid of your friends.' "

Once again, Tosca is quiet. Sometimes she moves her mouth as though trying out the next words. She doesn't say them to me.

"*Nuruzzu.* It's not a common name, is it?" It's I who break the silence.

"Not so common."

"One of the village women is called Nuruzzu. At least that's the name I heard the other women call her."

"Yes, she is Nuruzzu." Tosca looks at me then. Arranges her mouth in a crooked smile. "She is *the* Nuruzzu. Our friendship has lasted for a very long time. You see, for the next seven years after that day in the *caffè,* Nuruzzu stayed with me. And from time to time and for certain periods, many other of the Maqueda ladies and ladies from other quarters of the city also stayed with me.

"At first we lived on one floor of a derelict *palazzo* not far from the Quattro Canti. We made a life, Nuruzzu and I. Like brides, we set up house. We bought beds and mattresses and sofas and a dining room table. A gas stove we paid four men to haul from a dockside junkman. Pots and pans. Towels and sheets and blankets. We organized ourselves like an institution. Nuruzzu had her jobs. I had mine. We interviewed the women who desired to live in the house. Sent them for medical examinations. Filed the results. Issued clean, if used, clothing, bedding, a copy of the house rules, which included two showers a day. We instructed them in their daily housework. Found jobs for many of them. If they worked outside the house and continued to live with us, they tithed. Visitors only on Sunday afternoons and always in the *salone,* always in company. Some women came to stay with their children, with their mothers in tow. I took on the care of them. Of the little ones and the oldest ones. It was like being back at the *borghetto.* We set up a kindergarten for our own children and opened it to others whose mothers did not live with us. Nothing grand, mind you.

"People referred to the women as *i virgineddi.* The little virgins. Our apartment was known as The House of the Little Virgins. The sarcasm attached to the name was soon diffused into a kind of awe, though. *Awe* at the immense conceit of our undertakings, I think. As our ranks increased, I transferred us to a *palazzo* that was all our own. What Nuruzzu had predicted came to pass. We lived with threats and, more than once, almost died of the intended execution of those threats. An unyielding lot we were, though. Help came from unexpected sources. From rebellious factions within the clans themselves. Perhaps the greatest help came from our own fatalism.

"How amused we became by the high pitch of our recklessness. A recklessness that, over the years, earned a kind of underground fame for the house. Not as a refuge for the broken but as a place rife with small wonders. Wonder at our very existence in light of the clan's code of pitiless revenge. How had we saved ourselves? Why were we left to our own devices?"

She screws up her long, feline eyes to some far-off horizon.

"Blank spaces in the allegories," I say.

She nods her head.

"I never spoke to anyone of my finances. In draconian fashion, I bargained in the markets, grimaced each time I reached inside my pockets as though crabs lived in them. Haunting the secondhand shops for almost everything we needed beyond food, I began to scrimp the way I'd learned to do as a child. I can tell you that it was far more satisfying to invent some savory pap from scraps than it would have been to roast a joint each night. I feared the intemperance, the nonchalance of the palace. You see, I never stopped wanting to live in the *borghetto*. I suppose to this day, I've never stopped wanting to re-create it. The way the *borghetto* became after Leo's interventions. The careful measuring out of the daily bread distinguished from the feasting days. The balance. The washing and cleaning, the distribution of clothes and shoes. The security of supper. That's what we had in the House of the Little Virgins."

"It's not so different from life here," I say.

"No, not so different, though here we have more. More space. Surely we have more peace. I've never understood what incident or what passage of time caused my need to return to the mountains. I might have stayed the rest of my life in Palermo. It was a good life. It became a good enough life. I think it was when I began considering how much more could be done up here with all this land, all these rooms. I hadn't known that part of my mind had already been at work here at the villa. Fixing and restructuring, planting, building. Cooking.

"I didn't give my householders in Palermo a great deal of notice about my leaving. I put the running of the place in tried-and-true hands. You see, a year earlier Mafalda had come to live with Nuruzzu and me in the House of the Little Virgins. She had visited us over the years, observed us, once in a while, she would come to supper with us. And when I told her of my plan to return to the mountains, it seemed also right that I tell her about the lodge, the land, and all the rest. When I said that I would look for someone to whom I could entrust the running of the Palermo house, she simply said, 'I'll do it.' And she did.

"I left funds just as Leo had left funds for his peasants when he'd parceled his land to them. All the operational pieces were in place. To whomever among the *virgineddi* might have wanted to go with me—to begin again in the mountains—I bid welcome. I announced my plan at supper one evening, said I'd be leaving early the next morning. Without a word, Nuruzzu left the table, packed her things, buttoned her sweater, zipped up what she thought to be proper boots for country life, tied a kerchief under her chin, and, so prepared for departure, sat stiffly on the sofa to await the sunrise. Only she came with me."

"Came here with you?"

"Yes, here. We came home to this *place*. Nuruzzu and I. Mafalda stayed in Palermo for three years longer and then she, too, joined us here. But when Nuruzzu and I first arrived, Lullo still lived here. Lullo, the caretaker, and Valentino, his beautiful red-haired boy who'd grown up and was just married by then. The three of them lived and worked together in the villa and on the land. Though they'd labored with great constancy against the natural decay of things, theirs was a small bane against time."

PART IV

❧

Villa
Donnafugata
1963

"Switchbacking through the hills in a battered blue truck, we arrived, Nuruzzu and I and our driver, who was the owner of the truck. I sat up front with him.

"Nuruzzu arranged herself in the truck bed among the sparse piles of our belongings. It was the first time she had ridden in any sort of vehicle since the days when she'd been ported back to Palermo from her imperfect escapes. Steadying on her thighs a box of thirty cannoli from the Benedictines, Nuruzzu sang, screeched out into the mountain air she'd never before felt or breathed or ever thought she would.

"I don't know if I had fixed expectations of what or who I'd find at the villa. I just knew it was the right place to be. That it had become the right place to be.

"As the driver careened onto the long pebbled road, I took from the pocket of my dress the key that had lain among other keys in a long metal box for those eight years, the same yellow string still looped through its hole identifying it as the key to the hunting lodge. A talisman. The doors would be open.

"The accidental gardens flourished, the blown roses climbed, the pines soared and quivered in the hot gusts of a half-hearted breeze, and, as it had been on the day I first saw it, there was no sign of a mortal hand. I went to sit in the lap of the magnolia.

"I was there when Lullo and two ancestresses from Leo's hunters stumbled up, running from some back field, alerted by Nuruzzu, still singing, still screeching. As if he'd been expecting us, he shouted out a perfunctory *ben tornata a villa Donnafugata, signorina,* nodded to Nuruzzu and the driver, began carrying our things through the doors."

I watch her as she ploughs the bottom of a sea, searching for some lost shard. She looks about the gardens. Does she see herself in the lap of the magnolia? I can see her there.

"Taking Lullo's lead, we began immediately to call the place *the villa.* We loved the name *Donnafugata.* Fitting. Allusive. Ironic. Only we two would ever know how fine a name it was. Only Nuruzzu and I would know.

"Though detritus furnished every room, I think we did little more on that first day or the first days after that than bathe and eat and sleep. I remember that Lullo made a fire when Valentino and his wife came in from the fields at sundown. She is the woman, by the way, who looked into your eyes on that first day when you skulked about the kitchen. She is Annamaria. There was an unspoken and collective need to be, for a while, all in the same place, and so we piled sofa pillows and musty bedding 'round the fire. Feasted on the cannoli. I don't think we ate anything before or afterward. We drank tea and fed pieces of the pastry to the dogs. Though we hardly said a word, we laughed. While we slept that evening, Lullo made his rounds. *La Tosca è tornata.*"

"Let me explain that Leo had parceled, to some of the peasants from the *borghetto,* lands that adjoined the farms belonging to the villa.

These new landowners—just as had the new landowners who'd been deeded parcels near the palace—converted outbuildings into dwellings or built farmhouses, stone by stone. Each farmer lived on his own land. Each farmer worked his own land. Additionally each one of them worked, in some way or another, on the farms belonging to the villa that were the once mostly unproductive farms Leo had bequeathed to me. The farmers, rather than taking some share in the crops from the villa farms or even some share of the cash profits those farms brought in over the years, banked every lira. It was Lullo himself who oversaw the account. The account they'd opened in my name. The accumulated sum was not formidable, but when I added it to what I had, what was still being released to me monthly, there was a sufficiency. With the help of the farmers, Nuruzzu and I began to put the villa in order. And after we accomplished the fundamental interior and exterior improvements, we worked on the farms themselves. We bought equipment, made roads, laid irrigation pipes, planted orchards, enlarged the producing fields to include immense plots of fallow land. Once again, we did what Leo did. Do you remember my telling you that after he'd died I'd wanted to *be* Leo? To the farmers, I *was* him."

"And as Lullo never stopped expecting me to return, neither did all the rest. To welcome me, they came in pairs, in clutches. Some of them came alone. With none of them was there much to say or to listen to. As though we'd already caught up moments before. They brought wildflowers tied with hempweed. Oranges still on their leafed twigs. Jugs of wine and wheels of cheese. Braised lamb in an iron pot tied up in a white cloth. One afternoon a neighbor packed the makings of supper in a washtub, carried it on her head up from the village. She'd brought enough food for twenty and we laughed at the profusion of her gifts, told her she must stay, invite her own family to our table, and I think that's how being together began again. Without the burden of festival or mourning about us, we sat together and I was at home. I remembered how the peasants had placed jars of wildflowers on their single front steps when the *borghetto* was first reconstructed. How those flowers had symbolized their finally being *at home*. I did the same. I was beginning to draw circles, and I liked that.

"As I'd done with the Maqueda ladies back in Palermo, I made it known to the farmers that if and when any one of them—in sickness or in health—should desire to join Nuruzzu and Lullo and Valentino and Annamaria and me at the villa, the doors would be open to them and to their families. Too, I made known the details that would accompany such a decision. As there had been in Palermo, there would be rules, work commitments. There had to be.

"No one came scurrying over the hills dragging their mattresses. They were mystified. Timidity, I think. And that immutable sense of feudal correctness. As they would never have consented to live in the same place where their prince lived, so would they refuse to live in the same place where I lived. Once again, to them I *was* Leo. But also at work was the momentum of the short span of years that had passed since they'd become independent farmers. Coming to stay with me would be going backward. Backward into the old *borghetto*. Or would it? Did they prefer living separately? Were they nostalgic for their tribal life? Even if they were, perhaps their children or their children's children were not. Our joining together was well-reflected in all quarters. But in these thirty-two years since I've come home, the impedimenta of timidity and feudal correctness have fallen far away. It was indeed nostalgia for the tribe that took over, after all. Took over and thrived. *Almeno, finora.* At least, until now."

Nostalgia for the tribe. A lovely phrase, I think. Already I feel nostalgia for *her.* For these hours we've spent under the magnolia. Turning the last page of *Anna Karenina,* the curtain fluttering down to hide Pinkerton, weeping. Small deaths. She is speaking again.

"I said, *at least until now.* That's the story I wanted to tell you, Chou. Someone else will have to write the ending. A story without an ending and with some of its pieces missing, but nevertheless it's what I wanted to *try* to tell you. I am pleased that I did. I do hope that my superfluity of words has somehow compensated you for the uncharitable silence with which my countrymen greeted you a few weeks ago. My rudeness being as sincere as my kindness, I might well have done as they did. I am comfortable not knowing why I did not. Have I tired you over these days? Or have you grown so used to being the audience that . . ."

"No, I'm not at all tired. It's only that I think we all die a little when something good finishes. Something beautiful. When something beautiful finishes far more than when something painful ends."

"But therein lies the marrow, doesn't it? How each of us distinguishes the two sentiments. What we say is beautiful from what we say is painful. I think they're often quite the same. Truth is, we die a little for both of them. That's how we use up our time."

I stay quiet and she does, too, until she says, 'You'll find the dress that Agata fixed for you in your room. There will be guests for supper tonight. Old friends who grew up in the mountains but who live in Palermo now. One or two who live nearby."

"Has Fernando told you that we are leaving tomorrow morning? Heading for Noto, I think."

No answer. Not even a nodding of her head. "*Aperitivi* at nine in the *salone francese*. It's a room I don't think you've seen as yet and the light is quite marvelous there at that hour. I know how you love the light. It's nearly eight now. We should both be at our toilettes, don't you think?"

We rise, gather glasses and pitchers, place them in the wagon with some others to be taken to the kitchen. I run on ahead of her.

The born-again silvery-brown taffeta dress is arranged on our bed, pinched in at the waist, the skirt spread out as in a shop window. Without looking in a mirror, I hold it against me. Was it her dress? Or Simona's, or one of the princesses'? Imagining the afternoons, the evenings when the dress was new, when the dreams of those women were still new, when my own were, I hold it against me for a long time. I close my eyes and hold it against me until I find Tosca, barefoot in her organdy nightdress, flying over the cold stone steps of the palace to find her prince, and Simona with her bobbed hair set in tight waves wearing the gray dress sewn with shiny beads, and Charlotte and Yolande in white stockings embroidered with butterflies, and the peach-skinned girl whirling in the moonlight. I find the peasant women in thin cotton smocks tramping over the stones with wine jugs on their heads and babies tied to their chests and the Maqueda ladies with the wavy pomps dragging the tables and chairs together in the darkened bar under the whirring of the fans and Nuruzzu sitting on the sofa, her sweater buttoned up, her kerchief tied. The widows are there, too, screeching and washing their hair in the fountain, and so is Isotta in a satin gown, sipping cognac, negotiating with Death. There is another figure in my pageant. She is very small.

Almost all I can see of her are eyes, large, dark, and somber. Masses of curls nearly hide the rest of her face but I think she is me. I think all of them are me. I think all of us are one another.

I hadn't seen the note that Fernando had left on the bedside table. He writes that he's been back to the room to bathe and change, then gone on some mission to Enna with Valentino. They might be a bit late in returning, but I am to go ahead without him. We'll meet in the *salone francese,* he writes.

I undress, pour the heels of all the perfumes and oils and soaps into the tub, and twist the faucets open all the way, expecting the thin streamlets that normally fall from them. This evening water gushes hot and quick onto neroli, lemon, lavender, frothing them to an iridescent meringue. I scrub and think how I wish I had known the prince.

It's already past nine as I step into the silvery-brown dress. As though it was made for me. That's how it fits, how it feels. The long-cuffed sleeves Agata has cut away entirely, as she has the stiff stand-up collar. From the once demure bodice she has carved a deep heart-shaped décolleté, anchoring it with thin shirred straps. What she'd cut from the length of the skirt is now a wide sash to wind 'round and 'round the waist for a kind of corset effect. I crisscross the satin ribbons of my sandals. A rim of kohl for the eyes, a slick of Verushka for the mouth. No time to fix the hair still damp from the bath. A loose knot I make of its untidiness, leaving it to hang over one shoulder. I have no evening purse, no pearls. I cut short the stems of two creamy roses, wrap the thorned ends of them in a tiny tulle and lace doily that sits under a bud vase, and push the nosegay between my breasts. Thinking of Tosca and Flaubert and the rose petal between Roseannette's lips, I walk down the stairs to find the *salone francese.*

Opened only part way, I stand before the tall, chipped gilt doors. The leaving sun slashes pink across the room and tinges bronze the profiles of a small complement of men and women posed about a vast grouping of love seats and chaise longues flung with lengths of worn brocade that might have once been blue, as though the task of upholstering the lot had long since been abandoned. The men and women hold old-fashioned coupe-shaped glasses, speak in lulling voices, and the pink light flashes, falls away even as I stand there so that they and the stone-floored room with the cornflower-blue silk walls are lit now with only the quivering flames of candles massed on tables, mantles, sideboards. It is Cosimo who sees me as I enter, who comes toward me with his arms open.

"La Chou-Chou. *Buona sera.*"

Escorted and presented into their midst, I immediately wish I'd stayed in my reverie under the iridescent meringue. Here in the *salone francese,* I am an old prom queen misdirected into the sanctum of an Armani summit. Each one here is draped severely in black. Not widow black but chic black. Caught narrowly and left to puddle above the heels of alligator shoes, silk pleated-front trousers flutter down the long legs of the men. More black silk in T-shirts or open-necked dress shirts, longish, wide-shouldered jackets. Including Cosimo—who is dressed as they are all dressed—there are four of them. Two women wear short black jackets constructed with the precision and inflexibility of armor. Stiff peplums flare out from thin waists and hover above toneless derrières sheathed in tulip-shaped knee-length skirts. Bony bare sun-browned legs and narrow feet totter upon the heels of jeweled pumps. Tosca wears one of her blacks, a chiffon tunic that covers her up to her emerald in front and bares the burnt-almond Saracen skin of her back and shoulders. I am the single flaw in this living frieze and though I want to run out and away from it, I take the coupe-shaped glass of sparkling wine that is offered to me and drink to their collective health. They drink to mine. I can't recall even one of their names and I wonder about the Venetian, whether I'll ever see him again. I wonder who these people are. I wonder why Tosca didn't lend me a black dress.

One of the men, perhaps the eldest of the group, perhaps sensing my discomfort, compliments my dress.

"Do I recall, Tosca, that you once had a dress in that same wonderful color?" he asks of her while smiling at me.

"I might have," she says to him. And then to me, "As I've told you, Chou, we've all known one another for centuries. Of what we don't recall about ourselves, the others are always ready to remind us."

Forgetting the torment of the old prom queen, I look at Cosimo, think how fond I have grown of him. Too, I could soften to the eldest Armani whose *mise* and whose manner, closer up, is less studied than that of the others. When we are called out into the dining hall, it's one of the other Armanis, though, who crooks his arm, nods at me, *"Con piacere, signora."*

He is called Icilio, he tells me. I sit between him and Cosimo, who is already deep in discourse with one of the peplums. Across from me sits Carlotta, and next to her is Fernando's empty chair. Elijah, where are you? Tosca sits across from Icilio, and for a while I hope it will be to her rather than to me that he will intend the nasally delivered orations he'd begun on the way to the hall. Meanwhile I am distracted by supper.

Long terra-cotta dishes of *sarde a beccafico,* fresh sardines stuffed with fried bread crumbs and garlic and pine nuts and raisins and baked with fresh bay leaves and olive oil. There are trays of *panelle,* fritters made of chickpea flour; great metal dishes with sizzling black olives that have been roasted with lemon and garlic; there is *maccu,* fresh fava beans braised in olive oil and wild fennel, puréed and smeared on charred bread. *Fangottu,* monumental white china bowls, are heaped with pasta sauced with raw crushed tomatoes, olive oil, and shreds of pecorino still too young to grate. It is Saturday, and Furio is at table orchestrating the passing and tearing of his two-kilo sesame-crusted breads cleverly slashed so that, as they baked, they took on the form of immense golden crowns. There is lamb roasted with mountain mushrooms and wild herbs. Sausages and small potatoes wrapped in pancetta, speared onto wine-soaked twigs and grilled over vine cuttings, are piled onto wooden boards and carried 'round the table. Still no Elijah. I ask Tosca if she is concerned that Fernando and Valentino have not yet arrived.

"Not at all," she says. "You see, when Valentino goes to town, he does errands for everyone else who has neither time nor opportunity to go himself. The trip always takes a while."

"But it's nearly eleven and everything's been closed for hours."

"The deliveries," she says. "He must stop in five or six or more places to bring what's been commissioned. A coffee. A grappa. Some gossip. A hand of *briscola.*"

"*La signora* is missing her husband. This is lovely." It's Icilio who puts his large, smooth brown hand over mine. To comfort me.

"No, it's not that I miss him as much as that I wish he were here."

"Is there a difference?"

"This is our last evening at the villa. That's all. It's only that."

Icilio leans close to me, watches as I fumble trying to slide the sausages and potatoes from the twig. Setting down knife and fork, I turn to face him. It was that for which he'd been waiting. In a quieter but still grandiloquent tone he tells me that life is meant to *un armonia di amore, dovere e tradimento*. A harmony of love, duty, and betrayal. He says that each one is essential to the other. Not one of them can survive alone. No two of them can survive without the third.

He pauses then. A sip of wine. I'm still looking at him but thinking that I'm already struggling with the old prom-queen complex and now these damn sausages welded to a twig and he wants to be provocative, wants to talk about betrayal and harmony and the stuff of true love.

"Are you saying that rather than coming to supper this evening, my husband is elsewhere betraying me?"

"If he is not betraying you this evening, he will only have to betray you tomorrow morning unless, of course, he has already betrayed you yesterday. Love is not love without duty and betrayal."

"I see. Together, they make harmony."

"Excellent. You have understood." He sips his wine. Picks up his twig and bites cleanly and with finesse directly into the sausage and potato. Pats his lips with his napkin. "Of course it's true for you, as well."

I laugh perhaps a little too heartily, since one of the peplums swivels her blonded head toward me in what seems dismay. I think this Icilio is saying that my love for Fernando will not be a harmonious love unless I betray him. That it is my *duty* to betray him if I love him. Yes, I think that's what he's saying and, too, I think his is far and away the most brilliantly delivered seduction of my life. I tell him so. He thanks me. Refills my wineglass. Disposes of the lush scorched meat of another twig. Tells me how fetching are the roses tucked into my dress.

"Sicilians dwell in a sub-rosa world, you know. Under the rose. The implicit word. The gesture, cloaked. I will tell you another, more subtle, significance of sub rosa. A girl called Rosalia is our saint. We are *under the protection of Rosalia*. We trust ourselves to a virgin hermit and should she not be clever enough to save us, we can always turn to our goddess farmer. Do you know of our Demeter?"

"I do."

"Good. So you know, then, that we Sicilians, most especially we Sicilian men, believe in the power of beautiful women."

"I suppose I do."

"Pindar called us men in love with brazen warfare. Though I do like the sound of that phrase, alas, he was wrong, *signora*. Pindar was wrong. Or perhaps he was only half right. We are *mama's boys,* homespun, silver-tongued, Machiavellian. Everything we've learned, we've learned from women."

"A goddess-worshipping culture."

"Far more than that, *signora*. Far more than that. All Sicilians think they *are* gods. We pastoral Sicilians know that we are. Descended directly from Hera and Zeus and Poseidon and Hades himself—hardly a united family or one shy of terrifying characters—we understand and accept our wisdom and greed and infinite powerlessness as birthrights. Heredity. The gods lived right here where we live. They built temples, worshipped one another and themselves, wreaked havoc, murdered, loved, feasted, swindled, raped one another's wives, stole one another's children, surrounded themselves with beauty. They slept on beds strewn with wildflowers and drank their wine from alabaster cups. And, except for those—for the wildflower-strewn beds and the alabaster cups—all of us who have come after them have lived or are still living versions of the same lives they did. As you have undoubtedly noted, the past is not dead here. It hardly ever sleeps. That's why we are not much interested in change and not at all interested in changing ourselves. We are already perfect in the same imperfect way that the gods were perfect," he says as dishes of watermelon jelly are set down along with doilied trays of little peach tarts.

Elijah has yet to arrive. What with the sizzling olives, my discreet glances down the table at Furio—which only Icilio has noticed—the twigged sausages, all the Armanis, sub rosa and wisdom and greed and murder and swindling and alabaster cups, I've hardly had time to think of Fernando. Everyone is moving out into the gardens.

Tosca comes to whisper that Fernando is upstairs in our rooms. She tells me that he left word in the kitchen, asked that I be told he was tired. That he went to rest and to wait for me. That I shouldn't rush. I excuse myself and run up to him.

Fully dressed, Fernando sleeps. A *canarino,* a cup of water steeped with lemon peel, still warm, is on the night table. I sit beside him, stroke his forehead. The Venetian farmer is finally exhausted from nearly a month in the orchards and the fields. Banker's hands roughed, pale skin flushed to a dark ruddle, he has worked and, I suppose, played in a way he never had before. He stirs, murmurs something about grappa and Valentino, and I understand that with the lemon *tisana,* he meant to calm his stomach.

"I'm going back down to say good night. I'll be right back."

He sits up then. "I think we should leave this evening."

"But you're so tired. A good sleep and then we can be off."

"No. I want to drive in the darkness rather than the daylight. I'll get up and pack the last things. Let's just slip away."

"Are you sad to be going? Is that it?"

"It's not sadness. I don't know what it is, but it's not sadness. I've never had homesickness, but I think that's what I'm feeling. It's like when you say you feel *bittersweet.* I could never really understand what you meant, but I suppose I do now."

"Bittersweet. Life played on the minor keys. Small affirmations of beauty." I caress his face. "Will you betray me tomorrow morning, or have you already betrayed me this evening?"

"What?"

"I'll be right back."

When I return to the garden, all the torches and candles are spent. The household has retired. Even the Armanis have started back for Palermo or are tucked away in the villa. No, Icilio is still here. Sitting with Tosca near the magnolia. Still unseen, shall I slip away? Bid them good night? If we leave this evening, I'll not see her again. Icilio strikes a match and as it flashes, I say, *"Buonanotte, Tosca. Signor Icilio. Volevo solo dirvi buonanotte."*

Icilio lights a cigarette and, still talking, they stand, begin walking toward me.

"I was waiting for you; we were waiting for you," Tosca says. "Is Fernando feeling better?"

"Yes, I think so. I'll just get back to him, then."

"I'm going up as well. I can't seem to persuade Icilio to stay the night, though."

"If I can arrange it, I always prefer to spend Sundays in Palermo."

"Ah, Signore Icilio misses someone. Isn't that lovely?"

Tosca seems perplexed. A three-cheek kiss for Icilio. And, for the first time, one for me. Her hand on my face, she says, "You were welcome when you arrived and you are loved as you leave us."

She's gone. I stand with Icilio and we watch her until she reaches the door. I am still looking in Tosca's direction when he barely brushes my face, still warm from Tosca's hand, with his lips. He begins to walk away. I am nearly at the door when he stops, calls out in a stage whisper, "*Signora. Signora.*"

I swing 'round, press my back against the door.

"In another time, I, too, would have loved you. I would have loved you very well."

I climb the stairs to Fernando, wondering about Icilio's theory. I wonder about betrayal and duty. I wonder about love.

Fernando has packed our things, written a note to Tosca, one to Valentino, one to Agata. I trade the silvery-brown dress for jeans and boots. A fresh white shirt. I am folding the dress, tucking it into my case, when Fernando says, "Come here. Stay with me for a while before we go."

We lie down face to face on the bed, talk a little about the route. It takes a few minutes before we realize that we don't want to go to Noto at all. Or anywhere else in Sicily, for that matter. We want to go home. The quickest, fastest route back to Venice. Each one relieved to learn the other one agrees. We check ferry schedules. We can be halfway up the coast of Calabria by sunrise. In Venice for a late supper.

We carry our things down and I wait in the garden with them while Fernando goes to fetch the car, to drive it to a place closer than the distant villa gates where it has been parked since we arrived. I sit in the cleft of the magnolia. When I hear Fernando's approach to the little gravel lot on the other side of the villa, I begin dragging the bags across the garden to it. He comes to help me and, in a few moments, everything is stowed. I have never seen this side of the villa and so look about. Look up to a wide loggia that runs the whole length of the outside wall and has the same red marble columns that march along the loggia on the ground floor. It would be large enough to hold ten couples waltzing. Or just one. Or a daybed wrapped in opalescent curtains with a heavy satin border. Fernando has started the motor again. I get in, close the door quietly. As he maneuvers the car to face the private roadway, I look up at the loggia. I see a face in the upper window framed in a Gothic arch. A silhouette. A shadow. I see two shadows.

EPILOGUE

MARCH 2000
A Letter from Tosca

LUI É MORTO. HE IS DEAD. IT'S BEEN ONE MONTH AND THREE days since Leo died. Yes, you're reading correctly. I said *since Leo died.* It was Leo with whom I lived for these past years since his "resurrection." His reappearance. I imagine your perplexity. I hear you asking, *But why didn't you tell me?* Or perhaps, *Why did you deceive me?*

I could answer by saying, *I am Sicilian.* Tell you that mystery and even duplicity are my birthrights. That *chiaroscuro* is another form of storytelling. I could say that silence is not always meant to conceal but sometimes to enfold, to keep safe. Or I could propose that sins of omission may not be sins at all. Besides, what woman worth her femininity has ever told all of her story? Surely you have not, my darling friend. As the gods do, we reveal ourselves—if we reveal ourselves at all—to whom we choose and in our own good time.

It was in 1968, five years after I returned from Palermo with Nuruzzu to set up life here at the villa, when Leo came winding up the pebbled road one morning, flinging open the door of the old Rover while the motor was still running, unfolding himself from behind the steering wheel to stand there grinning at Agata and the women in the garden, holding a finger to his lips to silence them. He walked inside, listened for me, came to the door of the *salone francese,* where I was still trying to play *Saint-Saëns*. A long, lean spectre in sore need of a shave and a good scrubbing, he was wearing the same jodhpurs and riding boots he'd been wearing on the last evening that I saw him. And I was wearing his old suede jacket. The first words I heard him speak in fourteen years were, *It's a swan, Tosca. The music was composed to give the impression of a swan. There is no indication that an elephant approaches. Piano, piano, amore mio.*

No need to scream, Chou. I can hear you asking, *Why? Why did he leave you to suffer all that time? Why didn't he tell you that he was well?* The truth is, at that moment, I had little need for the *why* or the *how*. After the first great convulsion of stupor, there was a noise inside my head like a tumbril trundling over a cobbled street and after that, after looking upon him as he stood there in the doorway, there was an immense, a sublime reckoning. My only need was to continue looking at him, to run toward him, not unlike I did on that evening when I was fifteen. This time, though, he caught me in his arms, crushed me against his chest. This time, it was he who did the kissing. My face and my hair and my mouth. And then he swung me 'round and 'round, his hands clutching me under my arms, until I couldn't tell if I was seeing the end of some dream or whether the dream was only just beginning. We laughed, raised up screams and shouts of praise to the gods and yet we did not speak, words most often seeming paltry noise in times of pure joy. Still not saying much, I took the prince by the hand, walked him through the villa, showed him rather than told him what we'd done together. As we walked, we met up with all those people from our past—with darling Agata, with little red-haired Valentino who'd grown to be such a fine man, with Olga of the peach-skin cheeks, and with Cosettina, who kept crossing herself and touching

Leo's face as she would the face of St. Francis. Cosimo came running in from wherever he'd been causing his usual fuss and the two old mates held each other for so long that we finally had to separate them. And when we came to the kitchens, all the widows—even the ones Leo had never known before—made an intolerable cacophony of screeching and ululating, chanting and praying. The Tiny Mafalda was among them. She'd stayed apart from the rest who'd run to stand about Leo in an admiring circle. But he saw her, knew instantly who she was, and went to her. Lifted her into his arms as he'd done when she was six.

There is another beautiful woman who's waiting to welcome you home, Leo, I'd told him then. Besotted with emotion, trailing the household behind him, he let me pull him along through the garden. We stopped at the bakehouse door. Her face floured like a geisha's, Carlotta and two others were pulling out the second bake, shoveling the rounds into cooling baskets. I think Leo saw the scene rather than the people, because he just stood there and smiled. Then Carlotta whispered, *Papà*. She said it louder then and ran to him, finally screaming it, *Papà, Papà!*

There is another sin of omission that I must now confess. Carlotta is the Italian version of Charlotte. In her case, Princess Charlotte. When she came to stay with us soon after I'd returned from Palermo, she requested that we call her by her Italian name. Why didn't I ever tell you that she was Leo's daughter? You know the answer by now. I am Sicilian. She is Sicilian, too. But I will tell you, Chou, that even after all these years, I can still hear Carlotta screaming *Papà*. A case when words did not make a paltry noise upon pure joy.

. . .

Even before I was ready to start asking questions, Leo began to lay down the pieces for me. I will tell you that, for days and weeks, he carefully dosed out the events, trying to be certain that I'd taken in one part before he proceeded to the next. I have already dreaded reaching this point in my letter to you since the complications of what he told me—early on as well as over the long years afterward—and the further complications of what Cosimo told me are thick and tortuous. There are times when, even now, I lost my way inside the story. Yet, try to guide you through it I must. Else I might simply end my letter here. Which I may very well decide to do. But first I will try to reconstruct Leo's story.

Leo told me that it was Cosimo who'd saved him. Saved him from himself and then saved him from the clan. You see, Leo had arrived at the desperate conclusion to surrender himself to them. To present himself to the same man, this Mattia, who had come to whisper threats in his ear on that evening when he'd been summoned to meet with the clan. Leo had decided to do this even though he had received neither a word nor suffered the least untoward action from the clan during the three years which followed that evening. He'd been left undisturbed save by his own fertile conjecture. Yet, fear having worn him to a kind of madness, Leo had decided to remind Mattia of his promise.

Leo knew that Simona and the princesses were out of harm's way, perceived as they were so separate from him, but it was some injury to me, to the peasants, to Cosimo, that agonized him day and night. Though I think you never would, you might ask me why he simply didn't cease his activities, continue to help the peasants in less conspicuous, less antagonistic ways. Live out his life quietly with me. The story would have to have been about another man, Chou. *We're all who we are endlessly.*

At this time Leo was all but finished with the legal business of partitioning the land, of preparing the channels through which the peasants could sell their crops, of setting up accounts for them, arranging for twice-yearly withdrawals should funds be needed to supplement their first trafficking with profit and loss. He'd thought of everything. He'd made his arrangements for me, for Cosimo. And as though, with all this in place, his earthly work done, he was ready to pay for his deeds as Mattia had promised he would have to pay. Simply put, Leo told Cosimo that he would no longer wait for the clan to come to him but that he would go to them. The prince would no longer live perched on the rim of the well.

Leo informed Cosimo of the day on which he'd planned to go to Palermo to find this Mattia. He set down all his final desires, instructions, caveats. Left locked metal boxes and their keys in Cosimo's care. Transferred and consolidated to a single safekeeping the funds and deeds and jewelry that had been deposited in various banks. He was ready. In the meantime, Cosimo had arrived at his own desperate conclusion. As I write all this, I find myself thinking of Isotta. Of Leo's mother and how she set about arranging her affairs and then arranging herself for death.

Anticipating Leo's proposed journey to Palermo, Cosimo himself went to call on Mattia. I suspect the man must have been intrigued by Cosimo's request for an audience, which, in any case, was granted with ease. With no evidence of the bodyguards, the cohorts who Cosimo had thought would be present, Mattia saw the priest alone in a sitting room filled with lilacs. Callas sang from *La Traviata*.

Though neither of them could have been comfortable, they played the role of old friends, sipped coffee and whiskey and smoked the cheap Toscano cigars of which Mattia was fond.

As he was obliged to, the priest fired the opening volley. He asked Mattia why he hadn't yet taken Leo. Why he'd left him, it might seem, in peace for those past three years.

Has the Church taken to soliciting confessions? Another aberration from Rome?

Point one for Mattia. Cosimo proceeded. He told Mattia that Leo's work was very nearly completed. Cosimo began to offer details of the partitioning but Mattia waved his hand as if to say, *I know that. I know all that.* Cosimo then asked Mattia why he'd allowed Leo to continue with the very programs that the clan found so offensive.

Mattia answered, *Being men of honor, we've had our struggles over your prince, Don Cosimo. To make a martyr of him might have caused more grief than will the execution of his "programs," as you call them.* Mattia told Cosimo that he believed the clan's dilemma over the "disposition" of the prince might have inflicted a far greater punishment on him than would have the bullet through his heart that he'd so long been expecting. Cosimo verified that the sinister abeyance of word and action from the clan had indeed had its brutal effect upon Leo. It was then that Cosimo said, *I think it's time you killed him, Signor Mattia.*

Pretending tranquility, Mattia looked at Cosimo. Asked him if he had also thought about how and where they might dispose of the prince.

Una lupara bianca, Signor Mattia. When he's walking across the meadow to the borghetto. *There are stands of pines. Beeches.*

A well-delivered and properly cold-blooded recitation, Don Cosimo. Am I to understand that you have joined us in our displeasure with the prince? Have I missed something, some dissonance between the two of you? That would distress me. I mean, it would distress me to be uninformed. But yes, yes, white for a prince. Yes, that's good. But tell me, Don Cosimo, what is it exactly that you will gain by your prince's demise? Is it the puttanina *you want? She is beautiful, I admit. But I'd understood that you'd been having her since she was a child. Excuse me if I offend you. I don't mind telling you that I've thought about taking her for myself. Perhaps we could share her, Don Cosimo. Once the prince is no longer, what would you say to our sharing the* puttanina?

Cosimo knew that Mattia's discourse was meant to mortify him, enrage him. To take him off his game. Cosimo stayed the course and it was Mattia who was disarmed. Cosimo said, *I shall get to my motives for this* lupara bianca, *but first, Signor Mattia, would you please be kind enough to tell me what you will gain by prince Leo's death?*

Vendetta is not an intellectual concept. We, my brothers and I, will gain that particular form of peace of mind which a man of honor feels when he keeps his word. Leo said it himself that night. Don't you recall? You must do what you must do and so must I, he said. Leo has kept his word. We shall keep ours.

What if you kept your word to punish Leo, but what if you did it in a way that was, as you said yourself a few moments ago, "a far greater punishment than the expected bullet in his heart"?

Cosimo told Leo that Mattia openly displayed his agitation. Said that he kept lifting and replacing the telephone receiver that sat on the table between them.

Cosimo, we're both busy men. I thank you for your visit. In parting, let me assure you that I will give due consideration to your, to your words.

Cosimo said that Mattia rose, offered his hand to Cosimo but that he, Cosimo, remained seated and said, *Please, Signor Mattia, I've not yet answered your question. You wanted to know what it is that I will gain by the prince's demise. I think that's how you put it. The demise that I intend—the* lupara bianca *of which I spoke—does not have to mean his death. It can signify his removal, his exile, the end of all his freedoms. Another kind of death. It does not have to mean his physical death. You, as a man of honor, will save face, will keep your promise to punish Leo. Punish him even more than your threats and your silences have punished him already. The prince is not your enemy. He did not take from you; he did not call for rebellion; he mustered no one to move against you; he does not want what you have; he seeks neither power nor influence but only to help half a hundred men, women, and children who were hungry. The prince is also a man of honor, Signor Mattia.*

Mattia said nothing. As though in a trance, he closed his eyes. The only sound in the room was from Callas.

Cosimo spoke again. *He cares very little for his own life. Perhaps someday you will know how little. But I care for his life. Not to share it with him, not to stay in his presence, but to know that such a man still walks, however restrainedly, upon this poor earth of ours. That's the proposition which I came here today to present to you. Banish Leo, Signor Mattia. You decide when, where, under what circumstances, under what regulations. He will comply. The only other thing I beg of you is to leave the girl alone.*

The puttanina? *That I will not promise.*

Then my mission fails.

As though Cosimo were not present, Mattia paces, sits, paces, turns pages in a book that he does not look at, closes his eyes, mouths words that sound like prayer.

Get him away. By the time you've arrived back at the palace, instructions will be waiting for you. Get him away tomorrow. Tonight. Convince everyone of the lupara bianca. *You've been a priest for long enough to have learned to lie, Cosimo. Convince everyone, especially the girl. I shall oversee his exile while you remain at the palace to comfort the widow, the daughters. The girl. Should you try even to speak with the prince or he with you, I'll kill both of you. Likewise, should Leo make the most fleet-*

ing contact with the girl, I'll kill her. Send her to him in a box. And if he's still alive after he sees the way in which she died, I'll kill him, too. You tell him that.

Then it was Cosimo who rose to leave, offered his hand to Mattia. Though he did not offer his hand in return, Mattia said, *I thought I'd forgotten the stories my grandmother, my mother, used to tell me about when they were young. About hunger and cold and heat and work and about being thrashed, first thrashed and then raped, by the noble's capo, should they in any way displease him. I thought I'd forgotten those stories but, for some reason, today they all came back to me. Every one of them. Get him away, Cosimo. Get him away before I forget the stories once again. Oh, that jacket he always wears. Keep that jacket. Give it to the girl.*

Cosimo said that this last served to prove to him that Mattia's surveillance was complete, since it was true that Leo constantly wore the same suede riding jacket. But, wearing it, he rarely, if ever, left the palace grounds. The surveillance was carried on from within.

Cosimo asked, *Who is it, Signor Mattia?*

He said that Mattia began to laugh then. Laugh and shake his head. He showed Cosimo to the door.

So through the offices of Cosimo, Leo was exiled rather than murdered. Two questions are on your lips, I know. What would have happened if Leo, himself, had gone to Mattia? And without either Cosimo's intervention or Leo's surrender of himself, what would Mattia have done?

I have asked these of Leo and Cosimo. You might imagine how often. Neither of them, certainly not I, can know the answer to the first. There was always a vacillating consensus between the men that Leo, in his weakened state, might have presented a less-than-persuasive case for himself. To the second question, there seems no doubt of the outcome. Leo would have been murdered.

And so Leo had lived with me for three years in self-imposed exile in the palace and then, for fourteen years, he lived in the exile imposed by Mattia. You'll want to know where Leo was sent. What did he do? How did he live? And with whom?

Leo was taken to live on a farm whose wheat fields covered the length and breadth of a high plateau. The fields below the plateau were only a few kilometers from the western borders of the land he had just given away. So near and yet so far. A serpentine tactic, you might think, but as you will learn, it was not.

Alongside a large, extended family of tenant farmers, Leo worked as a laborer during the growing seasons. In the colder months, he helped to keep the barns and the farmhouse in repair. He was treated as the valuable worker and pleasant companion he showed himself to be. He slept in the cavernous loft of one of the outbuildings where he was not uncomfortable. He ate at the family table; his clothes and his bedding were cared for by the women of the house. He was invited to attend and to participate in what few outings and celebrations these simple mountain people enjoyed. Though they worked hard and lived simply, Leo said that this family did not seem to be poor. They seemed not to be living hand to mouth so much as they seemed to be living in the way they chose to live. An itinerant priest came to say Mass in a chapel in the fields each Sunday. They birthed their own children, buried their own dead. Small groups of the men and sometimes of the women went to market twice monthly to one or another of the nearest villages. Leo was often among them. But wasn't he recognized in the villages? you want to know. Though he wore a poor man's clothes, perhaps even took on a poor man's bearing, I think someone who had once known Leo would surely have known him in any guise at all. You must remember, though, the inexorability of Sicilian silence.

Several times each year, Mattia and his own family—his wife and grown children, grandchildren—would arrive in a colonnade of automobiles to spend a Sunday with this family on the farm. With Mattia's family. Yes, this exile that Mattia chose for Leo was none other than his matriarchal home, and the people with whom Leo lived and worked were all Mattia's relatives. Scrubbing, polishing, cooking, gathering branches and wildflowers, carrying barrels up from the cellar, Leo said that for those Sundays with Mattia, the family prepared as if for Christmas. He was their benefactor, their protector. The prodigal son.

Mattia would always shake Leo's hand. Look him hard in the eye. Rest his great, wide hand on Leo's back for a while. Ask him why his glass was empty.

Mattia punished Leo—would have killed him—for the blatant irreverence he showed to the clan's dictum. *But only secondarily was Leo to be punished for his real actions—his willful intervention of a centuries'-old system of hierarchy that kept the wealthy in comfort and the poor in misery. It was the affront more than the deed itself.* I shall not minimize the deed, though. You see, had all the landowners done what Leo did, the clan's revenues would have been mightily impacted. It was a far cleaner task for the clan to plunder a handful of cowering, effete landowners than it would have been to bleed pittances from thousands of historically starved peasants waving freshly inked deeds and hunting rifles. But once again, the upsetting of the hierarchy happened to be Leo's crime against the clan. The crime might well have taken on another form, his irreverance might have been demonstrated for some other cause. But what matters here and what seems so difficult to clearly state is that *it wasn't what Leo did so much as it was his affront* for which he had to pay. Leo's duel with the clan was not a philosophical one but one of deference.

Leo did not defer to the clan. Leo did not allow the clan to prevail. A mortal sin. Leo compelled the clan to make an example of him.

But if we return to the question of philosophy, you will see that, in his own way—by subsidizing his relatives who lived on the farm— Mattia had done the same thing that Leo had done for his peasants. The circumstances and the results were certainly different but, in the end, both men, both Mattia and Leo *had done the same thing*. I don't think it was until Cosimo sat with him, smoking Toscanos and drinking whiskey while Callas sang—I don't think it was until then that this truth impressed Mattia. The truth that the prince and the clan's chieftain had certain sentiments in common. Perhaps their very characters were not dissimilar, one from the other. And perhaps, just perhaps, Mattia began to think that, in his place, he would have done what Leo had done. Supposition, I know.

During all those years Leo never asked Mattia about time. About when or if he could leave the farm. Go back to find his own life. Nor did Mattia once broach the subject. I believe that Leo's exile ended when Mattia died. No one from the clans presented himself in Mattia's place, though Leo expected such. Waited for some unfamiliar automobile to move down the long gravel path. He waited for a year after Mattia's death, but no one came. Thus Leo believed that his debt was paid, that it was time for him to leave the farm. Though they were sad to lose him, the family always knew that Leo would not stay forever. I do not believe that any of them were ever told that they were keeping Leo prisoner for all those years. I think that Mattia must have asked them to give Leo refuge as a favor to him. Told them some story about Leo having fallen on hard times. That he'd needed to *stay apart* for a while. Perhaps Mattia told the family that Leo was a fugitive whom he'd promised to protect, this being more truth than fiction. Also, I do not believe that Mattia involved any other member of the clan in his decision to let Leo live. To his brothers, he might have claimed that some other faction of the clan was responsible for the supposed *lupara bianca*. It might have been one of those times when several factions took credit for a kill without anyone knowing which faction actually consummated the deed. He might have closed the issue of Leo in some other way and at some great cost to himself. But close it, Mattia did. However he settled it, though, the settlement included me. My safety. Mattia insured that no one from the rural clans either prevented my going to or tracked my existence in Palermo. This is not supposition.

Bread and cheese in his pockets and warm rain in his face, it was May, late May, when Leo said his farewells to the family, walked out over the fields and down the steep rocky crags to the half-made roads that led back home. He said that he never expected me to be at the palace, but that it was there where he must begin. Where he would begin his search for me. Someone would be there. Someone would know something of me. Would he find Simona and the princesses? Would he find Cosimo? He could say nothing to anyone of where he'd been. He would tell no one but me. But where would I have gone? Would I have so adjusted my life as to make his reappearance an intrusion? Did I love someone else, had I married someone? He arrived at the palace finding it all but abandoned, if not quite in ruins. He ran up the endless stones of the stairway to the entrance, beat the great tarnished lion's head against the massive door. He screamed, *C'è qualcuno?* Is anyone here?

But the door was unlocked and, his boots raising a hollow ruckus down the long uncarpeted hall, he saw Mimmo swishing a mop along the marble stairs. He called to him, but Mimmo kept on with his mop.

Leo called to him once again. This time Mimmo—without looking 'round at the ghost who sounded so like his prince—answered, *yes sir?*

Leo called him a third time. Still not turning toward him, Mimmo said, *You're late for lunch, sir, but I'll see what I can find for you in the pantry.*

I have my lunch, Mimmo, Leo said, pulling out the unwrapped bread and cheese, small spoils from a fourteen-year crusade.

In magnificent Sicilian arrogance, Mimmo leant the mop against the bannister, pulled a set of keys from the pocket of his trousers, and threw them over the bannister down to Leo, allowing himself only the swiftest glimpse of the ghost. Mimmo then picked up the mop and, looking down at the stairs, he said, *You'll find her at the hunting lodge, sir. She's grown even more beautiful, sir.*

When Leo was out of sight, Mimmo sat on the stairs and wept for wonder and for joy. This last event was told to me by Mimmo himself.

Do I anticipate you correctly? Are you wanting to know how the clan responded to Leo's return? We have established that Mattia—in a way that he may have kept concealed from everyone—closed the case on Leo. But when Leo reappeared—though he hardly went about the villages flaunting his resurrection—the clans all over the island would have known it within hours. Was there shock among them that one faction or another had not disposed of the prince as they'd so long believed? Had they, indeed, believed that at all? Did any of them surmise or suspect Mattia to have been Leo's savior? And, if so, would they be willing, or more importantly—being who they were—would they be able to refrain from vendetta against Leo now? Far stronger for the imposed calm of his exile, Leo claimed that they would. Cosimo agreed. But I, too, was stronger for my own exile. My own ventures with the clans. I had my own reasons to be-lieve that there would be no vendetta. As it turned out, all three of us were correct.

To a Sicilian, artful deception rarely invites vendetta since artful-ness demonstrates respect. And Mattia was nothing if not artful. Hence, he was nothing if not respectful to the clan. The clan, as it turned out, chose to acknowledge the respect rather than the dupe. The clan's acceptance of Mattia's dupe was not a form of surrender but one of resignation. An overburdened and humble resignation. A kind of draw. A Sicilian often prefers a draw over a win. A draw can be better than a win. Denying triumph to the opponent is more thrilling than one's tasting triumph one's self. A Sicilian's triumph is his denial of victory to his opponent. Leo allowed Mattia—and, es-sentially, the clan—his victory even if Mattia did not cause Leo's death. Mattia's and the clan's victory was greater than it would have been had they simply murdered Leo. Quieted him with that afore-mentioned bullet in the heart. Mattia made it possible for the clan to have more. Better than causing Leo's death, Mattia took Leo's life. I hope you will pardon my repetitiveness as I try to explain all of this, Chou. Perhaps I do so as much for myself as for you.

Leo chose the rooms at the top of the villa, enclosing himself there in a monkish way, never brandishing his survival as a trophy, a sign of success and, hence, appeasing, I believe, whoever might have been left with a yearning to kill him. It was Leo's delicacy with the pride and the egos of others, his gentility, his unprincely way of being that kept the balance of the draw and that would have made malevo-lence toward the aging prince seem vulgar.

The prince lived a reserved, almost shadowy incarnation for those years after he returned and until his second death. He rarely met with passersby, guests, those outside the family. Save members of the clan who visited him with an almost dutiful and, what one might think to be affectionate, regularity. Icilio, whom you met while you were here, among them. Icilio was Mattia's son, and it's possible that the father passed on a word or two about Leo to him. I do not know.

Cosimo had kept Leo's library. Cataloged in boxes strewn with tobacco to discourage mold and the indiscriminate hungers of winged creatures, Leo's books had been stored in the sacristy and be-hind the altar in the church of San Rocco. When I returned from Palermo, Cosimo and Mimmo transferred most of them to the villa. As much as Leo longed for me, I think, did he long for his books, and above all things, they remained his prizes. And so he read by his fire or in the shade of his loggia. He dined and drank modestly, if with pleasure. From time to time, he joined the household at table. He was always ready to meet with any of them, to talk about the smallest, the gravest of problems. He waited for me, listened to me, loved me. Reveled in my love for him. As we had once done on the far more in-considerable space of our dark red rug with the yellow roses, we made a whole world of those rooms. While I attended to the villa, he wrote, listened to music, played his flute. He rode for hours every day—in winter, going out just before sunset while in summer, leaving long before dawn. Over the years I never stopped asking to go with Leo on his rides, but he never once permitted it. The fear of vendetta rationalized away, still there remained some pale shade of terror in him for me.

Thinking him to be one of the household whom you'd not yet met, you must have, more than once, seen him in his arriving or de-parting. Also, it was Leo who complimented your silvery-brown dress on that last evening. When he shook your hand in greeting and introduced himself, it was as *Leo-Alberto*. As it always was on those rare occasions when he was among people outside of the "family," his wish was to remain unknown to you. But I will say that his reason for joining us that evening, at least in part, was so he might "meet" you. He knew, of course, of our talks under the magnolia.

As I look back upon these fresh pages, I fear I've told you much too much while, at the same time, I have once again left what must be bewildering vacancies in my story. I, too, am often still bewildered. But even if I could tell you more, I'm not certain I would.

I wrote repeatedly to Simona from Palermo, asking after her and the princesses. Though she always answered me, her letters were shadowy, stilted. I was hurt by what seemed her change of heart toward me. It was I who stopped writing. I'd kept silent for longer than a year when Carlotta wrote to tell me that Simona had died. A violent illness to which she willfully, swiftly surrendered. Sometimes I still wonder if Simona wasn't the wisest one of all of us and if her polite turning away from me was more a stepping back, a way to help clear my path of the past so I might do what she'd said I must do. *Find your own way home, Tosca.*

Carlotta had written that she and Yolande would stay on in Rome, where they'd been living when Simona became ill. She'd said any further plans were uncertain. I wrote my condolences and several subsequent letters but I never heard another word from them. Soon after I'd left Palermo and gone back to the mountains, I'd invited them to visit. Carlotta came alone. And she's never gone away. So the first and only journey Leo made after his return was to Rome. To visit Yolande. Cosimo went with him, and it's from him that I learned something of what happened on that day. Leo has never spoken of it to me.

Cosimo said that Yolande was ensconced in irredeemable spin-
sterhood in a glorious old palazzo in the Parioli, that she had agreed
to receive her father only after an hour of his pleading and cajoling
through the auspices of her majordomo, who spoke with him through
the *citofono*. I doubt that the prince expected his elder daughter would
run down the stairs and fall into his embrace screaming with rapture,
as had Carlotta. Still, his pride, what was left of his paternal instinct,
must have been sorely tried as he climbed the stairs to Yolande's
apartments. Venturing no farther than the palms and the gilt of the
anteroom and remaining unacknowledged, Cosimo stood like a second in a parlor duel while Leo approached Yolande, who'd sat—albeit
at its edge—on a small divan in the *salone*. She did not rise to greet her
father nor did she invite him to sit. With no preamble, Yolande asked
Leo why he'd come. Perhaps wondering himself, Leo stayed quiet.
Into the silence, Yolande proposed that his reason was, of course,
money. Akin to telling him that the cook would wrap a loaf for him if
he'd go to the back door, his elder daughter told him there were *certain proceeds* from *certain sales* that, if he would meet with her attorneys,
might be signed over to him. But otherwise . . . by then Leo could not
have spoken even if there were words he'd still wanted to say from
those that, over the years, he'd practiced, tried on, thrown off, tried
on again until he'd thought some had begun to fit. By the time she sat
there talking about proceeds and attorneys, I fear he could recall not
one of those words or *why* he'd wanted to say them. No one changes.
Yolande never touched her father nor he her. Leo turned to go,
restoring the rhythm of the princess's afternoon. Just as his leaving
had done always.

Illuminated by Leo's scrupulous observations, my will to provide
for the widows and the others at the villa leapt from cautious devo-

tion to obsession. Though life at the villa had proceeded nicely indeed, once he'd returned, once he was there, everything was better. It wasn't as though what was difficult or exhausting went away so much as it was that our collective affinities—what the widows and all the others and I had in common—were exalted. What you saw and felt while you were here with us, what held you in such thrall, was that. Was him.

It was nearly two years ago that Leo became ill. He chose not to submit to therapies and treatments. He trusted destiny to give him enough time. And so the illness had its way with him, seemed to be setting up to stay. It was then that Leo took things over. He did as his mother had done. For the second time, Leo arranged his death. Almost to the moment, he decided when he was ready to leave. Leo was his mother's son.

He never spoke of dying but rather about the sea, the sea that lay in wait for him behind the trees. In the sounds of his own tired, broken lungs and in the roar of his tortured breath, he heard the rasping of waves. He heard the sea. Hell imagined by a man who loves the earth? Rifles cocked, aimed from behind the yellow-leafed oaks? I never knew whether he feared or yearned for that sea. I still wonder.

Cosimo and I would spell each other and, often, both of us stayed whole days and nights together with him. We set up camp by his bed, warmed soup over his fire, roasted bread, fed bits to him as to a tiny bird. More than once Cosimo offered to hear his confession, but Leo said Cosimo already knew too much. And when Cosimo wanted to perform extreme unction, Leo smashed the vial of oil Cosimo held in his hand, saying that a send-off from him could only be to Hades, and they both laughed. They laughed, perhaps understanding that laughing was the right way to turn the last page on nearly sixty years of life lived, more or less, in company with each other. As Cosimo describes his love for me, theirs, too, was another kind of love.

I recall that when their laughter quieted and the silence was too big to fill with words, Leo reached his arms up to me. Like a baby wanting to be held. And so I held him. Rocked him. Noticing that the flesh of him seemed less even by the hour. He looked at me then and spoke to Cosimo. He told him that he'd rather kiss me with his last breath than kiss the cold, metal feet of an icon. The nailed feet of the crucified Christ.

Look your last on all things lovely, Leo quoted, quickly damning himself for not recalling whom. Deciding to make the phrase his own, he said it over and over again. *Look your last on all things lovely. Yes, I would rather kiss my Tosca.*

One evening, Leo told us that he would be pleased to say good-bye to his family. He, of course, meant the widows, the farmers. Especially those who'd been with us so long ago "when we were little," he'd said. He always called it that. The era of our lives before he went away. "When we were little." I told Agata of Leo's wish and she informed the rest. Asked them to collect early next morning. Gathering before sunrise, they lined up on the stairs, on the landing, in the corridor outside his rooms. Everyone came, Chou. The field workers, the gardeners, the artisans, the villagers. They came in generations— fathers and sons, grandfathers and their sons and their sons' sons, mothers and their children. Agata and I were still bathing him, tidying up his rooms while Cosimo revived the fire. Prayed. While they waited they sang. They sang all the songs from the harvest and the threshing. The ones Leo had taught the oldest ones among them. They sang all the songs of all the people who'd ever sown a field of wheat on this island. Singing all the songs of everyone who'd ever believed in a fistful of tiny seeds that, by the graces of the gods, might grow up into the sustenance to keep them all for just a while longer, they stood there. They sat there chanting and singing. Weeping. They were the *addolorati*. They were Demeter grieving for her baby girl. And Mary for her boy. Which I think is the same as grieving for ourselves. For the pain that lingers and the joy, flitting, teasing, that terrifies us more. Their sound was shrill and fierce and, in a way, a battle cry. They would not let their prince go quietly.

And when Agata opened the doors to them, they entered a few at a time, filed by Leo's bed, kissed the bumps his feet made under the quilt, or took his hand and held it to their lips. Leo asked nearly every one of them some question or another. Oh, you wouldn't believe the things he remembered about them, Chou! About their illnesses, their foibles. He remembered even their dreams. I think it was mostly their dreams that he remembered. How he wanted to talk! But when the breath wouldn't come, he'd whisper up his admonitions, his affirmations. He promised to look after them from wherever this next confounded journey was to take him. He promised over and over again that he would look after them. He kissed each one's hand. *As the peasants kissed his hand, he kissed theirs in return. That gesture no one had ever seen—the noble returning his peasant's kiss.*

That morning strengthened Leo, kept him alive a few days longer than both he and the looming black presence might have intended. Cosimo refused to leave Leo, save for his own abbreviated ablutions. He would sleep in a chair by the fire, otherwise sit there or pace back and forth and 'round and 'round, all the while talking to his friend, telling him stories. I slept on the bed next to Leo, my legs and arms twined in his as though, if I stayed still enough, he would forget

I was there, take me with him as though I were part of him. I *was* part of him. I am part of Leo, Chou, and I think that you know that as well as anyone ever has or ever will.

I woke one morning and before opening my eyes, I knew that he was gone. Cosimo had discovered him earlier, left me to sleep in his still warm arms while he went to see about things.

Only Cosimo and I buried him. And not in the cemetery but on the rise of the hill at the edge of the farthest field. In the place where he'd appeared one afternoon, years and years ago, when he'd come back from some extended business or other he'd had to settle in France and thought he'd missed the first day of a harvest. A lanky blond wazir swooping down from another place, tearing off his coat, impatient to get the scythe in his hand, hailing Demeter, praising the Lord God Almighty, fairly trembling with the joy of being back on his land, with his family. That's the place where the prince sleeps.

And it's from here that I am writing to you. *Io vengo qui con il crepuscolo.* I come here with the dusk. As soon as I can smell the darkness rolling in over the fields, I pack up my sack. Sweater, shawl, some good gin in Leo's father's boot flask. With the sack slung across my chest, dragging my chair behind me, I meet the goats on the narrow path, high-stepping the opposite way, going home to the other side of the mountain, the silky tufts on their foreheads blown back by the wind, their bells walloping madly in the blue-black cave the darkening makes, and we greet one another. All of us en route to our own peace up here on a hill in the middle of an island. An island in the middle of a sea, in the middle of the world.

Tonight wisps of cloud dandle a March half-moon that makes a silver sea of the wheat. On the ramparts above, wolves bay and, across the precipice, small fires dance here and there. Shepherds cooking their supper. Save me and my trappings, one could hardly put a date to this georgic hill, this high place where the old gods walked and slept, perpetrating ecstasies, wielding incubus. How little have three thousand years changed us!

I settle myself among the rock roses and the cushions of wild thyme and stay long after the light goes. I have always been enchanted by the night, by the sense not of ending, but of beginning that it brings. I sit here wrapped in my shawl which still smells of him, sipping, smoking, sifting through the years.

Sometimes I reach down to touch the stone Cosimo and I placed for Leo midst tufts of Demeter's marjoram. Like two aging picadors, we stalked the temple ruins one evening until we found a thin, worn slab of marble we knew Leo would like. Cosimo wanted to take it to the mason in the village to inscribe but I did it myself. I did not make a wonderful job of it what with my slanting, left-handed scrawl drawn with an old iron nail. Still, it looks right. It says,

LEO

The Last Prince

1912—2000

FINE

ACKNOWLEDGMENTS

I know it's true that *to understand and to be understood* makes our happiness on earth. In all my life, no one has *understood* more than my editor at Ballantine, Robin Rolewicz.

Intrepid, graceful, wise, Rosalie Siegel is my agent. More, she is my ideal.

Rosalia lo Forte, Dottor Gianluca Pazzaglia, Gilberto Barlozzo, Pina Pettinelli, Christine and Giorgio Crovato, Dottor Mario de Simone, Thomas Berendt, Heiner Oelman, Kristel and Elvio dal Bosco, Isis Elten, Regina Derna, Alessandra Criccomoro, Alberto Bettini, Annette Barlow, Rosalba and Marcello Mencarelli, Rosanna Giombini, Contessa Graziella Fiumi, Gioia Guidi, Doris Engleke, Sharona Guri, Franco Titocchia, Edna Tromans, Alessandro and Anna Repetto, Dottor Paolo Ceccarelli, Dottor Renzo Ceccarelli, Sergio Carli, Chiara Giacomini, Marge and Robert Feder, Diego and Linda Campanile, Roberto Anselmi.

Giancarlo Bianchini da Todi, l'ultimo vero principe.

ABOUT THE AUTHOR

MARLENA DE BLASI is the author of three previous memoirs: *A Thousand Days in Venice, A Thousand Days in Tuscany,* and *The Lady in the Palazzo,* as well as two books on the foods of Italy. She has worked as a chef and as a food and wine consultant, and lives in Italy.